DEMOCRATIC DISCORD IN SCHOOLS

DEMOCRATIC DISCORD IN SCHOOLS

Cases and Commentaries in Educational Ethics

Edited by

MEIRA LEVINSON
JACOB FAY

HARVARD EDUCATION PRESS
Cambridge, Massachusetts

Paperback ISBN 978-1-68253-302-4
Library Edition ISBN 978-1-68253-303-1

Library of Congress Cataloging-in-Publication Data is on file.

Published by Harvard Education Press,
an imprint of the Harvard Education Publishing Group

Harvard Education Press
8 Story Street
Cambridge, MA 02138

Cover Design: Wilcox Design
Cover Image: Qweek/E+/Getty Images

The typefaces used in this book are Minion Pro and Sabon LT

In memory of Brendan Randall (1966–2017)—scholar, educator, citizen, friend. Your insights, enthusiasm, kindness, and compassion are dearly missed.

Contents

Foreword

Schools do not exist in isolation. Democratic schools and classrooms can only thrive if they are supported by the communities in which they are situated. They need this support because good teaching sometimes causes what longtime civil rights activist and Congressman John Lewis calls "good trouble": exposing difficult and potentially messy conversations about equity and justice. Such conversations can reveal that young people in our classrooms are eager to explore these important civic conversations. However, outside of the walls of the classroom they can stir backlash from parents or the media, leaving educators vulnerable if they lack support from school administrators, their colleagues, and other community stakeholders. As longtime educators ourselves, we have seen firsthand disputes over curriculum, classroom practices, and school policies. It can get nasty.

Let us share an example. The town of Brookline, Massachusetts, where we both live, recently changed the name of one its schools in response to its reckoning with the town's historical connection to slavery. A slaveholder originally donated a slave as well as some land to the town. About 150 years later, Brookline erected a school on the site of the donated land and named the school after the slaveholder. The school carried his name for over a century. A few years ago, however, a group of parents and students protested that they should not have to attend or send their children to a school named after a slaveholder. Others pushed back, pointing out that slavery was inscribed in the names of streets and public buildings all over Brookline. Why should the name of the school be any different? School names matter because they often symbolize the core values of a community through whom they honor. The ensuing debate over the name change was thus predictably rancorous. People accused each other of political correctness, oversensitivity, insensitivity, or bigotry during community meetings and in the local press. In the end, our town decided to change the name of the school, a decision we both support. And yet, the impact of the controversy has provoked—or perhaps revealed—deep divisions that have lasted well beyond the spark. As the case studies and commentaries in this volume reveal, democratic discord in schools often call to the surface contested notions of values that Americans cherish—freedom, equality, justice. Sorting through them can be difficult and uncomfortable, yet doing so is absolutely necessary. This is the good trouble Congressman Lewis encourages us to engage in.

AN APPROACH TO EDUCATIONAL ETHICS

How are teachers, parents, administrators, school staff, school board members, policy makers, and students prepared to take up such challenges? Unfortunately, although we are all stakeholders in the education of the youth of our community, we have very little practice in preparing for the ethical decisions that suffuse our work.

Consider teachers, for instance, who likely engage in "200 to 300 interpersonal exchanges every hour of the working day."[1] That means, on average, teachers are making about 1500 decisions a day in response to those interactions. Many of these decisions will be ethical in nature, and they demand a repertoire of strategies to identify and act on ethical decision points. Educating teachers to think about the relationship between pedagogy and student learning undoubtedly helps with some of this decision-making. For example, teachers learn to draw on conceptual frameworks, textbooks, and (too often) standardized testing to inform the development of curriculum. While there is a lot of room for improvement, this education helps teachers make decisions about how to prioritize the content, what teaching strategies to draw on, and which resources to introduce to students. But these are insufficient for addressing complex ethical dilemmas, like those detailed in this book, that are inherent in the lives of schools.

The problem is not just that we haven't all studied ethical theory. Rather, as Herbert Kohl eloquently observes, educators must contend with the central question of how to put theory into practice—and put practice into theory:

> There is a complex and intimate relationship between theory and practice in the classroom. Theoretical ideas are tested every day by the complex and often unpredictable behavior of students and teachers, and by the constant influence of life outside of the classroom. Practicing teachers have to constantly adjust theory based upon their practice. The craft

> develops through experience and reflection upon that experience. What is hardest to maintain in the midst of the immediate demands of the classroom is the intellectual aspect of teaching, which though less apparent on an everyday level than the craft issues, still pervades and underlies every good teacher's practice.[2]

The case studies and thoughtful commentaries in this book do a brilliant job exposing the fault lines between theory and practice. In doing so, they bring what Kohl described as the "intellectual aspect of teaching" to the fore.

Lawrence Kohlberg was one of the first scholars to offer insight into the use of case studies in moral development education, in particular by showing that all of us could sharpen our moral thinking by wrestling with abstract moral dilemmas. The more we did that, the better we would be able to define our moral principles. This connects his work on moral development theory to schools, where such practice could take place. The field of moral development education has been further developed by an influential group of educators including Betty Bardige, Ted Fenton, Carol Gilligan, and Ralph Mosher, among many others.

Our decades of work at the international nonprofit educational organization, Facing History and Ourselves, where Margot was Founding Executive Director and Adam led the content development team, was profoundly influenced by this work—but with a twist. Building off Kohlberg's work using abstract dilemmas, Margot's insight was to focus, instead, on true-to-life moral and ethical dilemmas grounded in historical context such as Weimar and Nazi Germany or Little Rock's Central High School at the height of desegregation. These contextualized dilemmas serve as foundational texts for teachers and students to reflect upon in the classroom. Through both practice and research, we learned that deliberation on these historical dilemmas sharpens students' understanding of the past and helps them prepare for the moral and ethical choices they face in their own lives. This dynamic brings classrooms to life for both the teacher and the student.

It is here that our approach meets Meira Levinson and Jacob Fay's project. Their work provides an opportunity for educators to think about their thinking when confronted with moral and ethical dilemmas of education. Each case provides a standard text for conversation, professional learning, and discussion about the choices educational stakeholders make. Similar to the way we have explored historical dilemmas in our work, these cases can help develop educators' moral and ethical imaginations while helping them to anticipate the challenges they face in their personal and professional lives.

These cases and commentaries also illuminate real-life dilemmas of democracy, just as we did at Facing History, and as Adam does as cofounder of Re-Imagining Migration. Taken as a whole, they force us to confront difficult questions about the ethical dimensions of educating citizens and wrestling with difference, and doing so in ways that *sustain* a democracy. If we are serious about building the skills that citizens need to live together, what collective life can we build in schools to make sure we are indeed teaching and living democratic values? We need to engage students in the civic challenges of our time, including the fragility of democracy, racial and religious prejudices, homophobia, gender equity, climate change, genocide, individual and collective rights, and immigration. It is during these often uncomfortable classroom conversations that students first have the opportunity to practice the respectful give-and-take that is essential for self-government. As you listen carefully to students, you will hear them connecting the content of the classroom to their lives. Yet it would be folly to expect educators to simply be able to *do* this; they need practice and tools to help them reflect on the challenges of this work. We think this collection provides such an opportunity.

THE POLITICAL ENVIRONMENT AND OUR STUDENTS' LIVES

Such work is more important now than ever. We began by stating what should be obvious, that classrooms do not exist in isolation. Since the 2016 election, several studies have illuminated the way that the political divisions in US democracy are impacting students' experiences in schools. Reports indicate that the political climate has a direct impact on students' academic, social, and emotional lives, and that students are confronting increasing incidents of hate speech and violence.[3]

Some of our most vulnerable students feel it the most. A few years ago, for instance, Carola Suárez-Orozco and Marcelo Suárez-Orozco conducted a study focusing on how immigrant students believed they were perceived by Americans at large. They asked immigrant youth to respond to the prompt: "Most Americans think that most [people from the respondent's birthplace] are ________." Their findings were deeply troubling, as two-thirds of the children "filled in the blank with a negative term," often including detailed accounts of the prejudice they faced. "'Most Americans think that Mexicans are lazy, gangsters, drug addicts that only come to take their jobs away,' one 14-year-old boy wrote. Not only did many respondents choose words associated with criminality but many also chose terms related to contamination—'We are garbage'—and incompetence—'We can't do the same things as them in school or at work.'"[4] Research such as this shows that young people are internalizing the stereotypes around them, and hence we ignore democratic discord at our own peril. Too often we do not talk about the way the political environment shapes what is going on in schools until the stories spill back out into the community in soundbites captured in the press or distributed like a game of telephone across social media. We appreciate how cases like "Walling Off or Welcoming In" capture the way these attitudes ripple across a school community. At Re-Imagining Migration, the new organization that Adam directs with Carola and Marcelo Suárez-Orozco, they are already using this case with educators worldwide.

Educators cannot afford to be silent, or we risk perpetuating the mistakes of our past. A few years ago, we worked on a project about teaching the history of the civil rights movement in the United States. In the introduction to a book for teachers, Margot took the opportunity to reflect on the failure of her education to confront the civic fissures and struggles for change that divided her hometown:

> I grew up in Memphis, Tennessee . . . at a time when separate meant never equal. For it was in Memphis that simple childhood notions of logic and fairness were shattered. It was there that water fountains for "colored only" didn't spout water which reflected the colors of the rainbow as the child might expect but instead, as one learned later, stood as symbols of the unchallenged dogmas and practices of racism—dogmas that attempted to instill indignity, shame, and humiliation in some and false pride and authority in others, and practices that reflected centuries of unchallenged myth and hate.
>
> I grew up in Memphis at a time when black libraries housed books discarded from the white library; when there were empty seats in the front of the bus for young white girls on a shopping trip downtown, while those of darker skin color crowded the back of the bus on their way to work; when Thursdays were "colored day" at the zoo, and a rear entrance led to a colored section in the movie theatre balcony—if admission was allowed at all.[5]

While the experiences are Margot's, those stories shaped the way both of us think about education. The school's silence was deafening. Indeed, our students, teachers, parents, and school faculty bring the world into the school, and as much as some might try to reduce education to inputs from a standardized curriculum and student data to be measured, it just isn't that simple. Nor should it be. The lives of schools and the health of our democracy are intertwined.

These cases remind us all of that simple fact. They present messy ethical dilemmas without easy solutions that have real consequences for students' lives. We wish we had a classroom of students to share them with. In the exchange of ideas and the back and forth, we would discover what we really think. Those exchanges can feel like magic. However, it is important to remember that they aren't. One way to prepare for them is for teachers, professors of education, and their students to pick up this book and get talking.

Margot Stern Strom
Margot Stern Strom left the classroom to found Facing History and Ourselves as a nonprofit educational organization.

Adam Strom
Adam Strom is the Director of Re-Imagining Migration.

CHAPTER 1

Schools Of, By, and For the People

Both Impossible and Necessary

JACOB FAY AND MEIRA LEVINSON

During the summer following the inauguration of President Donald Trump, one of us was working with district superintendents in a politically divided state when an administrator shared a dilemma with which he had been wrestling. After President Trump's election, a number of residents in his school district put up yard signs reading, "Hate Has No Home Here. Love Lives Here." Some teachers posted the same sign on the walls of their classrooms without initially attracting any notable response. Some weeks later, however, other district residents planted a different sign in their yards: "Love for God, Love for Country, Love for Constitution." Like most regions of the United States, the majority of residents in this area profess to believe in God. We presume that many of those who posted "Hate Has No Home Here" thus also felt love for God, and likely perceived themselves as American patriots and supporters of the US Constitution. We presume that most of those who declared "Love for God . . ." would also claim that love, not hate, was at the center of their homes. Nonetheless, all residents understood how the "love" declared by the second set of signs was intended to be read as in contrast to the "love" promised by the first set. Soon after the new signs appeared, the superintendent started fielding student complaints about teachers' partisan bias in posting "Hate Has No Home Here" on their classroom walls. The superintendent had to decide whether to tell the teachers to remove the signs—and if so, on what grounds.

We expect that versions of the superintendent's story will feel familiar to many educators, policy makers, parents, and students not only in the United States, but also around the world. The particulars will differ, of course. As the cases that anchor this book illuminate, discord in schools and districts has erupted in response to a wide range of often unintentional provocations: the language children use during free play, class discussion, or lunchtime conversations; student activism around school walkouts and other protests; how teachers have responded to students' questions about current events during class and at a school assembly; a teacher's choice to wear a Black Lives Matter pin; faculty disagreement over what topics are appropriate to include—and how to teach them—in a social studies curriculum; districts' decisions to use digital surveillance techniques or to partner with law enforcement to keep some students safe while potentially increasing other students' vulnerability; or districts' policy responses to shifting political winds on social issues like immigration. There are no easy answers to the questions these instances pose for educators, policy makers, and citizens as they go about their work. Put simply, the intersection of democratic politics and education, particularly in a moment characterized by deep partisan discord, has made teaching children especially challenging.

Part of the challenge rests on our increasingly discordant political life. The past few years have witnessed rapid and contested shifts in civic and democratic norms.[1] Liberals, for example, shudder at the Supreme Court's rulings denying California the right to require that pregnancy centers give women accurate medical information in *NIFLA v. Becerra* and denying LGBTQ+ rights in *Masterpiece Cakeshop v. Colorado Civil Rights Commission*; they view both cases as the evisceration of fundamental norms of social equality. Conservatives, on the other hand, celebrate both decisions as refreshing refusals to bow down to elite political fictions and as triumphs of First Amendment freedoms of religion and speech. Immigration policy is another arena of dizzying, even extreme norm shifts. Immigration reform favored by liberals as a means to achieve greater inclusion has been replaced by conservative efforts, in the name of upholding safety and the rule of law, to crack down on undocumented immigrants, close borders, limit legal immigration, and exclude asylum seekers. These shifts challenge educators who attempt to remain nonpartisan in their work with students and families, as they wonder what common civic values they can safely uphold—and whether they can appropriately teach that any of these shifts, such as separating children from parents at the border, are not simply unprecedented, but also wrong.

Compounding matters is that these norm shifts are both taking place amid—and being driven by—an increasingly polarized and partisan political climate. For decades, partisanship and political polarization both in the United States and around the world has been on the rise.[2] Partisanship and polarization sharpens lines of difference within a society; those on opposing sides feel as if their opponents ignore, trample on, or twist fundamental American values into unrecognizable forms before their very eyes. As the superintendent's dilemma demonstrates, they also expand the bounds of political conflict such that even seemingly innocuous statements like "Hate Has No Home Here" are enveloped in a partisan valence. Finally, partisanship and polarization decrease people's willingness to engage across lines of difference, as they mistrust that their interlocutors will take their claims seriously or that anything positive will result. We see these processes at work both in our increasingly fragile, fractured media landscape, and in the demographically homogeneous "bubbles" that many Americans construct for themselves, making it rare for people to encounter those with profoundly different perspectives and life experiences. Schools have not escaped these changing political currents.

Hence, another part of the challenge of teaching children amid democratic discord has to do with the impossibly thin boundary between democratic politics and schools. Although educators may often wish otherwise, students bring their awareness of shifting norms into schools and classrooms. Some students seek condemnation of particular policies or political views, and/or reassurance that as refugees, immigrants, or minorities they still have a place in the classroom and in the United States. Many educators and school leaders have been eager to provide such reassurance—but then face the risk of backlash for seeming to take partisan stands that favor particular students. Other students echo claims that shifting norms have enabled—sometimes because they are simply curious, other times to express their own worries about and mistrust of particular groups such as immigrants, Muslims, refugees, or Hispanics. Educators struggle with these claims, as well. Depending on how students express their concerns, their claims may violate district and state antibullying policies. They may also violate civic democratic norms that schools have been committed to teaching for decades: norms of mutual respect, antiracism, civic equality, and religious freedom. But how can students be redirected or punished when they are merely reiterating language that they hear political leaders using at both campaign rallies and in the halls of state and national capitols?

It should not be at all surprising that democratic discord finds its way into schools, since, as Diana Hess and Paula McAvoy observe, schools "are, and ought to be, political sites."[3] Nonetheless, we believe it is important to make sense of the complicated ways in which schools are political. Schools function simultaneously as institutions *in* a democracy and as institutions that prepare students *for* democracy.[4] Nearly everyone, it seems, agrees that schools should be teaching students civic norms and dispositions that are necessary to sustain a democracy: to embrace ideals such as democratic equality and inclusion, and to enact these ideals by interacting with one another respectfully and civilly.[5] That's what we mean by teaching *for* democracy—preparing students to take on civic roles and responsibilities as they grow into adults. But what these norms are, what they mean in practice, and how they are best enacted are all deeply disputed, precisely because these are contested in contemporary democratic politics. That's what we mean by teaching *in* democracy; adults disagree with one another about what educators should be teaching and how they should teach it—and students do, too!

In other words, public schools—as well as teachers, administrators, and policymakers—are simultaneously subject to democratic politics *and* sites of the civic and democratic learning necessary for sustaining a democracy across generations. Hence, when educators confront dilemmas like whether to remove seemingly innocuous signs from classrooms, they must be both present-minded and future-minded. They must be aware of both the political climate as it currently is as well as the values that strengthen and invigorate democracy over time.

As more and more challenges like these emerge amid the current political climate—as rancorous, uncivil, and highly partisan as it is—it is easy to think that they are particular to this moment. But as much as this feels true, as urgent and frustrating as educating in *this* democracy is for an envisioned future democracy, it is important to recognize that the challenges we face now are also perennial issues in civic and democratic education. John Dewey noted nearly a century ago that rather than democracy being taken for granted, it must "be enacted anew in every generation, in every year and day."[6] In other words, a democratic society does not simply persist once it is established; it must be constantly reimagined and rebuilt by its citizens. Education, as Dewey made clear time and time again, is vital to democracy for precisely this reason. Our current moment is no different in this respect. The political turmoil and upheaval we are experiencing heighten the salience of particular issues and points of conflict—but the underlying concerns for democratic and civic education are timeless. Heeding Dewey's warning, we believe it is time to turn a fresh eye to meeting the challenges of democratic discord in schools in order to sustain our democracy.

REASONING TOGETHER

In our experiences as classroom teachers, we both came face to face with dilemmas like the ones we detail above and in this book. Whether it was deciding if a student could proceed with a civic action project that opposed same-sex marriage on Talmudic grounds or making potentially explosive choices about what to include in and exclude from a history curriculum, we have felt both the weight of the decision in front of us and the sting of the consequences that inevitably follow from the decision.[7] We know how it can feel like thankless work, where no choice can appease all comers. We know how educators worry about rocking the boat with their colleagues by bringing up controversial or political topics. We know that, as a result, they may make decisions behind their classroom doors, struggling through as educators are apt to do, perhaps second-guessing themselves, and all the while feeling alone in making their decision. We have both been there.

We believe, however, that it is important to reason through these difficult dilemmas together, with our colleagues rather than without them, in the faculty common room rather than behind closed classroom doors. With a polyphony of voices deliberating about a dilemma, it is likely that many different courses of action will surface, that reasons one educator may discount may be emphasized by another, and that values one educator may overlook are brought into consideration by a colleague. In short, reasoning together truly treats these dilemmas as challenges of *democratic* education.

One way we believe that this sort of deliberation can occur is through the use of *normative case studies* and case commentaries. In our previous book, *Dilemmas of Educational Ethics*, we defined normative case studies as "richly described, realistic accounts of complex ethical dilemmas that arise within practice or policy contexts, in which protagonists must decide among courses of action, none of which is self-evidently the right one to take."[8] Normative case studies turn on *realistic* ethical dilemmas; in other words, problems that are not of the "You find a wallet on the street; what should you do with it?" variety. Rather, the dilemmas that educators encounter are complex and intricately shaped by context. People's identities matter. Students' ages matter. The past history of students' or teachers' behaviors matter. Schools' histories matter. Social, cultural, and political contexts matter. Furthermore, the "answers" we come up with may be as nuanced as the cases themselves, as the case commentaries in that book and this one collectively demonstrate. When we invite people from different walks of life, disciplines, and professional backgrounds to deliberate about a case—historians and district superintendents, philosophers and middle school students, law professors and activists—we are rewarded with a profound range of responses. This is all to be expected; normative case studies are tools that aim to match the intensity and complexity of the decisions that educators actually make.

We think that normative case studies are particularly well-suited for deliberating about the challenges of democratic discord in schools. First, reasoning together about politically and ethically charged issues can cause tension to build quickly, to the point that collaboration—especially across lines of difference—seems counterproductive. It is easier and often more constructive to talk about a dilemma that is realistic, but not specifically one that the community is facing at that moment. Deliberation that is one step removed from an actual problem can help diffuse tensions. It can also help people recognize that even those with whom they may disagree about what to do in a particular dilemma are likely motivated by good intentions and recognizable values. Normative case studies can thus be tools that allow educators, policy makers, and parents to practice the deliberative skills they will need to use if and when they are faced with dilemmas in their community and in their own practice.

Second, normative case studies reflect a different approach to ethical theorizing, thinking, and acting. We are both political theorists. It is commonplace in our discipline to approach ethical dilemmas by first identifying a fundamental moral theory and then applying the principles of that theory to the specific dilemma. In our earlier volume, *Dilemmas of Educational Ethics*, we describe how we expressly reject that approach, favoring instead what we named *phronetic inquiry*: an approach that synthesizes theory and practice by combining philosophical insight, social scientific analysis, and practical expertise. Normative case studies are meant to facilitate such an approach; they immerse readers in rich detail and encourage people to think between and across disciplinary boundaries. We continue to maintain that this approach not only leads to answers about specific problems, but also develops people's ability to ask the right sort of questions regarding complex ethical dilemmas. In short, normative case studies are problem focused rather than principle focused.

Further contrasting our approach with that of traditional ethical thinking, sociologist Jal Mehta suggests in *Dilemmas* that the ethical work in which educators engage may be antithetical to that of political theorists. He observes how political theorists generally advance arguments about why one set of moral or political principles is better, all things considered, than another or any other set of principles. Educators, however, "do not have the luxury of prioritizing one such system" of ethical principles. They are engaged—daily—in the sort of problem-focused work we think normative case studies are meant to address. Thus, Mehta notes, educators and school administrators seek to diminish conflict between ethical principles, not incite conflict as arguments about better and best principles fundamentally incurs, and they value "solutions that will make multiple constituencies satisfied, even if not for the same reasons."[9] Not only do normative case studies encourage problem-focused thinking, but they also encourage collaborative, *democratic*, solutions.

In this moment, with our differences and disagreements constantly on display, we believe that prioritizing a multidisciplinary, practice-centered ethical approach is increasingly valuable. This is not to say it will solve all our problems. It would be unreasonable, for example, to believe that simply talking to each other will yield consensus on particularly challenging issues. However, at this point, Americans are finding it harder and hard to even talk to each other, particularly in a civil way. Thus, even if educators cannot always find the sort of wide consensus that a practice-centered ethics typically seeks, they might at the very least start to find common ground in a willingness to deliberate with each other. Agreeing to disagree is not without virtue, especially now. There is a good chance that reaching even this limited point enables people the opportunity to see that those they disagree with have reasons to believe what they believe—and those reasons may not be as terrible as one might initially assume them to be.

Our civic and political norms have been rapidly and repeatedly stressed by changes within our political systems. Schools have been directly implicated by this broader democratic discord. Only by acknowledging the fault lines inherent to educating in and for democracy, by engaging together across our differences, might we begin to revitalize some and reimagine others. Therein lies both the challenge and the promise of democratic education.

THINKING ABOUT DEMOCRATIC DISCORD IN SCHOOLS

At the heart of this book are eight normative case studies exploring the dilemmas of educating amid democratic discord at all levels of education policy and practice; each case is followed by commentaries by an array of interlocutors. While certainly not an exhaustive study of the challenges that emerge from the work of educating in and for democracy, the cases and commentaries we have selected both address some of the most pressing ethical dilemmas of this moment and explore enduring challenges of educating citizens in a democracy. Chapter 2, for example, considers how the fictional Jersey City K–8 can reestablish a positive and inclusive school culture after first graders build a block wall to "keep the Mexicans out," seventh graders are bullied by their peers for their support of Trump, and parents contest teachers' display of pro-diversity posters from the Women's March. Chapter 3 also considers challenging intersections among speech, safety, civil liberties, and peer dynamics as it explores Portland (Oregon) Public Schools' responses when students move their civic and political expression outside in a series of school walkouts.

In chapter 4, the superintendent of fictional Rosefield County School District has to decide not whether to allow students to walk out of school, but whether to allow sheriff's deputies to come *into* his schools. The sheriff's offer of anti-gang training and support in an increasingly violent area appeals to many—but others warn that inviting law enforcement into schools could increase racial profiling and imperil undocumented students by constructing a school-to-deportation pipeline. Chapter 5 explores a very different way in which schools try to protect students: namely, through the use of digital surveillance tools that track student keystrokes, automatically analyze their Google Classroom submissions and social media postings, and send videos of worrisome online search histories (about suicide, say, or school shootings) to administrators to review. The case invites readers to consider students' needs, rights, and responsibilities in the areas of digital citizenship, safety, academic learning, privacy, and civil liberties.

Because historically marginalized students and families frequently find themselves surveilled in and discriminated against in schools in which they are in the minority, a number of charter schools are adopting missions or practices—including dual-language programs, cultural or ethnic affiliations, or other distinctive elements—that are designed to cater to particular groups in *de facto* segregated settings. Chapter 6 delves into a Minnesota charter that serves Somali American families in order to illuminate the promises and challenges that self-segregation may pose to the development of future citizens.

Since self-segregation is neither always possible nor desirable, however, chapter 7 takes us back into a diverse school as the fictional Northern High School's tenth-grade social studies team debates potential topics for their annual debate curriculum. In deciding whether to prompt students to openly debate bathroom rights for transgender students, Northern's social studies teachers must weigh their commitments to professional neutrality, civic education, freedom of conscience, respect for persons, and students' social-emotional well-being. Chapter 8 shifts the lens from students' to *teachers'* capacities to engage with a challenging curriculum, as it details teachers' struggles in a fictional small charter school network as they attempt to scale up a middle school social studies curriculum about race in the United States. While the social studies director never questions the value of the curriculum in theory, she wrestles with whether relatively inexperienced, white educators are doing more harm than good trying to implement the curriculum in practice. Teachers are also at the heart of chapter 9, which considers the legal evolution of teachers' speech rights through a series of actual instances of teachers facing scrutiny for their choices to speak out about political issues, honk their car horns for world peace, or teach creationism in a biology class. The case raises important questions about when, how, and to what extent K–12 teachers should be able to interpret the official curriculum, take stands on democratic values, and challenge local political consensus.

Although these thumbnail descriptions are obviously brief, we hope that readers will see both the breadth of issues, policies, and practices that arise when we consider schools' roles navigating a discordant democracy, and also the common themes that run through many of these cases. We explore many of these themes in the final chapter of this book, where we also discuss how the cases and accompanying commentaries (which we discuss below) may be used in college, graduate, and even middle and high school courses, professional development workshops, and both formal and informal parent and community conversations. As the cases themselves demonstrate, dilemmas of educating both in and for democracy are hardly contained within school walls; they concern all citizens—parents, teachers, students, community members, school leaders, policymakers—and they are challenges we need to collectively and collaboratively come together to address.

CREATING A CULTURE OF COLLABORATIVE ENGAGEMENT

Given the breadth of issues and settings highlighted above, it is perfectly possible to read each case (and chapter) on its own, with no background preparation and without reading the other cases. We expect that many readers will take an exploratory approach to the book, starting with whichever case and set of commentaries seems most intriguing, timely, or relevant to their own practice. Although we have organized the chapters in an intentional way to pick up on themes from the previous chapter while also introducing new concepts and domains of shared civic life, we recognize that few readers are likely to follow our lead in every particular.

What we do strongly urge readers to do, however, is enter these chapters in a spirit of inquiry and openness to challenging conversations. Disagreement about what to do in these cases, what the right course of action is, or what values educators should aim to realize is to be expected. Nonetheless, creating a culture of collaborative, democratic engagement requires making room for many different voices and ideas. It is for this reason that we follow each case with commentaries written by a diverse array of scholars, educators, policymakers, students, and activists. In the pages of this book, readers will encounter the thoughts of moral and political philosophers, historians, anthropologists, sociologists, high school students, political scientists, teachers, a police commissioner, lawyers, philosophers of education, and school administrators, among others. They will hear from commentators who identify as liberals, moderates, conservatives, libertarians, critical theorists, and many other political stances.

We are particularly excited to include comments written by students. In talking with K–12 educators about *Dilemmas of Educational Ethics*, we are inevitably asked, "How can we use these cases with our students?" The examples of student-authored commentaries in this volume are one possible answer. Unsurprisingly, it turns out that students have a lot to say about the issues educators, policymakers, activists, and scholars worry about. Their voices are an important source of insight that adults often overlook—as the commentaries in this book clearly attest. We are thus happy that two groups of student commentators joined the conversations in this book.

Though the cases are all set in the United States for reasons of coherence, we have invited scholars from around the world to comment on each case. After all, the United States is not the only democracy struggling with partisan divisions, civic upheaval, political renegotiations, and disagreement over what it means to educate its citizens and residents. At the very least, the inclusion of perspectives from Singapore, England, South Korea, the Netherlands, Mexico, Ireland, Germany, and Australia can help those of us in the United States situate the challenges facing our own educators and schools within a global perspective. Given our interlocutors' engagement with these cases, we also hope that other readers outside the United States will find these cases and commentaries useful provocations to reflect on their own opportunities and obstacles in educating for democracy in unsettled times. More ambitiously, we hope that this book will become part of—even help enable—a global conversation about how schools and school systems can educate in and for democracy in a time of upheaval.

Finally, we hope that the range of ideas, values, and potential resolutions contained in these cases and comments will prompt an expansive conversation about the dilemmas of educating citizens and residents in a democracy. Readers will notice some overlap among the commentaries on any particular case, but they will also find points of sharp disagreement—even among those commentators who ostensibly agree that recognizing a certain value is critically important to resolving a particular dilemma. We believe that the sum of each of these parts is greater than the whole, that the different viewpoints expressed by the commentators surrounding each case challenge us all to re-engage with these difficult, poignant, and enduring dilemmas. We thus hope that these cases and comments provide a foundation for groups of educators, policymakers, parents, and students to reason together. We also hope that, like our first book, this work continues to push scholars to engage in a practice-centered, multidisciplinary ethics.

CHAPTER 2

Walling Off or Welcoming In?

The Challenge of Creating Inclusive Spaces in Diverse Contexts

SARA CALLEJA, TONI KOKENIS, AND MEIRA LEVINSON

It was the monthly meeting of Jersey City K–8's School Culture Committee (SCC). Rob Lewis, the school's social-emotional learning coordinator, had initiated the SCC to address a recent surge in divisive language among students. The teachers, parents, and school principal on the committee were eager to finish drafting guidelines for strengthening and evaluating school culture at JC K–8.

As always, they began by checking in on specific incidents that had divided the school and testing to see if protocols they had developed were effective at ratcheting down the tensions. "How has it been going with Danielle and her friends?" Principal Winters asked. "Are they still ostracizing Danielle because of her family's support for Trump?"

"I've been inspired by their willingness to be honest with each other during our Tuesday lunches," Rob replied, "but it is going to take a lot more time and work for their friendships to be repaired. Danielle's friends—especially but not only her friends of color—just aren't able to reconcile the fact that she says positive things about Trump. Teresa, in particular, still can't forgive Danielle for making that comment about 'criminal illegals' given what she knows about Teresa's cousin. And Danielle is just so hurt that her friends are holding her political views against her. They are all taking these statements very personally."

"It's hard not to take them personally!" Gregory Timms, a seventh-grade father, jumped in. "White students are the minority at this school, but they are treated like they are the unjustly privileged majority. Colin told me at dinner last night that there are kids in his class who won't work with him just because they know our family voted for Trump. He wants to switch schools, but we can't afford to move to a whiter district or send him to a private school."

"Well, we love Colin and hope he won't switch schools!" exclaimed Suzy, Colin's humanities teacher. "I think the problem is that many of Trump's statements are emotionally damaging to many of our students. They lack the coping strategies to depersonalize them."

"Right! How are kids supposed to react when they hear their classmates insinuating that they don't even belong in this country?" added Madison, mother of a first-grade student. "I believe in zero tolerance for bullying. The point of this committee is to make sure that JC K–8 has a culture we can be proud of, where no child is bullied or harassed. But in these instances, I feel like our kids are having to set boundaries because the school isn't doing it for them."

"I agree that our committee needs to set those boundaries more clearly, but I worry about characterizing these disputes automatically as bullying," Principal Winters intervened. "You know that by state law, we are mandated reporters for all incidents of bullying or harassment.[1] I don't think that we should be reporting and punishing Danielle, Teresa, or Colin's classmates; we should be teaching them how to work together and get along. Do we really want to criminalize what should be teachable moments?"

"But we have antibullying laws for a reason, and we can't overlook the harm that treating bullying or harassment as teachable moments could have on kids being bullied, especially those from marginalized groups," Madison responded. "That would do everything but create a safe space for students to learn."

"You faced a version of this teachable moment question in your class last week, didn't you?" Rob prompted Elena Morales, a veteran first grade teacher at JC K–8.

"Yes!" Elena eagerly began her story. "It was choice time, and a small group of boys began building a wall with blocks that spanned the width of the classroom."

"Oh, boy," muttered Suzy.

"Right," continued Elena. "At first, I thought nothing of it, but then they started chanting, 'Build the wall! Build the wall!'"

"No, they did not—" said Madison. Gregory shifted slightly in his chair.

"I could see that some of my students were feeling uncomfortable, and I immediately called a timeout. Normally, I don't interfere with the children's play. They need the freedom to explore, problem-solve, and negotiate differences on their own. But this time, something felt different. I just couldn't sit back and *watch*! I asked them, 'What are you boys working on, hmmm?' They said, 'We're building the wall to keep the Mexicans out!' They were so excited and proud of their work."

"I was so angry I had to pause for a few seconds and just breathe deeply," Elena admitted. "Then I thought maybe I'd just redirect them to a different activity—say, bring out the paints instead? 'Cause after all, they don't know the hate behind what they're saying. But then I felt like, you know what? They're in *my class* now! I'm their teacher. It is *my responsibility* to educate them and help them understand that we should embrace others rather than fear them."

"Right on!" Madison chimed in, and Suzy applauded. Elena continued.

"So, in front of the whole class, I posed the question: 'Why do some people want to keep other people out?' The kids had so many interesting comments. One child said, 'Because sometimes you just want to be alone or with your best friends, and so you have to say no to some people.' Another child said, 'Because you have to stay safe, and you don't know if strangers could be dangerous.' One of the boys building the wall said, 'Because the Mexicans will take our jobs!'

"I turned to that boy and I asked him, 'What is your job?' He looked at me with wide eyes and shrugged his shoulders.

"I quietly said to my class, 'Your job, boys and girls, is to come to school to learn. And while you are at school, your job is to be kind, to be caring, and to be respectful so that everyone has a safe learning space. Do you think anyone can stop you from being kind, caring, and respectful?' And they all said, 'Nooooooooooo!' So I said, 'Then nobody can take your job!'" Elena finished with a low chuckle and shook her head.

After a long moment of silence as people processed Elena's story, Madison spoke. "Thank you, Ms. Morales. You are teaching our children what really counts in life. To be kind to each other and to think about their actions. You didn't shame the boys, or talk about politics. You just guided them toward their better selves. I think this is the kind of teaching that all families value at JC K–8."

"Yes!" exclaimed Suzy. "You handled that amazingly! I would have gotten much more political, but you didn't even need to talk about the issue to correct the thought process behind the behavior. I can learn a lot from your example."

Rob interjected, "I think it is important to note that first graders have different developmental needs than seventh graders, Suzy. While Elena's response may have been just right for her students, a more nuanced and critical response would be appropriate for older children and young adults. Our policies should attend to the developmental levels of all of our students."

"Don't any of you see what is wrong here?" Gregory's voice was quiet but tense. "Those boys were playacting the policies of the President of the United States, and their public school teacher (a state employee, no less) leveraged her personal, moral, and political reasoning to stop them. That was a partisan move, through and through. The boys were creatively engineering a wall, and they were drawing on their knowledge of current events in the process! That should have been celebrated by the teacher, but instead their entire innovation was discouraged. If you wanted to make it a teachable moment, Ms. Morales, you could have taken the time to explain to them the difference between legal and illegal immigration. That would have been a good lesson!"

"Gregory has a point, everyone," said Principal Winters. "We can't censor student play or creativity just because it happens to disagree with our politics. Elena, I'm glad you checked yourself enough to not get angry with the boys, but perhaps there is a double-check required in an instance like this."

"Whoa," Suzy interjected, "are you saying that Elena should have allowed the boys to role-play being immigration officers at the border wall between the US and Mexico? And that perhaps some children in the class, say the Hispanic students, should have role-played trying to cross the border, and that Elena should have let that all play out?"

The room was quiet.

"I don't think that's exactly what I mean, Suzy, but I do think school needs to be a politics-free zone."

"With all due respect," Rob offered, "how can school be a politics-free zone? What happened in Elena's classroom—and with Danielle last month—shows us that politics will enter the school whether we plan for it or not. That's why we set up this committee, right?"

"Agreed," said Suzy. "The purpose of school is to prepare students to be citizens in a democracy. How can we prepare future citizens if we cannot talk about politics? We need to lean into these conversations, not back away."

"If we're going to 'lean in' to politics, let's have our kids study the First Amendment!" Gregory interjected. "In this country, offensive speech is protected. If you don't like what someone is saying, you have the right to ignore it! You can't censor something just because it doesn't agree with you. That's a freedom we fight for all around the world."

"But these are kids in school," Madison protested. "Adults can walk away from offensive statements, or people, but our children can't go anywhere. You said yourself that Colin wanted to switch schools but can't. I volunteered for this committee for a similar reason; I want Marquis to have a more positive experience here than I did as a student, when I had to endure all sorts of racist nonsense."

"We appreciate your commitment, Madison," Principal Winters affirmed, "and yours, too, Gregory. Madison is right, we have to be mindful of our state and federal bullying laws. We can't ignore statements and incidents that create a hostile learning environment and inhibit students' learning, especially since attendance is mandatory."

"Exactly," Elena interjected. "Free speech doesn't mean that schools shouldn't teach children how to be kind to one another! Maybe it's my 'liberal bias,' but I'm not going to stop teaching inclusion and social-emotional skills just because our national political discourse has lowered the bar below civility."

"I'm all for teaching kindness. Just don't confuse kindness with political ideology. Democrats don't have a monopoly on good character," Gregory responded. "Not to mention that your 'inclusiveness' seems to stop where conservative perspectives begin. Colin sees it in your classroom every day, Suzy."

Suzy stared at Gregory in bafflement.

"Those Shepard Fairey posters?"[2] Gregory continued. "The ones showing everyone *except* a white male as part of 'We the People?' They're obviously anti-Trump with those messages about how we 'are greater than fear' and have to 'protect each other.' Let me tell you, Colin notices that his views and people that hold them aren't welcome in your classroom."[3]

"Mr. Timms," started Suzy, "I hardly think that posters featuring women of color saying things like 'We the People protect each other' and 'We the People defend dignity' are inappropriate. They're simply inclusive. The posters are meant to show all students that I value them as people, and that we'll work together to create an inclusive classroom in which everyone's needs and rights are respected."

"Okay," Gregory responded, "so if you want to show students that you welcome and respect the rights of all people, would you be equally happy to put up a poster of a white man standing up for the second amendment?"

"Um," Suzy faltered.

Outside, the streetlights illuminated a steady snowfall against a twilight sky.

"So how do we think we can resolve these tensions?" Rob broke in, hoping to wrap up the meeting in time to get home and put his children to bed. "Are there any nonnegotiables that we can agree on as recommendations to the Jersey City K–8 community? We're almost out of time for today."

"We should support free speech and thought for *all* students," said Gregory.

"We need to ensure a safe environment where everyone is loved and cared for," said Suzy.

"We also need to stay politically neutral—or at least cultivate respect for different perspectives," added Principal Winters.

"And call out bullying when we see it," Madison added.

"How can we do all of that at once?" asked Elena. "How can we ensure that everyone feels safe, that no one is singled out, while also honoring contradictory perspectives—some of which actually serve to further marginalize people or intentionally leave them out? We can't start normalizing perspectives that fundamentally attack others' identities and beliefs, and still stand up against bullying."

"So do we have any policy takeaways?" Principal Winters asked in perplexity. "We can't keep going around in circles!"

What values, principles, and practices should the School Culture Committee prioritize in their recommendations for Jersey City K–8 faculty and staff? What boundaries should the school set on student speech, if any, in order to foster social-emotional learning, civil discourse, and friendship among students? How might they hold themselves and their students accountable for upholding school values, even when the intention of those values is contested in the broader political landscape?

Don't Avoid Politics: Develop a Civic Mindset

MAUREEN COSTELLO

The problem in Jersey City's K–8 is the problem of living in a diverse democracy: How do we maintain a culture of mutual respect while deeply disagreeing?

Our current political situation has exacerbated the school's problem, but it didn't create it. The problem arises straight out of democracy itself, and solving it should be at the core of a school's mission. Sadly, educational leaders have lost sight of preparing students for self-government and get caught in a thicket of side issues. These include concerns about bullying, about keeping politics out of school, about student safety, and even about the way in which democratic principles, like free speech, apply in schools.

Although all important topics in their own right, they distract us from the real problem. But let's be clear: Schools don't follow the same rules that apply to the public square. Schools must be safe places for all students, and not simply because safety is a nonnegotiable condition for learning. Bullying and harassment make schools unsafe and, in virtually all states, schools have significant legal obligations to prevent and respond to bullying. Teachers, as employees and agents of the state, have no free speech rights while standing in front of a class. Students enjoy greater First Amendment rights than teachers, but even these can be limited if they disrupt the educational mission of the school.

For many people—and in much of our public policy for the last two decades—the educational mission of schools is to teach basic skills like reading, writing, and math, and advanced subjects that will prepare children for college and career. This narrow vision is what allows some us to say that politics don't belong at school.

But politics—in the broadest sense—do belong at school. The essential and oldest mission of schools is to educate for democracy. This case invites us to think about what that really means.

EDUCATING FOR DEMOCRACY

I start with a few thoughts about what it doesn't mean. It doesn't mean that first graders should be given free rein to playact political policies they don't understand. Although direct instruction is a part of democratic pedagogy, it's a small part only. No, Elena shouldn't have launched into an explanation of illegal and legal immigration nor planned a lesson on the First Amendment, as Gregory demanded. But neither should she have redirected—and avoided—the issue she glimpsed in her classroom, which is that some children seemed uncomfortable because of the chant.

Learning to live in a diverse democracy means learning how to make decisions in an informed and thoughtful way. Decisions require knowledge, not just the "facts," but also knowledge of how other people see the issue and how they will be affected. They require deliberation and discussion. That's behind Otto von Bismarck's comment that "politics is the art of the possible." Few public issues are matters of right and wrong; they are complicated arguments about decisions that will have disparate impacts on people.

The boys' decision to chant "build the wall," was an opportunity to talk about the impact of speech on others and to hear some other points of view. Free speech doesn't mean, as Gregory would have everyone believe, speech without consequence. Words can be wrong, they can hurt, they can trigger reactions. Kids need to know that.

Democracy is about choices, and rarely are we offered perfect choices between an evil and a good option. Although many social studies classes put debate at the center of political discourse, that's a mistake; it emphasizes winning and being right at the expense of coming to good decisions for everyone. Good political discourse demands empathy, the ability to listen, and a questioning mind.

Children learn about democracy by living it in schools, the one place they're most likely to encounter ideas and interests that conflict with their own. Yet we all know that classrooms aren't democracies. Teachers have mandated curriculum to cover; more importantly, they have power. Good teachers need to be aware of their power, help children become good decision-makers, and deploy their skills to develop a civic mindset.

DEVELOPING A CIVIC MINDSET

Part of a civic mindset means talking about the big ideas that people living in democracies grapple with all the time, like how to balance individual rights against the common good. Even very young children, for instance, can engage in deep and interesting conversations about when it's okay to vote on something and let the majority rule and when it's not because it's taking away someone's rights or endangering them. Any child that loves peanut butter knows all about this when they learn about the classmate with severe allergies.

Elena confronted two impulses as she tried to paper over the episode in her classroom. First, the boys' behavior angered her personally. Second, she wanted to protect the children who were visibly anxious because of the chant. With a civic mindset, she would have also thought about how to use the moment to help her kiddos become empathetic listeners and make informed choices. The boys might still have decided their wall was to keep Mexicans out, but they'd at least think about the fact that they didn't have good reasons for their belief, and they might know that was hurtful to classmates. Maybe they would have decided to add a door.

Her decision to pause and think deeply was a good one. But I'm not sure Elena took enough time, because instead of facilitating a conversation she ended it by redirection when she heard something she didn't like.

As teachers, we're told over and over again not to inject our politics into the classroom. It's a lot like the injunction against religion, though: We should teach about politics, but not preach about them. For Elena this would have meant inserting herself into the discussion and modeling empathy. She could have simply said to the boys, "I feel sad when I hear that, because I know how it hurts my Mexican friends." That might have led to a discussion of who in the community is Mexican, and how generalizations can lead to stereotypes.

I'm sure Elena was also mindful of the feelings of her students from immigrant families. She rightfully didn't call on them to speak. Targets of hateful rhetoric shouldn't be compelled to carry the weight of presenting their point of view. But it is important that their perspective and humanity be present. That's where ally-ship comes in; Elena should be nurturing a classroom where friends and classmates can speak in support of those who are being bullied, harassed, or targeted.

With a civic mindset, Elena would have felt more confident leaning in. She would have already given thought to how to facilitate these tough conversations and keep them student centered, so that kids can practice democratic thinking and arrive at their own conclusions. To build empathy into the discussion, she might have invited other students—not those who looked distressed—to imagine what it might feel like if you were the one being excluded. And at the comment about Mexicans, she might have asked why they thought that and what evidence they had.

That would perhaps have been a riskier conversation, but it would have been real, and it would have given other children a chance to talk about what political conversations they were hearing. Elena would have a chance to talk about how people have different opinions and that it's important to hear all of them. She might also start teaching the unpleasant truth that expressing opinions means being accountable for them. That's a lesson both for people who say mean things and for those who speak truth to power.

CIVICALLY MINDED CLASSROOMS

Of course, a mind-set isn't just a matter of adopting a new attitude. For teachers like Elena to be successful, they need to be experts at democracy and clear about how to use their own power in the classroom. We expect teachers to master pedagogy and content; I think we need to require them to be experts at democratic ideas, dialogue, and decision-making as well.

Building classroom culture with a civic mind-set starts on day one. Ask students to help develop classroom rules or norms; plan learning experiences that require students to engage with divergent perspectives; model the listening and thinking behaviors you expect students to adopt; create lots of opportunities for interaction and participation. And teach students to make informed choices, which means learning when to take charge and when and how to release responsibility to kids.

Teachers need skills and a mind-set, and schools need supportive leadership. Jersey City is on the right track with its School Culture Committee that includes parents, teachers, and the principal. Research shows that leadership makes a difference: Where school leaders put the kibosh on discussions of politics and leave teachers to their own devices, divisiveness and polarization often fester. In those schools where leaders express support for all students, affirm the value of civil discourse and understanding across lines of difference, and give teachers guidance and support, outcomes are much more likely to be better.[4]

We cannot and should not aim to declare schools politics-free zones. If schools can't teach about political thinking and engage on political issues, kids will learn their skills from memes, social media echo chambers, and unreliable news sources. If we avoid politics, we fail completely at the central mission of education, which is to nurture the skills we need to argue better, compromise, and work together to solve problems.

Maureen Costello is the director of Teaching Tolerance, a project of the Southern Poverty Law Center. She has been an educator—in the classroom and at the helm of national educational projects—for nearly forty years.

The Distinction Between Difference and Divisiveness

Andy Smarick

There are two different civic educational goals in play for the parents and educators in this case study—both important for teaching students how to have healthy discussion about public issues in a pluralistic society. The first is understanding how and why our governing system prioritizes free expression of differing views. The second is making sure young people possess the skills needed to participate fruitfully in such a system.

These two matters are distinct, and adults involved in teaching need to keep that in mind. Unfortunately, the characters here mostly fail to separate them. As a result, they are ill equipped to teach their students the virtues of difference and the vices of divisiveness.

IDEAS AT ODDS

Adults need to teach children that the collision of ideas isn't just inevitable; it's also necessary for progress. This is obvious in the sciences. Galileo, Kepler, Newton, Einstein, Darwin, and many others made arguments that ran against the grain. Thank goodness they did. The Enlightenment didn't teach us to never disagree; it instilled in us curiosity and offered processes for resolving conflicting positions.

The same is true, maybe even more so, when it comes to issues of public policy. There will never be unanimity of opinion on most issues. Our varying cultures, histories, religious traditions, experiences, and political philosophies—the very things undergirding our nation's great diversity—give us different guiding principles and cause us to prioritize values differently. This is actually an asset when it comes to litigating and adjudicating issues. Since most policy questions don't have a single "right" answer (What's the correct tax rate on investment income? How much should be spent on roads vis-à-vis public transit?), we enter our different opinions into the political process, debate them, and ultimately reach a compromise.

There are numerous reasons we assiduously protect individuals' right to possess different views and then to hash them out publicly. Great decisions often result from the "wisdom of crowds"—wildly divergent ideas are thrown together, and a robust conclusion emerges on the other side. Any one of us can be mistaken in our facts or reasoning; a confrontational process helps fix our errors and strengthen our arguments. Educators have a responsibility to teach students that these benefits can only come about when we're allowed to disagree.

But educators also need to explain the enormous costs associated with *not* allowing differing opinions to be expressed. Disengagement, frustration, and then fury are the consequences of prohibiting people from taking contrarian positions. If silenced, they internalize that their views don't matter and that they have no agency in their own lives or in our collective work. People are angriest when they feel powerless. Indeed, Dr. Martin Luther King Jr. famously said, "A riot is the language of the unheard."

Those in power can also contribute to the suppression of free exchange. Authorities are typically most comfortable with the status quo and will always try to stop dissenters from making waves, even when it is with the intention to prioritize peace and order. This is why Frederick Douglass famously wrote, "Power concedes nothing without a demand." Dr. King's celebrated "Letter from Birmingham Jail" was, importantly, a response to a "call for unity" from white local leaders who thought the Civil Rights protests in their city were "unwise and untimely." The case study explains that the committee had prioritized "ratcheting down the tensions." But sometimes, an unpopular position can be the most important one; indeed, Dr. King's letter lauded the change-inducing force of "creative tension."

For all of these reasons, students must be taught that tamping down political difference comes at a steep price. Even if it is done with the best of intentions, for example (using Suzy's language) to create "a safe environment where everyone is loved and cared for," much is lost. If anyone can invoke the protection of their sensibilities—"You can't say that because I find it offensive"—to counter an unwelcome argument, then conversation grinds to a halt. A pro-life student will silence a pro-choice student and vice versa. A student who wants more free trade will stifle the views of a classmate who wants less and vice versa.

If adults are able to pick and choose which positions are impermissible, then we allow their political preferences to shape what's discussed. Perhaps Gregory would be willing to stop students from speaking badly of President Trump. Elena seems willing to stop students from supporting immigration controls or gun rights. Limiting discourse often means privileging certain political preferences.

The uncomfortable but necessary approach related to the content of such discussions is to recognize that the vast, vast majority of political views are in bounds and that, when dealing with the substance of those views, educators should aim primarily to help their students become more informed. Obviously, free speech has limits, so some views are clearly out-of-bounds, such as advocating violence. Schools should be firm about those lines. And the information gathering guided by educators should be developmentally appropriate; a first grader expressing a view on immigration shouldn't be assigned readings about territorial sovereignty under the Peace of Westphalia. But perhaps an eleventh grader should.

The point here is that students are future citizens of our diverse nation. History teaches that the free exchange of ideas—including of controversial views—enables us to improve as individuals, produce smart collective decisions, preserve the character of our different communities, maintain a sense of personal efficacy, uproot injustice, and more. Downplaying difference can undermine these important outcomes.

HOW TO ENGAGE IN THE SYSTEM

But educators also have to teach students how to behave in our governing system—and here we can draw a distinction between difference and divisiveness. We can't be shy about passing on democratic norms and teaching the responsibilities of citizenship. Of course, this includes voting, volunteering, and being informed on matters of public importance. But it also includes using moderate language, treating political opponents with respect, and remaining mindful of our own fallibility—Elena alludes to this when stressing the importance of the bar of civility. In practice, this requires adults to separate political positions from how they are expressed and model this for children.

A student must not be told she cannot believe in limits on immigration. But she should be taught that racial epithets aimed at immigrants are wrong. A student must not be told he cannot believe in the Second Amendment. But he should be taught to be sensitive to the views of victims of gun violence. Students cannot be told that Trump or Clinton was the right vote. But they should be taught that calling your opponent's supporters "deplorables" is wrong, as is giving insulting nicknames to those running against you.

The opening anecdote from the case study offers educators an opportunity to explore two aspects of the behavior-related components of civic responsibility. Danielle and her friends are at odds over her family's Trump vote. But our nation can't survive if we turn those who voted differently than we did into permanent, mortal enemies. So students need to be taught the right ways and wrong ways to support a candidate, to talk about your candidate's opponent, and to discuss the major issues of the day. Danielle's family's support of Trump wasn't inherently wrong; her use of "criminal illegals" was.

But students also need to be taught that political tolerance demands our recognition that people of goodwill can reach different conclusions and that "they" could be right and "we" could be wrong. Danielle's friends weren't inherently wrong to oppose Trump's election; ostracizing a friend whose family voted for him was.

Along these lines, Rob's celebration of the students' "willingness to be honest" is inapt. Danielle's cruel language and her friends' retribution might both be "honest," and the feelings beneath them might even be deep-seated. But civic responsibility in a pluralistic democracy demands more than honesty. On that score, Danielle and her erstwhile friends came up short.

WHAT NOW?

By distinguishing political difference from bullying, Principal Winters offers the best way for a school community to simultaneously teach students about our governing system and how to behave in it. In simplest terms, kids need to learn how to disagree without being disagreeable.

Winters' argument that "we should be teaching them how to work together and get along" should not be read as "they must all agree" or "they mustn't express their differences of opinion." Working together and getting along doesn't require homogenizing or silencing. Civic virtue and political tolerance enable us to get to *unum* while preserving our *pluribus*.

Gregory is right that free speech and thought are essential. But students need to be taught why chanting, "Build the wall!" among a diverse group of classmates is a problem. Suzy is right to worry about "emotionally damaging" language. But we should not deem every political statement at odds with our personal views to be an affront.

In sum, respect for difference is the key: Showing consideration for others by moderating our behavior while accepting, even appreciating, views that diverge from our own.

Andy Smarick is the director of civil society, education, and work at the R Street Institute. He's a former president of the Maryland State Board of Education, deputy commissioner of the New Jersey Department of Education, aide at the White House and in the US Congress, and cofounder of a charter school.

Courage and Wisdom in Handling Political Speech

YUN-KYOUNG PARK

The dilemma that Jersey City K–8 School faces is quite familiar to me. It reminds me of my experience as a high school teacher and as a teacher educator in South Korea. There I learned firsthand that, whether we like it or not, the classroom is a place where students express different political perspectives and conflicts between those views often and inevitably arise. This is especially true in modern, pluralistic democracies. I believe that rather than avoid those conflicts, educators and schools ought to help students develop the willingness and ability to communicate with their peers who hold different political viewpoints than their own. Facilitating such growth is necessary for schools to be able to fulfill their democratic purpose.

THE COURAGE TO TEACH WITHOUT AVOIDING CONFLICT

Educational theorists often talk of schools as microcosms of society where students learn about democracy. Educators are vital components of this picture. They should encourage students to take an interest in political and social issues, teaching them that different people can have different points of view on these issues. They also should teach students that a democratic society is a place where dialogue and negotiation are both necessary and possible between members with differing political perspectives. In so doing, educators help students understand that democracy is a journey in which members of a society put their heads together to solve the problems at hand, despite their differences.

However, out of concern that broader political tensions may infiltrate their classrooms, some educators want their classrooms to be spaces completely free of any political issue. Unfortunately, such an approach may do more harm than good. Rather, they should be more proactive in trying to provide their students with opportunities for political dialogue. In fact, while many of the students who participated in a three-year research study I conducted on citizenship formation wanted to discuss or talk about current social or political issues, they also complained that they had few opportunities to do so.

Therefore, the good news is that JC K–8 is already on track when the School Culture Committee focuses on *how* they deal with political and social issues in school, rather than *whether* they should deal with politics in school. As the committee members in the case suggest, their goal is to identify the principles that guide how they handle political speech and its associated challenges. And they clearly recognize that their school cannot be a "safe place" for students that simply prohibits the open discussion of political issues in the classroom. But the consequences are very real. While responsible adults hesitate and struggle to come to a consensus, students—like Danielle and Teresa—experience real conflict with one another without filtering their behaviors or words they have acquired from their everyday lives.

Further, JC K–8 provides another important lesson for educators, even as they struggle. Schools and teachers should never remain passive and wait for teachable moments to appear by chance. Rather, they need to be more proactive in educating their pupils about the political issues in the real world. In other words, when members of the School Culture Committee at JC K–8 claim that school should be a "safe place for all students," we have to focus on the true objective of such a claim. As part of a democratic education, a safe place must function as an environment where students freely explore their own political perspectives. Educators should use their authority to protect this important civic development. If they do not, the idea that schools are safe places for civic development is nothing more than overprotective rhetoric, enabling educators to avoid their educational responsibilities.

THE WISDOM TO ENSURE A SAFE POLITICAL DIALOGUE

What should we do to make school a safe place where political dialogue is allowed? To begin with, educators should enable students to express their opinions to others with different points of view. For this to happen, there must be a minimum level of trust among students that rests on the certainty that no one will have to suffer just because they hold different political perspectives. In other words, the School Culture Committee should agree on the rule that anyone can freely express their political opinions without having to suffer any disadvantage for doing so.

The students at JC K–8 are still relatively naive in terms of political perspective. Their perspectives will change and gradually mature through experience and education. To help their political growth, we should expose them to many experiences of exchanging different opinions with others. In many cases, however, a student may be considered partisan or seen in an uncomfortable light by others for the simple offense of expressing a premature perspective that is still developing. If educators allow the calcification of politics writ large into their classrooms, students' efforts to continue interacting with different others cannot likely endure. Therefore teachers, who have an influential position in the classroom, should never play the role of judge on any politically controversial issue and never allow personal bias to interfere with evaluating the individual opinions of their students. Rather, they should serve as advisers who help students develop their naive or immature political perspectives into mature perspectives through educationally reflective processes.

But another question still remains: Should we allow students to say anything in a political dialogue? Part of what the JC K–8 committee is wrestling with is the fact that broader civic and political norms are currently in flux. But educators can—and should—approach this challenge without having to simply accept that whatever happens outside schools should determine what happens inside schools. While schools are political spaces, they are also educative spaces.

To begin with, dialogue is a form of free communication between people with equal rights. The most important prerequisite for a political dialogue is that we should never allow any form of violence that undermines the existence or identity of any participant in the dialogue. In addition, while we should allow everyone to support or oppose a particular policy, we should never tolerate any form of humiliation or insult to be directed at any individuals who may be affected by the issue under discussion. For example, while students should be free to support or oppose the objectives, content, and methodology of a particular immigration or welfare policy, an educator should not tolerate hatred directed at immigrants or marginalized people. When a student mixes up policy and people, or mistakes inhumane speech that undermines human dignity for a political opinion, educators should intervene with the aim of redirecting the student's thoughts, speech, and behavior back toward the policy or system.

When school does not fulfill its role as a place to educate mature citizens of a democratic society, it goes against not only its educational purpose but, as I have learned from my experience, it also goes against what students actually want. Students want to learn more about the emerging issues of their society, and they are ready to learn more to see if their thoughts withstand scrutiny or not. It is high time that responsible adults muster up more courage to help students navigate these difficult conversations. To overcome hardships in the future, we must help young developing democratic citizens gain more experience with reflection.

To this end, school must teach students that democracy is a political promise between many different others. The promise is based on the premise that a society's members trust each other enough to believe that everyone wants to find solutions for the challenges facing their society, even when we deeply disagree about what those solutions should be. But we do not live as members of the same community because we hold the same views or thoughts. Rather, we must exchange our opinions and develop them together because we live in the same society. This last point is the basic prerequisite of democracy, and as institutions tasked with training future citizens, every school needs to help students understand this fundamental requirement. Educators, then, may need to reinvent themselves to serve as wise and courageous guides for their students.

Yun-Kyoung Park is professor of social studies education at the Cheongju National University of Education in South Korea. She is the coauthor of Understanding and Practice of Multicultural Education *(Seoul: Jeongminsa, 2018) and the award-winning book* Civic Education in Korea *(Seoul: Dongmunsa, 2010), and now focuses on understanding the citizenship formation of adolescents and teacher professional development.*

Handling Matters of Friendship

Myisha Cherry

Three incidents pose a challenge for the Jersey City School Culture Committee. First, the divisive political climate permeating the broader society has seeped into the school. Second, students at the school are acting out controversial policies, holding and expressing political views, and excluding other students based on these views. The committee is unsure whether to characterize these behaviors as bullying or harassment, given their political dimensions. Third, the committee is also challenged with how to appropriately respond as an educational institution. Do they use the incidents as teachable moments or report them? If they are teachable moments, what should be the content and method of the lessons? The committee's challenge is complicated by the fact that students' developmental stages are wide ranging. It seems that no single solution will fit all.

However, there is yet another challenge. While the incidents at Jersey City have educational aspects (such as whether to allow kids to build a wall in class), they are also interpersonal in nature (for example, helping kids to repair a friendship). Solutions for the educational aspects may not translate to the interpersonal ones. Because teachers are often more equipped to handle the former, I will focus on the interpersonal dimensions of these incidents and examine how and to what extent teachers can help.

THE FORGIVENESS ANGLE

Recall that Danielle and Teresa's friendship is under threat. Danielle's family is not only Trump supporters, but Danielle has expressed positive things about Trump to her friends: friends who are also targets of Trump's political rhetoric. Danielle's friends respond to her comments about "criminal illegals" not just as political expression, but as a violation of the norms of friendship. Danielle knows about the immigrant status of Teresa's cousin. She also knows that Teresa cares about her cousin. Danielle, as a friend, should care enough about Teresa to be mindful of what and who Teresa values, *and* she should respond with care given her knowledge of her friend.

We do not know who introduces forgiveness, but the teachers' dialogue indicates that it is the preferable solution. From what Rob describes, the fact that the incident remains unresolved turns on a lack of forgiveness. He even suggests that the problem between Danielle and Teresa is unresolvable unless Teresa forgives Danielle for her comment. However, this view is anchored in the assumption that there is only one type of forgiveness available—*unconditional* forgiveness. Unconditional forgiveness does not require repentance or atonement on behalf of the offender. This view holds that forgiveness is a gift that Teresa gives to Danielle. No other conditions need to be met.

Although unconditional forgiveness is not impossible, this *gifted* forgiveness may not promote the aims the parties want to address. Because they continue to engage in weekly meetings, we are led to think that Teresa, Danielle, and the other students want to continue in their friendship. Repair is the goal. Unfortunately, these meetings have not led to any progress. It is likely that they have been unsuccessful because they are relying on the wrong kind of forgiveness to achieve their goal. Promoting unconditional forgiveness may be counterproductive at worst and unsuccessful at best to the aim of repair.

Why? If Teresa unconditionally forgives Danielle it is not clear how this will repair important elements of the girls' friendship. Danielle and Teresa will still disagree on the nature of the wrongdoing. Danielle may continue to hurt Teresa or others with expressions of her political beliefs. Teresa may not be able to trust Danielle with knowledge of her family and beliefs, thus limiting the depth of their relationship.

In order to repair the friendship, the teachers need to rethink what forgiveness requires. In other words, they should aim for *conditional* forgiveness. That is, if Teresa is to forgive Danielle, it may require that Danielle acknowledge wrongdoing on her part and make a commitment to not do it again. Teresa's change of heart is important, but the teachers also have to focus on Danielle's change of action. The committee will have to not only value honesty but also consider what tools they can use to get Danielle to see how she is hurting her friends.

Importantly, this can be separated from the political tensions that complicate the conflict between Teresa and Danielle. Forgiveness need not be a matter of settling what view is right or wrong. Danielle could still feel justified in her political views. Forgiveness does not mean she has to revise them. Forgiveness is rather conditioned on her having begun to understand how her actions have hurt those she cares about, and on her seeking ways to not hurt her friends again—even while maintaining her beliefs.

If this sounds tenable, then it is best to not focus solely on Teresa's inability to forgive Danielle, but also on Danielle's inability to act in ways that could lead to Teresa's forgiveness. The teachers' goal should be to encourage and even facilitate the satisfying of the conditions necessary for forgiveness to proceed.

THE ELECTIVE NATURE OF FRIENDSHIP

Danielle does not understand why her statements are hurtful to her friends. While it is understandable that she is also hurt that they are holding her political views against her, is it morally permissible for them to do so?

If people could hold applicants' political views against them in hiring practices or university admissions, it would be discriminatory and therefore illegal. They would be acting unjustly by failing to provide equal opportunity to all despite their differences. One's political and religious views are most often irrelevant to performing a job or earning a degree. However, interpersonal relationships like friendships are entirely different. Friendships are, at their core, discriminatory. We choose to be friends with some and choose not to be friends with others. And we do this based on reasons like their moral and political views.

Friendship is an elective relationship. I can choose to be friends with Luvell who also adores NBA player LeBron James. I may choose him as my friend for this reason. If he decides to hate LeBron James, I am justified in holding his basketball beliefs against him. And I can refuse to be friends with him as a result. Likewise, Luvell's changing basketball beliefs may influence his desire to continue to be friends with me.

Similarly, political beliefs can be reasons to friend or unfriend someone. Individuals may find it preferable to befriend those with whom they share similar perspectives on economics, immigration, and religion. While it could be argued that the person who is only friends with those who share their political views is choosing to live life in an ideological bubble, it is not morally impermissible to choose and not choose friends based on these preferences.

Danielle is justified in being hurt that her friends are holding her political views against her. She may not want her friendship to change. But the elective nature of friendship suggests that her friends are not morally wrong for doing so. Friendship holds the seeds of its own corruption. We can provide reasons for others to choose us as friends. But morality does not require that we *remain* friends once those reasons are no longer satisfied. There may be a temptation to urge Teresa and others to remain friends with Danielle despite her political views. But perhaps the best outcome that can be reached is a peaceful coexistence rather than friendship.

COEXISTENCE AND OSTRACIZATION

The teachers are rightly worried about Danielle feeling ostracized. But they must also realize that as an alternative to forgiveness, peaceful coexistence will likely involve a degree of ostracization. When an individual is no longer a friend, they are no longer part of another's social world. They are shut out of others' personal lives, excluded from party invites, and perhaps even ignored. This is the dark side of the aftermath of friendship, but it is not unethical. A person who has never been friends with them is also on the receiving end of the same behavior. In other words, the Jersey City teachers may have to accept some degree of ostracization as a consequence of the failure of Teresa and Danielle's friendship.

But there is a darker, morally impermissible side of ostracizing that they should address if it occurs. Teresa could spread rumors about Danielle, taunt her, wish for her downfall, or refuse to respond to her when it is morally called for. It is this behavior that teachers should discourage. But ostracizing is not always the same as bullying or harassment. If Teresa were to ostracize Danielle in a way that denied her access to goods that should be available to her as a student at Jersey City, there is a moral failure. However, friendship is an elective relationship. Mutual respect and cooperation should be part of the school culture. Teachers should encourage these values. They can encourage friendship, and they can encourage forgiveness—but they cannot force or expect them. More importantly, they should not think that friendship and forgiveness are the only possibilities for a peaceful future.

Myisha Cherry is an assistant professor of philosophy at the University of California, Riverside. Her books include The Moral Psychology of Anger, *edited with Owen Flanagan (Rowman and Littlefield, 2018) and* Unmuted: Conversations on Prejudice, Oppression, and Social Justice *(Oxford University Press, 2019).*

Creating Safety While Embracing Discomfort

Thea Renda Abu El-Haj

The educational tensions with which Jersey City's School Culture Committee is wrestling resonate with questions I repeatedly face in my practice as a professor of education. I have come to understand these tensions as inherent in two critical commitments I hold as a teacher: to value and include each individual student, and to create a community in which we critically analyze and act against the structures of oppression that frame our schools and society, including in our classroom space.

These commitments may appear to contradict each other, as an example from my own practice shows. Years ago, I was teaching an undergraduate course in educational foundations. Our topic for the week was creating queer-inclusive schools and classrooms. I can still see Ryan, who identified as white and Catholic, stating that because homosexuality was "against my religion," schools should not address the issue at all. Given my commitment to the equality and dignity of all persons, I felt confident insisting that we were not debating the rights of any group of people to belong in our schools and society. Rather, given that education is a human right for all people, our job was to discuss what substantive inclusion could look like in our schools. Yet even as I felt, and continue to feel, crystal clear about this stance, I asked myself: What about Ryan? Did my pedagogical stance contradict my commitment to value and include every student?

The case study of Jersey City's SCC raises similar apparent contradictions. How can JC K–8 claim to value and include all students when students like Danielle or Colin feel their viewpoints are excluded? On the other hand, how can the school protect the safety of oppressed groups if it takes a neutral stance toward speech and actions that embed oppressive messages? These educational dilemmas entail two presumed contradictions: first, between teaching as a neutral or a political act, and second, between safety and exclusion. In what follows, I unpack these apparent contradictions in relation to the core question at the heart of our educational endeavors: what does it mean to prepare students to be citizens in a democracy?

EDUCATION AND NEUTRALITY

One of the core tensions articulated by the Jersey City SCC is between a view of public education as a "politics-free zone" and one of education as being inherently political. This apparent tension rests, however, on a misunderstanding. Education is never politically neutral. Educational decisions entail values. From what we choose to include in and exclude from the curriculum (What materials are included? Whose perspectives are represented?), to how we structure classroom communities (Authoritarian discipline or democratic processes?), to how we organize our schools (Tracked or diverse classes? Inclusion or separation of children with disabilities?), we are making inherently political decisions.

If I entertain Ryan's views on an equal footing, for example, I convey to my students that perspectives that refuse to accord queer people full equality and dignity as persons are of equal value to those that do. That is not a neutral position. It is a position that entertains the possibility that denial of some people's equality and their human rights is acceptable. Similarly, Elena's response to the boys in her class who stated that they were "building a wall to keep the Mexicans out" was not an attempt to shut down a political or policy debate about immigration; rather, she was addressing the particular political climate within which these young children have learned their play. Elena's spontaneous lesson was her attempt to educate her young charges about the dangers of this climate in language that first graders could understand.

Recent political discourse that invokes "Mexicans" or "Muslims" as "criminals," "terrorists," and dangerous outsiders—discourse promoted by the sitting US President—has stoked fear of *entire groups* of people. It has led to a significant increase in harassment and hate crimes directed at individuals who are perceived to belong to these groups. Teaching that does not support students to discern racist and other oppressive speech and images is not neutral; it is at least negligent about, and often complicit with, injustice and oppression. There is no neutral teaching position. As educators who are committed to preparing students to be members of a diverse *and* just democracy, we must therefore be upfront with ourselves and others about the values driving our work.

EDUCATION, SAFETY, AND DISCOMFORT

Another tension articulated by the Jersey City SCC emerges from competing ideas about creating safety in educational settings. At the most basic level, creating safe schools has been codified into NJ's antibullying law that requires schools to act immediately upon verbal or physical harassment and intimidation. Although aimed at stopping the bullying of any child, this legal, zero-tolerance policy was crafted as a much-needed remedy to dangerous physical and emotional aggression directed at individuals because of their group membership (such as race, religion, sexuality, national origin, gender, disability)—aggressions that create hostile climates for learning. As Principal Winters points out, educators need to do more than just stop overt acts of bullying: calling others racial epithets, or grabbing another's breasts or genitals. Rather, creating safe learning communities requires educators to take action well before zero-tolerance antibullying legislation would kick in.

So what constitutes a safe space for learning? And whose safety must be guaranteed? I would argue that a space is safe for learning only when educators and students alike commit themselves to seeing and acknowledging the dignity, equality, and humanity of all persons. This requires educators to create an environment in which no individual's full personhood and right to belong are challenged. I read the recent protests on campuses across the United States to speeches delivered by Charles Murray—a person who has repeatedly argued that white men are "intellectually, psychologically, and morally superior"[5] to people from minoritized communities—as acts of civil disobedience (arguably also modes of speech in their nonviolent forms) that reject political discourse that denies our common and fundamental human equality and dignity. Entertaining views such as Murray's in academic settings provokes ire precisely because these views, by denying the equality and dignity of some members of the learning community, threaten their safety by questioning their right to belong.

The question, in my mind, is not whether institutions must choose between free speech and safety. The question is whether, in the face of speech that expresses, for example, racist ideas, educational institutions take a clear stance on the side of supporting the equality and dignity of all persons. This does not necessarily mean always taking a zero-tolerance approach to offensive speech. However, it does require that individual educators and their institutions critically address, unpack, and stand against those ideas with clarity and fortitude in order to create a safe learning community that stands on the side of justice.

What does this commitment mean for Colin, Danielle, and Teresa in the case of Jersey City's SCC? On the one hand, it means that schools must create spaces that are loving and compassionate toward all of these children and their peers. Educators must find ways to hold up each child's strengths, to model that each individual is valued in and of herself. And, schools must actively teach children how to address conflict and how to talk across differences. These skills are essential, not supplemental, educational imperatives.

However, creating schools and classrooms in which compassion, care, and inclusion for each individual is a paramount value does not mean accepting oppressive opinions and viewpoints. Schools have an extra burden to protect those who are members of groups facing structural oppression, and to teach all children to critically assess speech and ideas that embed racist or other oppressive language and ideology. Teresa's anger and hurt over Danielle's invocation of "criminal illegals" must rightfully be addressed in relation to the broader speech contexts in which this image invokes racially minoritized immigrant groups.

In this respect, creating safe learning environments also entails sometimes creating discomfort. Colin and Danielle must feel they are valued members of their school community while simultaneously being challenged—even being made uncomfortable—when they express racist, sexist, or homophobic perspectives (even if, and perhaps precisely because, these views are held by the current US president). This is not an argument for creating a thought police for safe schools. We must distinguish, however, between discomfort that results from having one's assumptions challenged—which can be a critical component of deep learning, and should hence be experienced by all children, including those who are members of oppressed groups—and discomfort that results from having one's very membership or human worth challenged.

Again, therefore, educators who aim to prepare students to be active members of a diverse democracy should confidently teach students to feel discomfort with ideas and actions that trample on the rights of others to be treated as full human beings with dignity. In so doing, they can also be confident they are creating safe and inclusive schools for all students.

Thea Renda Abu El-Haj is an associate professor of education at Barnard College, Columbia University. Her most recent book is Unsettled Belonging: Educating Palestinian American Youth after 9/11.

Creating a Democratic School in a Diverse Community

JAMES A. BANKS

Jersey City K–8 School is facing numerous challenges in creating a culturally inclusive school that exemplifies and teaches democratic values. There are, however, a number of research-based approaches they can take to strengthen their school culture. First, teachers, parents, and administrators should work together to define and embrace values such as justice and equality that are central to the American Creed. Second, the school can sponsor cocurricular and extracurricular clubs, as well as cooperative learning groups, that help students develop bonds across racial, ethnic, and cultural lines. Third, JC K–8 should review and adopt multicultural curricula that help elementary and middle school students develop more positive cross-racial attitudes and modes of interaction. The challenges are too great for any single intervention to promote a truly inclusive and democratic school culture, but these three approaches taken together can make significant inroads into achieving a school that lives up to the best of American civic values.

VALUE EDUCATION

One of the central missions of the public school is to socialize the nation's youth so that they will internalize and enact the idealized values of the nation-state. In order to do so, schools must identify and deliberately endorse a set of values that will guide their policies, practices, and decisions. Jersey City K–8 faces a major problem because its teachers, parents, and administration have failed both to embrace a common set of democratic values and to confront the inherent ambiguities and even contradictions among these values. For example, Principal Winters and parent Gregory Timms seem not to understand that freedom of speech must be limited and balanced with concerns for civility, equality, recognition, and the safety of all students. Furthermore, they should recognize that special attention should be given to groups that have been historically victimized and marginalized. The freedom of speech of the students who built the wall must be considered within the context of providing civic equality for the Mexican American students in the school who might be emotionally harmed by the symbolic meaning of the wall. Research and wisdom of practice indicate that hate speech and expressions, if not negatively sanctioned within schools and the larger society, can escalate to discrimination, violence, and in extreme cases to genocide.[6]

The teachers in JC K–8 should therefore implement value education lessons and activities that will help their students to develop a set of clarified values that are consistent with American creed values that can guide purposeful and reflective citizen action. Teaching students a method or process for deriving their values within a democratic classroom atmosphere can best attain this goal. Students should also learn how the consequences of their values and related actions would affect other racial, ethnic, and cultural groups and individuals who have different political affiliations. It is important for all of the participants in JC K–8, including the principal, the teachers, the parents, and the students, to understand that their value choices and decisions must be defended within the context of American creed values such as human dignity, justice, democracy, and equality.

IMPROVING INTERGROUP RELATIONS

The incidents described in this case study indicate that there is a high degree of ethnic, racial, and political polarization within JC K–8. Serious action needs to be taken to create more harmonious ethnic and race relations among the students, teachers, and parents. One simple yet effective approach is for the school to create *superordinate groups*, that is, groups with which students from all racial and ethnic groups can identify and in which they can all participate. Sports teams, the marching band, Spanish Club, and Campfire are examples of crosscutting or superordinate groups. Research and theory indicate that when students from diverse cultural, racial, and language groups share a superordinate identity—whether as musician, debater, or athlete—cultural boundaries weaken and cross-group friendships blossom.[7] JC K–8 should thus turn its attention to creating rich co- and extracurricular opportunities for all students in the school.

The teachers in JC K–8 can also implement interracial cooperative learning groups, which have been shown to have significant positive impacts on students' racial attitudes, friendship choices, and academic achievement.[8] Gordon Allport's contact theory posits that intergroup relations improve when individuals from different backgrounds: (1) are in cooperative rather than competitive relationship with one another; (2) experience equal status; (3) have shared goals; and (4) experience their contact as sanctioned by authorities such as the principal, teachers, or parents.[9] When implemented well, interracial cooperative learning groups in class can achieve all four of these criteria. They must be deliberatively structured by teachers to do so, since otherwise students from both privileged and marginalized groups are likely to reinforce the status of the higher-status group.[10] But when structured appropriately, research shows that they facilitate friendships among students of color and White students, enhance the academic achievement of students of color, increase student motivation and self-esteem, and help students to develop empathy.[11]

CREATING AND IMPLEMENTING A MULTICULTURAL CURRICULUM

Constructing and implementing a multicultural curriculum could also help to decrease the tight ethnic and racial borders within JC K–8 and to improve intergroup relations within the school. Since the 1940s, a number of curriculum intervention studies have been conducted to determine the effects of teaching units and lessons, multicultural textbooks and materials, role-playing, and other kinds of simulated experiences on the racial attitudes and perceptions of students.[12] This research indicates that the use of multicultural textbooks, simulations, multicultural media, and cooperative teaching strategies that enable students from different racial and ethnic groups to interact positively can help students develop more positive racial attitudes. These kinds of materials and teaching strategies can also result in students choosing more friends from outside racial, ethnic, and cultural groups. Curriculum interventions such as plays, folk dances, music, and role-playing can also have positive effects on the racial attitudes of students in elementary schools.[13]

A major goal of the transformative multicultural curriculum is to help students understand how knowledge is constructed, how school knowledge usually reflects the perspectives of the mainstream and dominant groups within society, and how the experiences of minority groups are often marginalized within textbooks, within the school curriculum, and within society writ large. I have developed a typology of approaches to transformative multicultural curriculum reform that helps teachers think about ways to enable students to view concepts and events from the perspectives of both mainstream and minority groups, and to take action to reduce prejudice and discrimination within their schools and society.[14]

The contributions approach often found in schools focuses on heroes, holidays, and discrete cultural elements. The additive approach incorporates concepts, themes, and perspectives related to diversity into the curriculum, but does not change its basic structure. In the transformative approach, however, the structure of the curriculum is changed to enable students to view concepts, issues, events, and themes from the perspectives of diverse racial, ethnic, and cultural groups. There is also a social action approach, which allows students to make decisions on important social issues and take action to help solve them. The transformative multicultural curriculum—which exemplifies both the transformative and the social action approaches—teaches students to know, to care, and to act to increase social justice within their schools and communities.[15]

In most elementary schools, events and concepts such as the discovery of America, the westward movement, and the struggles of the pioneers are taught primarily from the perspective of European Americans. The transformative multicultural curriculum helps students to understand how these concepts have very different meanings for European Americans, Indigenous American groups, and for the African Americans who came to America in chains. This curriculum also teaches students how to construct their own versions of events such as the westward movement after they have examined them from multiple ethnic and cultural perspectives. By engaging in transformative multicultural education, JC K–8 can help students and their families understand and appreciate others' perspectives about both historical and contemporary events, which may also reduce racial prejudice and discrimination.

CONCLUSION

The surge in divisive language among the students at JC K–8 is symptomatic of larger structural problems related to race, culture, and political affiliation within the school and the community. These problems will not be solved by tinkering with isolated variables within the school, such as focusing on divisive language or the building of a wall by first-grade students. A comprehensive plan designed to change the structural variables within the school is required to improve the school's racial climate. I have identified some of the variables within the school environment that require change, including developing a focus on value education that will enable the various actors within the school community to make decisions consistent with American Creed values, and creating superordinate groups to break down racial borders and facilitate cross-racial and cross-ethnic relationships. Creating and implementing a multicultural curriculum and implementing cooperative learning strategies that will foster positive interracial contact will also facilitate positive structural changes within JC K–8.

James A. Banks holds the Kerry and Linda Killinger Endowed Chair in Diversity Studies and is the founding director of the Center for Multicultural Education at the University of Washington, Seattle. He is a past president of both the National Council for the Social Studies and the American Educational Research Association, an AERA Fellow, and a member of the National Academy of Education. The author or editor of more than twenty books on multicultural education, diversity, and citizenship education in a global context, he most recently published Citizenship Education and Global Migration: Implications for Theory, Research, and Teaching *and* An Introduction to Multicultural Education, Sixth Edition.

CHAPTER 3

School Walkouts and Civil Disobedience

NICOLÁS RIVEROS, NICK FERNALD, AND JACOB FAY

On the morning of November 14, 2016, over 400 students from at least ten middle and high schools in Portland, Oregon, walked out of their schools to "tell adults and people who actually voted in this election" that "Portland Public Schools [PPS] does not stand with racism, we do not stand with sexism and we do not stand with Islamophobia."[1] The purpose of this protest was explained by some of the students as an attempt to "counteract some of the divisive rhetoric" witnessed during the presidential campaign.[2]

Over the course of the day, students marched through the city, chanting slogans like "No Trump, No K K K, No Fascist USA," "Not my president," and "Whose streets? Our streets!" At one point, they sat silently in the middle of an intersection to commemorate the death of Michael Brown, an eighteen-year-old shot by a police officer in Ferguson, Missouri, in 2014. Some supporters joined them, while other passersby chanted at students, "We won, you lost!"[3]

The November walkout was not the first protest Portland students initiated regarding the 2016 presidential election. The previous spring, Latino students from at least five PPS schools organized their own walkout to speak out about their growing feeling of fear as Donald Trump emerged as the Republican nominee. Partly inspired by students from nearby suburban Forest Grove, who walked out of their classes to protest the hanging of a "Build a Wall" banner in a school hallway, the

Latino PPS students also used the walkout to denounce structural racism in schools and to declare that school administrators had been "failing to address the issues minority students" were dealing with.[4]

Nor was the election the only target of student activism in Portland. Seventh and eighth grade students from Astor K–8 marched outside their school in October 2016, upset upon learning that after a year in which math classes had been staffed only by substitutes, the recently appointed teacher was being relocated to another school. A month earlier, students from Lincoln High hit the streets demanding that the Portland Public Schools Board of Education include a ballot question in the November election for a construction bond that would help repair deteriorated school facilities. In previous years, students walked out in protest of schedule changes replacing art classes with extra math instruction, marched in support of striking teachers, stepped out of class to urge boycotts of standardized tests, and rallied against the war in Iraq.[5] PPS officials have thus been confronting student activism for quite some time.

ON STUDENT WALKOUTS: APPROVAL AND OBJECTIONS

District and school administrators face a number of difficult decisions when responding to student demonstrations. Many worry about what might happen to students who take their civic activism into potentially chaotic public spaces. For example, before the November walkout, the principal of Wilson High sent a note to parents stating that while he hoped "the deep and old wounds that have been torn open in our society once again will help our children now see, and do more, than perhaps my generation has done to deal with the systems of oppression, the marginalization of LGBTQ community, women and minorities, that exists in America," he could not recommend to parents that students participate in the walkout. "Given the last few nights of protests and the raw emotions that the political campaign and election surfaced, I think the risks far outweigh the benefits for students."[6] Indeed, broader demonstrations across Portland had resulted in more than seventy arrests, violent confrontations between marchers and local police, and even one shooting. The principal invited parents instead to have conversations with their children about the intended demonstration, and offered alternative activities to be held inside the school premises.

Nor were such concerns confined to administrators, or even just adults. The Portland Metro High School Youth Alliance, for example, did not endorse the walkout despite opposing the election results. Calling attention to the unrest and violence of the larger protests in the city, this group of youth leaders issued a statement on Facebook: "We want to strongly encourage everyone NOT to participate in the walkout on Monday. We value each student's voice, and right to protest, but we don't want a powerful message to get lost in something that lacks clarity, organization and a consistent message."[7]

Defining to what extent a student walkout is part of the students' learning experience is also problematic. While students might be strengthening civic skills when they protest, some school leaders see student protests as conflicting with the academic goals of schools. For example, during a 2013 walkout in support of a teacher strike, one principal argued that "missing valuable instructional time to support teachers is not the best way to honor their work."[8] Other school leaders, however, have lauded their students' organizational skills and claimed that "students exceeded Civic Club expectations" for *adults* in their commitment to civic engagement.[9] During the Lincoln walkout, likewise, one teacher sent an email to the student leader recognizing what they had achieved and commenting that the walkout was "most definitely a CAS experience (or even project!)."[10] A local blogger agreed: "Chances are they [students] learned more today about becoming a good, involved citizen than in their entire school careers." He therefore argued that "PPS officials should NOT count this as unexcused absences."[11]

Varying levels of student support for walkouts also shed light on a deeper concern: the impact of student demonstrations on school climate. After Forest Grove students walked out to protest the "Build a Wall" banner, one student published an op-ed in the *Portland Tribune* to express his concerns about the fallout. Despite lauding its "noble and worthwhile cause," he felt that the walkout engendered a "with us or against us" mentality that ultimately "morphed into a vendetta against the administration and people who support Donald Trump" and "further polarized and increased the divide between students at FGHS."[12] Rather than encourage conversation among students across social, racial, and political differences, he argued, the walkout may have precluded such conversations from happening.

Still, demonstrations are not necessarily the driving force behind deteriorating school climate. In many cases, they are a reaction to preexisting fractures in a community, highlighting how unwelcome, marginalized, and voiceless some students feel. Well before the banner incident at Forest Grove High School, for example, students documented multiple experiences of inequity: "My own counselor assuming I take the easiest classes because that's what 'my people' do," hearing Mexican and Latino students called "useless farm workers," and being tracked into English language development classes on the basis of Hispanic surnames.[13] In response to such experiences, students met with both school and district leaders but felt their concerns continued to be ignored. As one student put it, "We had two unsuccessful meetings where we took the appropriate steps . . . I thought (the walkout) was a wake-up call that the school district really needed."[14] From the perspective of these students, the school climate was already toxic, and the walkout merely brought the problems out into the open.

Students may thus interpret actions to disallow or enable protests as conveying a message about students' value as members of the school community. On the one hand, schools that dismiss or oppose student protests run the risk of reinforcing some students' experiences of marginalization and disempowerment, particularly if their protest is in response to those same experiences. As one walkout participant explained, "the whole leadership is pretty much Caucasian, all the teachers are pretty much Caucasian, and it's like they only care about half of the school."[15] On the other hand, students that do not want to participate in a protest, or are actively opposed to it, might also feel excluded by their peers and teachers. Actively supporting a protest—especially on the part of faculty—can be seen by some students as a rejection of their beliefs.

Making matters even more complicated, questions about climate and safety are entangled with the question of whether or not students are engaging in protests voluntarily. Students may be under significant peer pressure to protest. A parent wrote to the school district after the September 2016 walkout protesting Lincoln High's poor physical facilities: "My son was shocked by this walk out today. He texted me in a panic and was so confused. He felt forced to take part in it and felt it was what his teachers wanted since they were with him."[16] The sense of "with us or against us" that the Forest Grove student writer called attention to is also a form of peer pressure.

Pressure might also come from groups who see themselves as allies of students. Following the election, PPS informed parents that the Portland Police Bureau had approached the district with concerns that organizations like Portland Resistance were encouraging students to participate in protests. For the police, this brought up the issue of safety—particularly given the violence of the postelection protests. Portland Police Sergeant Pete Simpson explained, "Our hope would be that anybody in these events will understand that everybody needs to follow the law, and the kids shouldn't feel like they can do something against the law because these grownups are doing it."[17]

At the same time, claims that adults have unduly influenced student protesters should be treated with a healthy degree of skepticism. Walkout opponents frequently use this tactic to undermine students' standing as political actors and to delegitimize students' own arguments. Students are aware of this, and often fight back eloquently. As one PPS student lamented during the walkout supporting teachers' contract negotiations, "It saddens me that people think the teachers' union is using us as pawns. I would hope that they had more trust in the youth. I go to school with some of the most brilliant people I've ever met, and I wish they could realize that."[18]

Finally, student demonstrations typically provoke parental reactions that are as varied and intense as the reactions of students. Some parents believe that students have the right to speak out, and express pride in their children's political activism.

The mother of a twelve-year-old anti-Trump protester, for example, affirmed that "it's really important for them to learn how to express themselves and voice their opinion."[19] After the Astor K–8 march, similarly, a father shared that he was "proud of the kids for protesting the right way and wanting more for their education."[20]

Other community members, however, question students' capacity to understand the political context, and draw a line about the issues they should be allowed to protest given their age. Others question students' motivations for participating in school walkouts, suspecting students of getting involved just as an excuse to skip class. They also critique protest as antithetical to civic education. One parent posted about the November protest: "High School Students are children! Our child attends PPS and the teachers even talk of the 'value' of protesting. It is absolutely ridiculous! We are a Nation of Laws! Portland looks to be a city of poorly educated crybabies!"[21]

HANDLING OF RECENT WALKOUTS: CONSIDERATIONS AND EFFECTS

PPS district and school-level officials have tried a variety of responses to student demonstrations, including physically preventing students from walking out of school. During the 2016 September walkout over school conditions at Lincoln High and other PPS schools, the district approved a lockout at Benson High School. As over 800 Lincoln High students approached Benson and called on students to join their protest, they were met by school resource officers and posted signs reading "No one In. No one Out." Officials justified the lockout on the grounds of student safety.[22] As the assistant superintendent put it: "Six hundred students out in the streets created panic in many of us." School leaders were simply unsure what they should do: "we have not been trained in what to do in situations where so many students are in the streets during a walkout and the liability in which we put ourselves and the District if someone gets hurt."[23]

The lockout was criticized by students, parents, and other activist groups as a "rash and unnecessary action" that "violated the civil liberties of Benson students."[24] Community members also noted telling racial and economic differences between the two schools—Lincoln is predominantly White, while Benson has many students of color—and raised suspicions that this factored into how prospective student protesters were treated. Even a school board member declared, "It gives every appearance that the district was allowing the students at our wealthiest and whitest school to stage a walkout and a cross-city protest . . . but when it comes to one of our poorest and most diverse schools, the response is a lockout and a police line."[25]

Still, safety remains a compelling concern for district officials. In November 2016, having been informed of planned demonstrations for the days after the election, PPS sent an email to parents recognizing "the right of students to demonstrate regarding their beliefs and concerns" but also pointing out that "the safest place for students is in school engaged in their classes." While not going as far as another lockout, PPS declared that students who walked out would receive unexcused absences, that K–8 and middle school students should remain in class unless a guardian checked them out, and that students protesting would be responsible for their own safety. They also made it clear that the walkouts were neither district-sanctioned nor school-sponsored events, and no staff should participate in them.[26]

School districts elsewhere around the country, however, have taken much more supportive approaches to student walkouts. In response to postelection school walkouts by middle and high school students, for example, the Des Moines, Iowa, school board emphasized students' rights to free political expression. "[A]s the elected governing body of this school district each of us took an oath right next to this flag to uphold those rights even when it allows for the expression of opinions that differ from our own." The district thus committed to "not stand in the way of students peacefully expressing their concerns," and to "support that walkout with limits and boundaries that would better ensure the rights and safety of all of our students."[27]

School officials in Seattle also favored supporting student walkouts in the aftermath of the election, although for different reasons. Although students participating in the protest would receive unexcused absences, the district's spokesperson observed that "Kids are hurting. They do not need to be punished. They need to talk about it."[28] Demonstrations, on this account, provide an outlet for student expression that district leaders value, but cannot necessarily accommodate within its schools. In line with that position, the district also declared that school staff should observe the student demonstrations "for safety and security reasons."[29] This corresponds with recommendations from the Readiness and Emergency Management for Schools (REMS) Technical Assistance Center, which notes that when school personnel accompany students who are staging a walkout, they can monitor student safety, mediate between students and law enforcement and other first responders, and help defuse demonstrations.[30]

PPS AND FUTURE WALKOUTS

The Benson High lockout in September 2016 proved to PPS leaders that they needed to rethink district policy about student demonstrations. Lincoln High's principal thought the events signaled the need for "common protocols, guidance and support when handling these issues to ensure that students are treated equally and equitably across our city."[31] After the incident, PPS' interim superintendent wrote a letter to students committing to a review of the district's planning, policies, and communications for similar cases.

Along with the district's need to revisit their position on and handling of student walkouts, momentum for further student activism and demonstrations has continued to build. The Portland Student Action Network (PSAN), noting students' increasing political energy, declared on the group's Facebook page their intent to develop a "long-term movement making tangible change on a local level."[32] They issued a thirty-five point list of demands that includes, among other concerns, discipline reform, action against bigotry in schools, and affordable health care. PSAN followed up by organizing three demonstrations over a four-month period, starting with a January 2017 protest against incoming Secretary of Education Betsy DeVos.[33] In February, PSAN organized a rally and march in memory of Quanice Hayes, a black teenager shot and killed by Portland police. In April, they launched an ongoing campaign calling for the removal of armed school resource officers from Portland Public Schools. PSAN also sought out school administrators directly, organizing students to attend school board meetings throughout the year to formally present their demands.[34]

As student activism increases, so do concerns about student safety. In February 2017, Portland police resorted to using pepper spray and nonlethal rounds in clashes with protesters. They also arrested seven adults and six teenagers, including a fourteen-year-old. Three months later, two men were killed and a third seriously wounded while trying to protect a Muslim teenager and her non-Muslim friend from the hateful tirade of a fellow passenger on a public train in Portland. At a free speech rally the week after the murders, counterprotesters—many of whom identified as members of Portland's antifascist action group, Rose City Antifa—launched bricks and rocks at the rally goers, sparking another violent confrontation. The wave of political violence prompted *Politico Magazine* to label Portland the most politically violent city in America.[35]

In light of these many considerations, how should district and school officials in PPS respond to student walkouts and demonstrations? What priorities should they set when it comes to ensuring students' political freedom, emotional safety, academic (including civic) learning, and physical well-being, and how can they realize those priorities in real time? To what extent can school and district leaders in other cities learn from Portland—or might PPS learn from other districts—given the widespread nature of student walkouts (which were documented in more than twenty-five states between November 2016 and March 2017 alone)?[36]

Students' Perspectives on How Schools and Districts Should Prepare for and Respond to Walkouts

Jonathan Boisvert, Keegan Bonds-Harmon,
Innocense Gumbs, and Jalissa Mixon,
with guidance from Arthur Baraf

Although for some Providence high school students it was just another day, for others, January 20, 2017, was a day to start a change. For those of us who walked out of school for Donald Trump's inauguration, our experience was educational and motivating. It brought students from various schools together to express our outrage over the president-elect's proposed policies and hateful rhetoric. As we walked from our schools to the Rhode Island State House, supportive people honked their car horns, waved, and chanted. We were using our political voices, and people were listening.

Our schools did not support our walkout, nor did they impede it. We suggest this was appropriate; for reasons of both political neutrality and liability, schools and districts should not involve themselves in student protest. At the same time, however, we argue that districts should provide students multiple opportunities for civic education and engagement. These should include opportunities for students to analyze and take action about a wide variety of contemporary issues.

YOUTH VOICE IS IMPORTANT—FOR YOUTH *AND* FOR THE COMMUNITY

As young people, we are in the process of developing our voices and our ability to express ourselves politically. But we can only develop these skills and habits of civic engagement if we are given the opportunity to practice them. What we are allowed to do or say impacts who we are and who we are becoming.

Unfortunately, young people often feel like we are considered a joke. We hear messages from adults that we aren't worth being listened to. Yet, many youth today are more "woke" to the injustice going on in our world than many adults seem to be. We use digital technology and social media to gain new insight into what is happening in the world. When supported in investigating the issues we care about, we are capable of reflecting on this knowledge and our morals in order to take a stance and take action. Although we are still young, and our minds are still growing, we are capable of thinking and acting morally.

Our protest against Trump's inauguration demonstrates this. The protest gave us a sense of pride, leadership, and efficacy. We told our city that we can exercise our right to engage politically, just as much as anyone else can. We showed that we can be trusted to peaceably take a stand for what we think is right. Young people, from Providence to Portland and everywhere in between, should be able to take political action—including staging walkouts—and then come back to school and learn more.

Our protest also demonstrated our commitment to the community. When we protest, we are telling society that we care about Providence, our nation, and our world. We are fed up with how things are now, but we want to help change them for the better.

We believe that schools need to demonstrate the same commitment to us. When schools stifle our freedom of speech, they send the message that others' rights do not apply to us, that our voices don't count. When schools enable students to protest, on the other hand, they tell us that our community values us as we tell our community that we value it. Since we spend most of our time in school, it is important for schools to support us in developing our political voices.

HOW SCHOOL DISTRICTS CAN REDUCE LIABILITY, MAINTAIN NEUTRALITY, AND STILL PROTECT STUDENTS

Although schools should allow students to engage in political action like walkouts, they must also have a realistic approach to their liability when students leave the school. Districts should not be legally responsible for young adults who are making their own conscious decision to walk out of school and protest for something they believe. Furthermore, they should take steps to make that position clear.

To keep itself free of liability, a district should communicate with teachers and administrators that they should not explicitly show support for the protest, as this could create a perception that the adults are supporting particular political views or the action as a whole. School staff should be politically neutral. Also, the school should not advertise the event, such as displaying any imagery or making any statements that could be perceived as support. Nor should school personnel attend the protest, even under the guise of keeping students safe—although they might provide certified first-aid training and other safety guidance to the students themselves.

Finally, the district should clearly communicate to parents and guardians that schools are not liable for students who decide to walk out. For example, the school could communicate: "The walkout will commence on . . . We cannot be responsible for the safety of the students as soon as they leave the building." Knowing this, the parents/guardians will be able to help the student decide whether participating in the walkout is a good choice. Permission slips, on the other hand, aren't necessary because it defeats the purpose of the school letting us exercise our freedom of speech. We don't need permission from an elder to exercise our rights.

Even while they distance themselves from the protest itself, schools and districts should help ensure their students' safety by communicating with other adults who will be there. Schools should communicate with police and emergency management personnel, for example, that there may be children at these protests and to watch out for them. This can increase student safety at the protest should something go wrong. Schools can also communicate with protest organizers to ensure that they are aware of the children in the hopes that they will not be hurt or harassed while there. They should advocate for student safety precautions, asking other organizations for their support. Finally, schools should contact the parents and guardians of students who walked out so they know where they are and can make decisions about how to keep their children safe. By playing the role of *communicators*, schools and districts can help keep students safe without violating their neutrality.

SCHOOLS' BROADER RESPONSIBILITY FOR TEACHING CIVIC ENGAGEMENT

Schools' and districts' responsibility for creating civically involved students shouldn't stop at keeping them safe while protesting. Many people think about politics as abstract concepts that don't directly relate to ourselves or those around us. But politics affects everyone on a day-to-day basis. Therefore, educators must demystify these systems and teach students how to live in the real world in which political and civic life matter.

One way that schools can do this is by providing students the opportunity to learn about issues that affect them or others in their communities. For example, in our community in Rhode Island, students care deeply about issues such as immigration, abortion rights, LGBTQ+ rights, and mass incarceration. We want the opportunity to analyze these topics in our classrooms. Through analysis we become more educated and more motivated to take civic action in a wide variety of ways.

Furthermore, as we learn about social issues and political struggles in schools, we may be inspired to protest and rally, but we may also take other approaches to making positive change in our own community. Districts should help students understand that political action and involvement can take many forms. Activism can manifest in obvious ways, such as running for office, organizing or joining activist groups, and planning protests. But activism also means starting community gardens in low-income neighborhoods, distributing opportunities in equitable ways, and passing the mic to the voices you may have overshadowed. When schools enable political discussion and debate and help students make connections to their local communities, young people are empowered to take many paths toward working to make a better society.

Finally, when students are taught to civilly discuss and debate political issues, we grow academically, emotionally, and personally. We have found in our political discussions that we gain persuasive skills as well as challenge our own viewpoints. In our political philosophy class, we have been transformed by debating with peers. Using scenarios such as the trolley problem, and framing the conversation around "What would you do?" helped us to better understand our own morals. These scenarios illustrated broader concepts, connected to specific political issues, and prompted reflection and debate that was incredibly helpful for us in establishing our beliefs in politics and morality.

In summary, politically charged issues impact the lives of youth, and students deserve to have the opportunity to talk about them. We should not be asked to leave our political identities and futures at the classroom door. Schools and districts can contribute powerfully to our civic learning even as they stay politically neutral and limit their liability during student protests. The empowering notion that we can voice our views and make a change fills us with excitement, motivation and hope for the future.

Jonathan Boisvert, The Met High School class of 2020, is training to be a software developer and IT guy. He has a side passion for politics, ethics, and the show Black Mirror.

Keegan Bonds-Harmon, The Met High School class of 2020, is a small business owner, artist, and fashionista.

Innocense Gumbs, The Met High School class of 2020, has a passion for teaching, wants to grow up to be an elementary teacher or ELL instructor, and is starting to learn the piano.

Jalissa Mixon, The Met High School class of 2020, has a passion for midwifery. In her free time, she likes to study ethics and think about politics, current events, and community engagement.

Arthur Baraf is a veteran high school principal, a Students-at-the-Center Distinguished Fellow, and creator of the Student-Centered Learning Podcast. He taught the moral philosophy seminar in which these high school sophomores wrote this commentary.

Citizens Now

Responding to Youth Voices and Choices in Real Time

MICHELLE J. BELLINO AND NATALIE R. DAVIS

This case raises questions about how schools and districts should respond to youth civic actions when they disrupt formal instruction and place students' safety, civil liberties, and social cohesion in tension. When confronted with controversy, schools often attempt to opt out of politically charged conversations and double down on standard curriculum. Yet for many young people, issues such as police brutality and the repeal of DACA profoundly impact their daily lives. From these youths' perspectives, schools' silence makes them *less* safe places rather than spaces of refuge. By refusing to engage with current politics, students charge, schools exacerbate societal tensions rather than remedy them.

Young people's voices need to be front and center in guiding schools' and districts' responses to youth demands. Even though youth actions occupy center stage in this case, we rarely hear directly from young people about their own goals, assumptions, and expectations for the tactics they are employing; nor do we hear how they conceive of their interactions with school actors and policy. This matters, first, because young people are not merely citizens in the making, as many civic educators assume. Rather, young people have the right and capacity to contribute in real time to policies that shape and constrain their everyday choices.[37] Second, youth voices matter because they will help us get past the binaries of participation or nonparticipation and understand the wide variety of ways in which young people experience, enact, and resist civic agency.[38] By centering student voices within the curriculum itself and strengthening youths' capacity to respond to and improve their social worlds, schools can empower young people to contribute their ideas and actions towards creating stronger, healthier communities and more equitable and just policies.

SCHOOLS AS SPACES OF CIVIC POSSIBILITY

Youth develop civic attitudes and values in the context of their daily experiences in and outside of schools.[39] By shaping students' relationships with authority figures such as teachers and administrators, for instance, schools contribute to young people's broader perceptions of systems of power.[40] Every school must thus address an essential question in civic education: how much should young people be positioned as compliant subjects versus critical, autonomous agents who might question and challenge the structures that govern their society?[41]

We see competing answers at play in the different ways that Portland Public Schools actors considered disciplining or incentivizing student involvement in demonstrations. Schools' responses speak to different models of citizenship and to a range of ideological roles assigned to democratic education.[42] Those who attempt to suppress student movements promote a passive conception of citizenship, communicating that political engagement is dangerous and irrelevant to the academic work of schools. Schools that waive punitive consequences, by contrast, embrace a more agentic conception of citizenship. They become enabling environments for students to practice and experiment with various forms of participation; these are tangible goals for citizenship education rarely realized in schools.[43]

Yet even this more agentic approach does little to offset concerns about students' physical safety, coercive participation, and polarization within the school community. The principal of Wilson High School recognizes this tension, seeking a middle ground by fostering alternative spaces for expression within the school. Would more structured responses such as teach-ins, class debates, or community dialogues funnel productive conversations back into classrooms? Or would students lose the power to express and enact their personal political commitments if they were confined to school-sanctioned events? We suggest that the only way for school staff to answer these questions is by engaging openly and directly with students.

WEIGHING THE RISKS AND BENEFITS OF (IN)ACTION

Students' own voices also need to be made more central because even though their substantive message is widely agreed to be important, it gets obscured by adult worries about students' means of expression. Remarkably, few people in the case seem to question the value of the local, national, or global issues around which students are rallying. School actors seem to agree that educational access and quality, systemic racism, and the overtly xenophobic and divisive rhetoric that surfaced during and after the presidential election should incite in all citizens a desire to act. Nonetheless, parents, teachers, and district administrators in the case all worry that students' tactics of initiating walkouts and joining public protests puts them at risk of arrest or violent confrontation with police, muddles social justice goals, interrupts instructional time, and further divides the community.

Here, the focus of discussion on the *medium* rather than the *message* inhibits adults from talking with students about the issues themselves. It also portrays school accountability as pertaining more to disciplining students' actions than to responding to the substantive concerns raised by young people. Finally, it gives the impression that protests inevitably threaten safety and stability, whether they are chaotic and violent or conducted with care and organized around principled, strategic goals such as nonviolence. Dismissing the medium without attending to the message suggests that parents and teachers are more discomforted by protest than engaged with the authentic concerns of the youth involved, who may have carefully and collectively thought through their rationale for employing these tactics.

Students confront both risks and benefits when deciding whether to participate in these movements. Equally importantly, however, *non*participation also brings risks and benefits. While joining student walkouts poses possible physical and academic risks, abstaining from walkouts might entail greater socioemotional threats of invisibility and exclusion in school and the community. Meanwhile, the potential benefits of participation—such as increased public awareness and responsiveness—should be weighed against the benefit of uninterrupted academic learning time stemming from nonparticipation. Marginalized groups in particular often confront risk embedded in the status quo and thus feel compelled to act, knowing that taking action replaces one set of risks with another.[44]

FOSTERING CIVIC DIALOGUE IN RESPONSE TO STUDENT MOVEMENTS

We thus propose shifting the terms of the debate from controlling student demonstrations to harnessing opportunities for youth-led engagement. Instead of fearing student activism, PPS can leverage youth civic engagement to cultivate a democratic school culture that normalizes and encourages civic dialogue across difference. Capitalizing on these opportunities can take the form of direct instructional tie-ins, community dialogues, and youth-led action campaigns.

Social studies teachers in particular can draw on a variety of contemporary and historical cases to foster curricular links between student movements and the broader social and political issues they represent. Students organizing against the border wall or advocating for DACA could immerse themselves in units on the history of US immigration policy or the nonviolent principles grounding the African American Civil Rights Movement. By learning about past and present efforts, young people can master important academic content and skills. In the process, they might also come to understand the collaboration, choreography, and sacrifice necessary to mobilize groups and secure long-lasting changes.

By engaging with youth about their own goals and tactics, as well as teaching about other contemporary and historical social movements, educators can help students collectively consider how agency and power are exercised through social movements in a democracy. Portland Public Schools cannot directly reinstate DACA or amend gun-control laws. But the PPS school board could take measures to increase student inclusion, ensure consistent access to quality teachers, and set equitable policies across the district. As schools help students build collective knowledge about pathways for impacting change, young people may decide to focus strategically on these more local issues. Or, they may still choose to address national and global concerns, but with a greater awareness of the symbolic aspects of their protests. Alternatively, students might ask schools to help them engage directly with national and global decision makers.

By teaching youth about ways that civic activists vocalize dissent and foster social justice other than through protest, educators offer students an opening that might offset social pressures to either participate or abstain. Students can use their newfound knowledge to align their goals and tactics with one another. This grants youth the agency to decide how to employ their collective voice without necessarily positioning their peers as either activists or disengaged. Students will ideally learn to think simultaneously about resistance and resolution, positioning themselves as agents of change—not only through expressions of noncompliance but also as problem solvers.

Too often, students critique injustice and inequity in classrooms without being offered opportunities to consider how to respond to oppressive conditions. Young people are engaged and enraged by the problems that surround them. They may feel overwhelmed and powerless to impact change, or they may organize walkouts and protests because these are the only tactics they know about for bringing about positive social change.[45] Educators can help students develop a stronger sense of political efficacy and structural inclusion by incorporating critical and transformative approaches to citizenship education into the curriculum and the regular school day. In so doing, they challenge existing social and structural arrangements and position young people as civic agents capable of cocreating their worlds.[46]

Portland Public Schools has a chance to put these principles in practice. Doing so requires listening to young people's understandings of equity and justice, and to their everyday experiences with inequity and injustice. It also requires foregrounding the roles that ordinary citizens can play in shaping a more equitable and just society.

Michelle Bellino is an assistant professor at the University of Michigan School of Education and codirector of the Conflict and Peace Initiative. She is the author of Youth in Postwar Guatemala: Education and Civic Identity in Transition *and coeditor of* (Re)constructing Memory: Education, Identity, and Conflict.

Natalie R. Davis is a postdoctoral research fellow in the School of Education and Social Policy at Northwestern University. Her work explores critical intersections between teaching, learning, and the sociopolitical development of children from nondominant communities.

The Goal Is Civic Learning

Principles for Administrators in Times of Uncertainty

Sheldon Berman

Demonstrations and walkouts are dramatic events in the life of a school community. While testing the management skills of building and district administrators, they also present a powerful opportunity for students to learn about productive civic engagement. If not handled well, however, they can polarize students and staff and risk the safety of those involved. How adults prepare for and respond to these events can have a significant impact on students' civic learning and on the school's culture and climate.

When students walk through the schoolhouse door, they do not forfeit their right to either free speech or peaceable assembly. However, schools may establish limitations to maintain order. US Supreme Court decisions, in particular *Tinker v. Des Moines*, have upheld this balanced approach. As demonstrated in Portland, every walkout or protest is unique, and context matters. Although there is no one best response, experience provides some guiding principles to either preventing or handling a walkout in a way that is most productive for students and for the school as a whole.

CIVIC LEARNING

The first principle is that the primary goal should be to promote civic learning and encourage thoughtful civic engagement. America's public education system was founded on the belief that the survival of a democratic republic depends on an educated, informed, and active electorate who can make reasoned and sound judgments that benefit the present and future populace. The only way to achieve that goal is through education that teaches positive civic participation. Schools facing a potential or actual walkout should engage students in dialogue about thoughtful and meaningful approaches to freedom of expression, the right of assembly, the rights and responsibilities embodied in dissent, and the democratic processes that promote change.

Rather than framing the incidents as confrontations with students, administrators should seize the opportunity to listen carefully to students' concerns and help them think through various approaches they might take. This includes considering the consequences of each approach, as reflecting on the potential impact of their actions—both positive and negative—is an essential aspect of civic learning. Each situation is an opportunity to affirm student voices and to teach the processes and tools that are available to citizens for addressing grievances or making a public statement of concern.

COMMUNICATING WITH STUDENTS

The second principle in dealing with walkouts or demonstrations is that school leaders should maintain positive relationships and open communication with students rather than resorting to coercion. Administrators should show they value student voices by providing a forum for students to express their views and encouraging students to work with them in addressing their concerns. Students need to feel comfortable coming to administrators and teachers to discuss their plans, trusting that they will be heard and that administrators have the students' best interest in mind. This level of communication may prevent a walkout or transform a potential walkout into a positive learning activity.

Sometimes, students do not approach the administration in advance, or they respond to an event spontaneously. It is at those times that relationships and communication matter most. Administrators and teachers can maintain communication with student leaders as events unfold, protect student safety, and perhaps prevent acts of violence.

COMMUNICATING WITH PARENTS AND COMMUNITY

Third, parent communication is essential. If students are planning a walkout, parents need to be informed and have the opportunity to talk with their children about their potential participation, ensuring it is voluntary and considered rather than coerced through peer pressure. If students walk out spontaneously, parents need to be informed as soon as reasonable about what happened and how the administration handled the situation.

Walkouts also affect the larger community, particularly if students leave school grounds. Communication with the media through press releases, interviews, or a press conference helps the community to understand what happened and why, and to understand the steps that the school administration took or will take. All communication needs to be coordinated with central administration to ensure the district is consistent in its message.

Some parents and members of the community will not agree with the administration's approach to the walkout. However, getting ahead of the situation through proactive communication will help most of them understand both the circumstances and the school's rationale. It will also give the students a fair opportunity to have their voices heard in a larger forum and demonstrate how the school is working to promote an understanding of democratic rights and responsibilities.

CONSEQUENCES FOR STUDENT PARTICIPATION

The fourth guiding principle is that actions have consequences. Students have many options to express their perspectives without violating school rules. They can publish their views in a blog or newspaper, gather before or after school, circulate petitions via social media, or hold a rally during lunch. The school may choose to convene an assembly, vigil, or march, thus enabling all interested persons to participate in a school-sponsored activity. The district may allow parents to sign students out of school as an excused absence to participate in a demonstration.

However, students who walk out during school hours leave class without permission and disrupt instruction for everyone. Unless a walkout is a planned part of a school-sponsored event, leaving class to demonstrate is an act of civil disobedience. Students should learn that civil disobedience brings consequences, such as having their absence treated as unexcused. At this point, communication with students and parents is critical in helping them grasp and accept the academic implications of a walkout. It is important for students to understand that any school-imposed consequence is not meant to be punitive but rather is inherent to the meaning and significance of the walkout.

ROLE OF STAFF

Fifth, school staff should promote dialogue about the issues that are provoking the action and about democratic participatory processes, but they should not enlist students in their own causes or advocate for their own political beliefs. Particularly when students or community members disagree strongly about an issue, staff members must find ways to foster mutual understanding by enabling students to express and think through divergent views.

There are additional reasons for staff neutrality. Not all students will agree with either the reason for the protest or with walking out as a viable way to address a grievance. Staff participation in a walkout can accentuate the polarization among students and staff. Moreover, staff members who leave their class to participate in a walkout may be characterized as abandoning their jobs and violating their employment contracts.

For liability reasons, some district protocols prohibit adults from being present in a student walkout. These protocols convey that the school neither condones nor condemns the walkout, that staff are neutral nonparticipants, and that the school is not responsible for student participants once they leave school property. If staff accompanied students in these districts, they would be seen as supporting the students' actions; the school or district might also be held liable if students were injured, injured others, or damaged property.

However, other districts believe that school personnel can and even must accompany students to exert a constructive influence and promote student safety. Trusted adults can provide guidance to student leaders, communicate with police, mediate between students and police, defuse difficult situations, and prevent escalation. These adults are present not to support the cause of the students but to maintain peace and protect students from experiencing or causing harm. Some states specify that individuals who are present to help manage the situation cannot be held liable unless they were negligent in responding.

Any staff members asked to accompany students should be administrators who have authority in these situations, such as the principal, assistant principals, or school resource officers. At times, schools may seek assistance from guidance counselors or selected teachers who have significant influence with students. In districts with protocols that allow staff presence at a protest, it is important that everyone understand that these adults are not endorsing the cause but are there to promote safety.

COMMUNICATING WITH POLICE OR SECURITY

Lastly, walkouts and marches are public events that require the attention of security personnel. It is critical that administrators communicate with school resource officers, district security, and local police as soon as they are aware that a walkout is being considered. When authorities understand what is happening and why, they are less likely to inadvertently escalate a situation. Ideally, administrators already have a collaborative relationship with security or the police, and they are accustomed to working together effectively.

Although the reasons and circumstances surrounding a walkout vary greatly, these guiding principles—focusing on the goal of civic learning, maintaining communication with all parties (students, parents, the community, and the police), establishing clear protocols for participation by staff, and ensuring students understand the implications and consequences of their actions—can turn a challenging situation into one with a constructive outcome. These principles should be shared with staff, parents, and students in student handbooks and through staff training prior to an event rather than as postmortem reflections. Finally, in keeping with these principles, it is essential to debrief the walkout or other event with students so that they reflect on and grow from the experience.

> *Dr. Sheldon Berman has served as superintendent of schools for twenty-six years in Andover, Massachusetts; Eugene, Oregon; Jefferson County, Kentucky; and Hudson, Massachusetts. He has authored two books,* Children's Social Consciousness *and* Promising Practices in Teaching Social Responsibility, *as well as numerous articles on social responsibility, social-emotional learning, service learning, universal design for learning, special education, virtual education, education reform, and ethical leadership.*

Don't Just Protest

Make Real Change Through Public Work

Harry C. Boyte

The student walkouts in Portland illustrate patterns across the country and around the world. Young people are eager to make change on issues from national politics, such as the election of Donald Trump, to questions close to home, like the absence of art supplies or permanent math teachers in schools. The approach they know is protest, fueled by fury and despair. Jasmine Adams, who organized a sit-in at Oberlin College in 2016, voiced a generational view. "*Whatever* you do at Oberlin as a person of color or a low-income person, it just doesn't work!" she said. "I have to be political in whatever form or fashion because I have *nothing else to do*."[47]

Protest is usually ineffective. Protesters assume that decision makers have the capacity to solve the problem, which is often not the case. They believe that the best way to move authorities to action is through confrontation, which in fact may simply deepen intransigence. Finally, protest produces an "us versus them" mindset, as the Forest Grove student wrote in the *Portland Tribune*.

There is, however, a better way. Public Achievement, a youth civic education and empowerment initiative that I and others founded in 1990, provides an alternative to protest and polarization. Its aim is to teach young people the grassroots skills and citizen-centered politics I learned in the civil rights movement, including while working for Martin Luther King's organization, the Southern Christian Leadership Conference. In the twenty-eight years since we started it, Public Achievement has spread to communities across the United States and in more than twenty countries around the globe. Offshoots based on what we call public work have taken many forms.

I believe young people and the adults who support them could learn three important lessons from these experiences.

REAL STORIES OF CHANGE

First, teach students about people like themselves who successfully made a difference in the community. This will help youth move from merely protesting injustice to making constructive change.

In the freedom movement, I found teachers in many places. Oliver Harvey, a janitor at Duke University, where I went to college, lead an organizing effort among maids and janitors to improve wages and working conditions and also to gain more respect. Harvey was a great civic educator. He drew on his own past campaigns organizing cross-racial coalitions of tobacco pickers, textile workers, and disenfrachised voters, to teach me how to work with others to make change. Most importantly, he taught what I would later call *everyday citizen politics*, which begins with understanding where your opponents come from and looks for positive possibilities even in one's enemies. The maids and janitors at Duke, for example, framed their organizing in terms of their desire to further the university's own mission. They succeeded as a result.

I was similarly inspired by Bayard Rustin, a friend of my father, who organized the March on Washington in 1963. Drawing on his own youthful experiences with alliance building against fascism in the 1930s, Rustin framed the march as a way to win over "middle America." He pointed out that most people did not actively oppose the civil rights movement; they were mainly indifferent. Attacking people for what they "should" be interested in, Rustin argued, would alienate potential allies. Instead, invite middle America in by drawing on their own hopes and dreams. Martin Luther King's "I Have a Dream" speech brilliantly expressed Rustin's strategy and vastly expanded the civil rights movement. These kinds of examples can help young people see how to shift from "us versus them" protests to collaborative public work.

PUBLIC WORK

Public Achievement is based on a framework of politics called *public work*. Young people work as teams on issues they choose that make a public contribution, undertaken in nonviolent and legal fashion. Students are thus conceived as cocreators of schools and communities, not as citizens in waiting.

This is a shift from both traditional civics education and service learning. Students learn that democracy is an ongoing way of life created by citizens, not simply a sporadic exercise in voting or helping others. Government is a potential partner, neither the solution nor the enemy. Politics is the way to engage other people to solve problems and build a commonwealth of shared resources, not a way to create winners and losers.

The frameworks of civics and service are not wrong, but the public work frame expands people's political imaginations. It generates commonwealth projects, creating shared resources and cultural change. Public work also highlights the civic potential of educators, support staff, and school and district leaders to promote and sustain youth civic empowerment through their own work.

At Anderson Elementary School in Minneapolis, for example, a team of eight fifth- and sixth-grade boys was angry about the state of their bathroom. The stalls had no doors. Toilet paper and other supplies were missing. Obscenities covered the walls. They named themselves "the Bathroom Busters."

Two coaches helped them map out the power relationships and politics around the issue. They were dealing with a highly inefficient bureaucracy. The principal had been unable to get the central school district to paint the bathrooms for four years, in part because unions had to give approval.

The racially diverse group of children learned how to create alliances and communicate their concerns (many were English language learners). Youthful determination combined with good coaching to achieve results many thought were impossible: the stalls were fixed, and the walls got painted.

The next year, however, graffiti reappeared. Caesar (his real name) chose to work on the problem again. His team met with other children and asked, "What can we do to prevent graffiti?" They created a mural from many kids' ideas. As it took shape, the bathroom became free of graffiti and turned into a symbol of school pride. Many visitors came to see this Public Achievement project. All were taken to the bathroom and heard from Caesar, who became publicly known for his eloquence on the issue. "This is our property," he said. "We have to take care of it!"[48]

CIVIC SKILLS

Finally, experiences like the Bathroom Busters teach civic and political skills. These include communication through one-on-one meetings, writing, and public speaking; collective evaluation and reflection on experiences; and *power mapping*, analyzing who has interests in and influence over an issue.

Concepts and skills of public work can be taught in diverse communities around the world. The Institute for Democracy in South Africa (IDASA), which played a crucial role in ending apartheid, decided to deepen its democracy education efforts beyond voting or advocacy. After working with Public Achievement in Minnesota and learning about public work, IDASA's democracy education director Marie Ström and her team adapted these approaches to African realities. "Being an active citizen is not just about demanding things from government. It is also about doing the work of democracy in everyday settings," Ström wrote. "For this to happen, citizens need to develop the skills to engage with others across lines of racial, cultural, economic and ideological differences. They need to be able to take action themselves on public issues from education and crime to economic development and HIV/ AIDS . . . in partnership with government as well as on their own."[49]

Powerful examples emerged. Nomthi Skhosana, from the low-income community New Eersterus, went through IDASA's training program. She developed skills and a new way of looking at her role as a citizen. Skhosana got a team together and created Vukani, a community development organization working with women, youth, and children. It undertook many projects, from creating an after-school program for HIV/AIDS orphans to a project to bring running water to the community. Throughout these projects they used tools like one-on-one meetings and power mapping. "With a power map," she said, "you can find a way to tackle any problem . . . identify potential allies and figure out strategies for building power to bring about change."[50]

In sum, public work provides young people a pathway from protest to constructive politics. If young people in Portland and elsewhere learn such organizing skills, knowledge, and dispositions, they will likely stage fewer walkouts. Most important, they will develop the confidence, hope, and capacity our society needs for a democratic awakening.

Harry C. Boyte is founder of the international youth civic education and empowerment initiative Public Achievement. His newest book is Awakening Democracy Through Public Work: Pedagogies of Empowerment.

Chicago 1968

A Historical Perspective on District Responses to Student Activism

Dionne Danns

Student protests have a long history of transforming schools and society—from student-organized antislavery protests in the 1830s that led to the founding of Oberlin College to the Birmingham Children's March in 1963 that reignited the Civil Rights Movement. Portland Public Schools (PPS) student protests against racism, sexism, and Islamophobia evoked by Donald Trump, and their walkouts to improve education and school facilities, are thus in line with the history of student activism in the US. In fact, over 27,000 students in the Chicago Public Schools (CPS) walked out of or boycotted school in October 1968 over the combined issues of racial injustice and educational quality. Both the scope and the focus of CPS students' activism were broader than PPS students have thus far achieved. But partly for that reason, student activism in Chicago in the late 1960s may provide an instructive (and cautionary) lens through which to consider the potential growth, risks, and possibilities of student protest.

Chicago high school students in 1968 had a list of concerns that would likely seem quite familiar to PPS students in 2018: inequitable academic tracking, unfair disciplinary measures, overcrowded schools, poorly designed and insufficiently challenging curriculum, and ineffective school leadership. One Sunday in mid-October, twenty-five student leaders from city high schools convened to clarify their grievances. They issued a list of demands that included calls for more homework, the creation of black history courses, holidays for black leaders, and the hiring of more Black administrators, counselors, and teachers. The next day, 27,000 students boycotted over a dozen schools, and they threatened continued boycotts on subsequent Mondays.

After deliberating with colleagues, Superintendent James Redmond responded to the student demands at a press conference three days later. By many measures, Redmond's response was extraordinary, as it essentially affirmed many of the students' positions. Redmond promised to create new assistant principal positions at predominantly black schools and to increase the number of Black history courses offered. He also promised a $5 million increase to the school budget the next year to improve school facilities. At the press conference, Redmond stated:

> We have heard your demands, we are concerned about many of the same problems which are contained in them. Your Board of Education, your teachers and your administrators are trying, within the money available to them to improve all the schools. Accept our commitment to improve the schools and consider your mission of dramatizing our needs accomplished. Return to your studies and do your part in furthering your necessary education by remaining in the classroom. . . . The demands which are made are not reason for staying away from school.[51]

Redmond's response to the students was telling in its balance of acknowledging problems while also trying to rein in protests. On the one hand, Redmond hoped his relatively quick response, and his efforts to meet their demands within the limits of the school budget, would convince students that he heard them and was taking their concerns seriously. He also hoped to placate teachers and administrators by acknowledging that they were aware of the problems and were working to improve students' education. On the other hand, Redmond made it clear that he believed students should end their boycotts and return to school. He issued stern warnings against future protests, threatening during the press conference to take students to juvenile court for truancy, and even to utilize circuit court to charge "indifferent parents" of students who boycotted. Redmond similarly instructed school officials to enforce attendance laws for students and encouraged principals to suspend or even expel student protesters.

Although Redmond hoped to end the protests by addressing the students' demands quickly, 20,000 students boycotted city schools the following Monday, October 21. Additionally, 500 to 700 Black teachers joined the students at the second boycott. These students and teachers viewed Redmond's press conference as mere verbal window dressing. They intended to continue protesting until they saw actual solutions to their problems.

In response, Redmond took a more purely antagonistic approach to the protesters. At a board meeting following the second boycott, Redmond instructed principals to dock boycotting teachers' pay unless they provided proof that their absence was due to illness or personal business. Students nonetheless staged a third boycott on October 28, but their numbers dropped precipitously, to under 10,000. Parental and student support for the boycott waned, especially as media reported vandalism, violence, pulled fire alarms, and walkouts on additional days other than the planned citywide boycotts. Student suspensions and arrests also took a toll on continued boycott support. As students began to see the actual cost of boycotting, many lost interest.

When students shifted tactics to a sit-in a week later, Redmond could act immediately, since the students remained on school grounds. He warned students that they would be arrested, and ended schools an hour and fifteen minutes early. These measures, along with police presence and the arrest of twenty-six youth at various schools, thwarted the sit-in.

Student activism has always come with consequences for those involved. Many of the protest leaders in Chicago and elsewhere were arrested, expelled, or suspended. Some had to finish their education elsewhere. At the same time, however, Chicago students' actions led to increased black school leadership and black history courses. They, like other students before and after them, found that they could have an impact on their school curriculum, leadership, and other issues by taking a stand for what they believed was important to their educational and community development. They had the right and the ability to transform opportunities for others, and they successfully transformed themselves in the process.

The situation in Chicago certainly differs from that of Portland, but it is instructive nonetheless. Chicago Public Schools, like other districts in the 1960s, had to confront well-organized, large scale protests that evolved after numerous protests at individual schools. It demonstrates the potential for student organizing, particularly when the responses of administrators at individual schools are ineffective, or those administrators are not in a position to meet the demands of the students. Chicago also demonstrates the ambiguity and potential growth of protests. It provides a lesson related to the need for a quick and effective response, and the patience and recognition that these responses may not work right away.

Portland school administrators need to respond quickly to student demands for school improvement with words and action. Often students are initially ignored, which leads to walkouts. For walkouts associated with issues outside of schools, administrators have to balance their responses to various constituencies. Give students an opportunity to have in-school forums to discuss their grievances. This could eliminate the need for a walkout. Get parents involved in working through the student's grievances, and work with teachers to create educational activities around civic engagement. Finally, students have a democratic and constitutional right to protest. In some instances it is the only way their concerns can be heard. Hard-line responses should be a last resort, regardless of what one thinks of the student demands. School officials should listen to student concerns, address them as best as they can, and show students they are respected. Student protests are highly educational, potentially transformative, and a necessary part of civic engagement. When viewed from that perspective, school leaders can find constructive ways to make these perceived disruptions an opportunity to provide meaningful discussions with students.

Dionne Danns is an associate professor and the department chair of Educational Leadership and Policy Studies, and associate vice provost for institutional diversity at Indiana University Bloomington. She has authored or coedited three books: Something Better for Our Children: Black Organizing in Chicago Public Schools, 1963–1971*;* Desegregating Chicago's Public Schools: Policy Implementation, Politics, and Protest, 1965–1985*; and* Using Past as Prologue: Contemporary Perspectives on African American Educational History.

Just Protest

Juan Espindola

When confronted with dilemmas such as those Portland Public Schools (PPS) must grapple with in this case study, the easiest course of action for educational authorities is to discourage walkouts (for example, by threatening that absences will be unexcused) or even forbid them (for example, by locking students in or out). Officials who take these steps may be well-intentioned. But they are often wrong to do so. This is not because walkouts themselves are intrinsically virtuous; they are not. Rather, it is because stymieing walkouts is likely to exacerbate extant forms of educational injustice—injustices to which the walkouts are often an implicit or explicit response.

In particular, schools are obligated both to provide adequate civic instruction and to construct inclusive classrooms. The failure to fulfill either duty of educational justice morally disqualifies those schools from prohibiting or discouraging walkouts. In other words, lockouts, not walkouts, stand in need of justification. This is true even when the problem of political violence comes onto the scene. By shifting the burden of justification, I show how student activism merits more breathing space, and how teachers and school authorities ought to work with activists rather than shutting them down.

CIVIC INSTRUCTION

One set of arguments in the case study values walkouts for their civic qualities, that is, for giving students a civic training of sorts. When students protest against the relocation of a teacher, or the substitution of an art class for extra math, they exercise this kind of civic agency. Educational stakeholders worry, however, that such an engagement comes at the cost of valuable instructional time, presumably for non-civic subjects. How seriously should we take this worry?

The answer depends on whether schools such as Lincoln High or Benson High (or for that matter, any school) promote civic instruction in an adequate way. As things currently stand in the United States, few schools provide rich opportunities for civic engagement. There is little evidence in this case showing that schools in PPS do so, either, despite one administrator's vague allusions to alternative civic programming. If anything, schools and districts across the country are inclined to do just the opposite. In response to corporate, legislative, and even parental pressure, schools increasingly sacrifice subjects and activities, such as civic instruction, that are not perceived to be instrumental in helping students improve their SAT scores or gain a competitive edge in the job market.

Students merit high-quality civic instruction, however, and they have a right to construct it for themselves if their school does not provide it. Civic instruction is an irreplaceable part of the curriculum because it alone gives students the skills and knowledge to participate effectively in public affairs. Civic participation, in turn, is essential for collective self-determination—the basis on which fundamental decisions about education policy must rest, including how to allocate school time between civic and non-civic education. Thus, if without the walkouts students are likely to lack any kind of civic instruction, then school authorities must countenance these protests as an imperfect instance of civic learning.

While in a sense this way of framing the problem imposes a limit on authorities to restrict walkouts, in another sense it gives them some leverage to do so by providing more fruitful civic instruction. The point of civic education is to help youth acquire knowledge, hone skills, and display attitudes that will assist them in becoming competent and responsible citizens. Walkouts may achieve some of these goals by energizing students and by giving them a voice and an ephemeral experience of what acting in concert with others is all about. But walkouts achieve little in other important regards. They may be unable to help students sustain interest in, and apply their knowledge to confronting pressing public issues that affect them. Walkouts may also be a double-edged sword by failing to foster a sense of self-efficacy if students perceive that their protest is ineffective. Thus, if officials address the civic deficit in schools by promoting more structured and empowering kinds of civic instruction (for example, by offering students orientation about the best way to get involved in the work of community organizations), then they may rightly restrict walkouts. But absent such civic education initiatives, these officials have no legitimacy to limit walkouts.

INCLUSIVE CLASSROOMS

In addition to giving students the opportunity to become at least rudimentarily engaged in the affairs of their community, walkouts are valuable for giving voice to disadvantaged students experiencing an injustice of some kind. They are a channel for grievances when other avenues may be occluded. (The two motivations—civic engagement and resistance to injustice—may of course be related, but it is important to realize that they do not necessarily go hand in hand). In Forest Grove High School, for example, disadvantaged students felt unfairly treated and disrespected as a result of insidious practices involving tracking, stereotyping, and discrimination. Deprived of mechanisms to render the school accountable, they demonstrated to oppose these racial and ethnic injustices that disadvantaged them.

Walkouts are often the only channel available to disadvantaged youth to articulate these grievances, and therefore should not be restricted or even discouraged (as through unexcused absences). This is because schools' authority over students should be understood as a form of social contract. As with other social contracts, those under the school's rule must not be arbitrarily subjected to practices they have not acquiesced to and that unfairly disadvantage them. To the extent that schools enable by action or omission the educational injustices committed against disadvantaged students, they lack moral standing to prohibit or discourage walkouts. In other words, it would be morally objectionable for teachers and school authorities to suffocate or impede walkouts when they have failed to discharge their duty to build inclusive school environments. It is no exaggeration to claim that obstructing walkouts would make them complicit in educational injustice.

The discomfort of some (likely more privileged) students, and the loss of instructional time (benefiting whom?), must also be weighed against the potential gains to disadvantaged students from schools becoming more accommodating and just as a result of their protests. These gains need not have immediate or obvious distributive consequences. The sheer validation of the demands of aggrieved, disadvantaged youth is valuable in and of itself because it is an expression of respect for them.

The obvious implication of these ideas is that school personnel must be honest, serious, and effective about creating inclusive school environments, with practices ranging from empowering minority families to making faculty aware of potentially unjust and disrespectful school practices. This is to the student's benefit but also, more pragmatically, to that of school authorities, since if they are able to show that they have ways of ending discrimination, then they have some leeway to place legitimate (but reasonable) restrictions on walkouts.

POLITICAL VIOLENCE

Protecting students from the threat of political violence—which is both unpredictable and possibly uncontrollable even through the exercise of public force—may be schools' strongest justification for preventing student walkouts. Nonetheless, even when the potential for violence has been duly taken into account, school authorities must make a convincing case that lockouts are justified, and the threshold of justification must be set high. This is because the risk-benefit calculations behind walkouts and lockouts are both complex and responsive to school intervention in a variety of ways.

First, schools that restrict walkouts should be required to show that violence is truly likely or even imminent. The reason to impose such a stringent standard is that without it, school authorities would have at their disposal exceedingly broad grounds on which to restrict any demonstration that came their way; the concern, as in First Amendment jurisprudence, is that unsubstantiated appeals to the risk of violence may have a chilling effect on the expression of ideas. Second, schools must show that there are no alternative means of guaranteeing the personal safety of students, aside from prohibiting or restricting walkouts. This will be challenging, since not only do such alternatives usually exist, but these alternatives will also advance instead of undercut the school's mission of fostering critical thinking. For example, school authorities can teach students about the risks of protesting in situations with the potential for violence, and they can offer guidance on how to cope with those risks (for example, through cultivating skills of emotional self-regulation). High school students may not be as mature as adults, but they are *sufficiently* mature to understand and to learn how to behave in those situations.[52] In fact, only by giving them the benefit of the doubt to exercise such complex civic judgment are they likely to develop it.

In sum, if the case for lockouts has nothing to say about how to compensate for the positive role of walkouts in bringing into full light the deficits of educational institutions from the point of view of civic education or justice or both, it may be guilty of throwing the baby out with the bathwater. Lockouts stand in need of a robust justification. I suspect that more often than not, school authorities will be unable to provide one.

Juan Espindola is a CONACYT research fellow and an assistant professor in the education program at the Center for Research and Teaching in Economics (CIDE) in Mexico City. As a political theorist and author of Transitional Justice After German Reunification: Exposing Unofficial Collaborators *(Cambridge University Press, 2015), he also researches private schooling and educational equality.*

CHAPTER 4

The Price of Safety

Gang Prevention, Immigration Status, and Law Enforcement in Schools

TATIANA GERON AND MEIRA LEVINSON

"The public comment session is now over." Rosefield County School Board Chairwoman Jen Antiglione looked out across the municipal building auditorium. The Board usually didn't have much of an audience for its meetings. Today, however, the auditorium was packed with teachers, parents, students, school administrators, community organizers, and small business owners. They all wanted to weigh in on County Commissioner Michael Lonergan and Sheriff Anthony Fiorelli's proposed anti-gang partnership with the schools.

The evening had opened with a moment of silence for three Rosefield students, two from North High School and one from South, who had been killed just in the past six months. Marisol Sanchez, Ana Willis, and Rodrigo Mora's murders were devastating confirmations of the rise in gang violence that was setting the suburban community on edge. No wonder people had become emotional over nearly two hours of public testimony for and against the proposal.

"In compliance with state law, I propose that the Board go into executive session to discuss matters of security and public safety. Do I hear a motion?"

"So moved," board member Lena Gonzalez affirmed.

"Second," Marie Austin chimed in.

"All in favor?"

William Santos and Patty Sullivan joined Gonzalez, Austin, and Antiglione in raising their hands in assent. The five school board members then moved toward a small conference room across the hall from the auditorium. Superintendent Jack McMahon followed, as did school district attorney Joseph Ryan and the board secretary.

"Chairwoman Antiglione?" Juan Ramirez, a junior at North High School and the board's student representative, asked. "Can I participate in this session?"

"It's not a personnel issue, so the bylaws permit it," Antiglione pondered, as Ryan nodded. "Sure, please join us, Juan. It's great that you're so committed to this work."

Once everyone was settled, Antiglione turned toward McMahon. "Superintendent, could you please recap the outline of the proposal?"

"Of course." McMahon cleared his throat and glanced at his notes. "Rosefield County Sheriff's Department has received $500,000 from the Department of Justice for gang prevention initiatives. A portion of this money is earmarked for community programming. Given that gang recruitment has been occurring on school grounds, and gang affiliation has become a school issue, Commissioner Lonergan and Sheriff Fiorelli are proposing a partnership between the sheriff's department and the school district, to be funded by the DOJ grant."

"I think it's worth noting here the nature of the school issue," Ryan interjected. "No violence has been committed on school grounds, but we know that gangs have been recruiting at North and South High, and Marisol and Rodrigo were targeted after resisting recruitment efforts."

"Marisol, Rodrigo, and Ana are three out of seven murders in Rosefield this year," added Austin. "Considering the testimony we've just heard about how our students and teachers have been impacted by the violence, and how many families are asking the schools to get involved in prevention, this is a really fortunate opportunity that the DOJ is finally taking an interest in Rosefield."

"But we need to consider what this program entails," Santos cautioned.

Ramirez nodded in agreement. "Superintendent, could you please go over the details again?" Ramirez asked. "I got a bit confused during the public comment session."

"That's not surprising, Juan, given the number of different ideas people proposed. I'm not sure they realized that the program design is already established. Anyway, it's the same program they've been using over in Danforth County," McMahon explained. "You heard the sheriff's testimony. Gang affiliation is down by almost 40 percent among kids in Danforth schools, and it stays down throughout high school. Plus the teachers love it—the exit surveys are through the roof."[1]

"My niece is the guidance counselor at Danforth Middle. She says it's improved the school environment and the kids' attitudes towards police,"[2] Austin affirmed.

"The commissioner and sheriff want to bring that success to our district," McMahon continued. "Sheriff Fiorelli would assign one deputy to each of the middle and high schools. They would teach gang prevention curricula to students—you know, communication and refusal skills, conflict resolution, that sort of thing.[3] They'd also run a Recognize the Signs professional development for teachers, which trains school personnel in respecting cultural diversity, dealing with disruptive students, and identifying and supporting at-risk kids.[4] We'll work with teachers to refer students to a support group, and hook these kids up with mentors and summer jobs. The point is to give students a positive path and a sense of community through a full Rosefield County partnership."

"Thank you for that very clear summary, Superintendent," Antiglione took over. "Now, we know neither the commissioner nor the sheriff has been exactly . . . discreet about the program so far. They want to move quickly with the money they've received, and they've been open with the community about their proposal. We've heard from a number of people tonight, and it will be up to Superintendent McMahon to issue a recommendation for us to vote on in our next meeting. In the meantime, though, I think it would be useful to get a sense of where people stand."

"I think it's just what we need," Gonzalez enthused. "It's crucial that we respond to community concerns and get teachers more informed and involved. I can see how this could really slow the growth of gangs in Rosefield. I don't know why they've chosen our county and kids, but we've got to unite to stop them."

"We know why they've chosen us," Austin commented. "We're an easy target—an all-American community with no defenses up. The problem is these Central Americans, coming from places with a gang culture and taking advantage of our immigration policies or just crossing the border illegally."

"Hang on, Marie," interrupted Antiglione. "I hear you making some pretty big assumptions about families in Rosefield."

"I'm not just talking about families, Jen. So many kids are coming by themselves! You heard Principal Lane testify that South High School absorbed thirty-four new unaccompanied minors just this spring. North took in seventy-two. These kids come here, usually without conventional family; even their sponsor might be someone they don't know. They come to our community not knowing the language or culture. They're vulnerable, and these gangs preach protection.[5] Schools need to provide them with resources to stop the cycle of violence. This is what this program would allow us to do."

"I'm not convinced," Antiglione countered. "Five years ago, we voted to remove sheriff's deputies from our schools in order to disrupt what we saw as the potential for a school-to-prison pipeline. Superintendent, you were a major champion of that measure—you know how much work it took to change people's mindsets about discipline. But teachers and parents are finally on board, and it's paying off. District suspension rates have dropped by over 70 percent, and our graduation rates are up. Now we want to welcome law enforcement back in?"

"You sound exactly like Principal Adams," McMahon lamented. "She called me this morning as soon as she heard the announcement and told me under no circumstances did she want Fiorelli's deputies back at North High School."

"I don't understand why not," Gonzalez queried. "The officers aren't going to be involved with discipline this time. They're running enrichment programs. Besides, think of Marisol, Ana, and Rodrigo. Circumstances have changed in Rosefield. We need to protect our students."

"I think we have different ideas of protection, Lena," Antiglione responded. "Have you forgotten all the research we looked at? Having officers in schools substantially increases the number of students involved in the criminal justice system.[6] I'm especially worried about our students of color. The sheriff talked about looking for warning signs of gang involvement—how is that different from racial profiling? Deputies assume any young Latino is involved in gangs, and they look for any reason to arrest them. This issue was brought to our board last year!"

"Not to mention that Fiorelli's office is working in partnership with Immigration and Customs Enforcement," Santos broke in. "He's part of a nationwide network of counties whose members have been trained to enforce immigration law as part of the 287(g) program. Under the partnership, sheriff's deputies have been trained to act in the same capacity as ICE officials. They can detain and even carry out deportations."[7]

"Really?" Sullivan asked, shocked.

"Yeah," Santos affirmed. "You know how I assist Rosefield Unidas with their legal services? We're working with one family right now—their nephew was suspected of being gang affiliated and was picked up by the sheriff's office. The charges were bogus and were dropped. But because of the partnership with ICE, they still detained him when they found out he didn't have papers.[8] Now we're fighting to release him from a detention center."

Ramirez shifted in his chair uncomfortably.

"I can't see how putting ICE-trained officers in schools, where they will come into contact with undocumented students and unaccompanied minors who are suspected of gang involvement, is going to end well," Santos continued. "We talk about a school-to-prison pipeline, well, you could be setting up a school-to-*deportation* pipeline if we have these officers literally walking the hallways."[9]

"I hear your concern," Austin responded. "But most of our students aren't at risk of deportation, while they *are* at risk from gangs."

"Yes, we need to protect all of our students from violence, right?" Sullivan attempted to compromise.

"I agree," Gonzalez jumped in. "The *testimonios* we heard in the public comment section were pretty powerful. Families are struggling, fearing for their children's safety. They need schools to supplement what parents are doing at home.

Kids have a lot of hours in the afternoon to get themselves in trouble, and it gets worse in the summer when their parents are at work all day. Remember what Mr. Ramon told us earlier—the mentorship and summer internship programs felt like an answer to his prayers. I'm sure you could figure out ways to help the kids you're concerned about," Gonzalez concluded. "But please don't ruin the chances for other students."

"Especially when you're focused on students who are here illegally in the first place!" Austin added.

"I'd like to respond to that comment," Ramirez spoke up. "For starters, Ana was my lab partner, and Marisol was a friend of mine. This issue hits me hard. But, as some of you know, last year I decided to be open with my school. I started a student group called Undocumented and Unafraid. I'm an undocumented immigrant. I wanted to speak up about the challenges that come with being undocumented and try to change how students like me are perceived in the community."

Ramirez looked from Austin to the rest of the group. "Part of the reason I felt comfortable doing this was because of how committed North High School and the district have been to respecting students like me and families like mine. Taking school resource officers out of schools, using restorative justice practices instead of zero tolerance—our district did all that. Because of this, school has always felt like a place I could be safe, be myself."

"You've done quite a job," Sullivan said, smiling at the student representative.

"Thank you. But honestly, if this program goes through and sheriff's deputies are in schools every day next year, well, I'll definitely have to disband our group, I won't plan on running for student representative . . . honestly, I don't even know how I'll feel about coming to school at all."

"But you've put in so much work!" Sullivan protested. "That would be terrible."

"It might not be worth the risk." Ramirez responded.

"And it's not just Juan," Santos reminded the group. "There are lots of undocumented students who likely have similar stories, even if they aren't getting top grades and serving as school board rep. They deserve our protection and respect, too."

"Exactly," Ramirez nodded. "What I'm trying to say is, if you bring sheriff's deputies into school, it isn't safe for us anymore. I'm not saying that we don't do anything. I'm not sure what to do. But I do think we have to leave law enforcement out of it."

"Juan, I really appreciate you sharing your story," said McMahon. "I promise that, no matter what, our commitment to families and kids won't go away. No one's going to be asking about students' immigration status under my watch—that's illegal, anyway, thanks to *Plyler v. Doe*. We welcome all students. And all student information is protected, that's what FERPA is for."

"Well, Superintendent, law enforcement isn't bound by FERPA," cautioned Attorney Ryan. "And I'd be careful about promising anything on behalf of the sheriff."[10]

Antiglione could hear the custodians unpacking their vacuum cleaners for the night shift. "All right," she sighed. "Any last considerations?"

"I know you said that Principal Adams is opposed to the partnership at North," Gonzalez remarked, "but we should also pay attention to Principal Lane's testimony. She thinks it could make a really positive difference at South."

"I'd also like to remind the group," said Austin, "that the Private Industry Council and the Boys and Girls Club have already signed on as partners to the Commissioner's plan. Community members are mobilizing, whether or not the school board votes to approve."

"Sure," Santos responded, "but it's up to us whether we invite the sheriff's deputies into our schools. Not all money is good money, Jack," he said, turning back to the superintendent. "We need to set our own priorities, not rush into a partnership just because the resources are there."

"It all seemed so simple when the Commissioner first announced the plan," Sullivan said, dejectedly. "Now I don't know what to think."

The board fell silent. Antiglione decided to wrap things up. "We all have a lot to think about, I guess. Superintendent, we'll need a final recommendation from you next week, so we can gather our thoughts in time for the vote."

McMahon felt his head spinning. Should he choose to recommend the partnership, or not?

Education and Deportation

Serving Students in an Era of Intensified Immigration Enforcement

Jennifer M. Chacón

The 1982 case of *Plyler v. Doe* famously established the right of unauthorized migrant children to receive a free public school education. The Court reasoned that although a state could legally distinguish between those who were lawfully present and those who were not, it was "difficult to conceive of a rational justification for penalizing these [undocumented] children for their presence within the United States,"[11] especially given "the importance of education in maintaining our basic institutions and the lasting impact of its deprivation on the life of the child."[12] Although *Plyler* has been challenged over the years, the case has proven resilient. Lower courts readily use the case as the basis for enjoining legislation—including California's Proposition 187 and a Georgia law requiring public schools keep track of students' immigration status—that burdens the right of noncitizen children to an education.

But schools have never been a completely safe haven. Two contemporary developments in particular suggest that educators will need to engage more actively in preserving the security of immigrant children. The first trend is the emergence of a mode of school discipline that both emulates and leverages the tools of the criminal enforcement system. The second is the rapid rise of an aggressive immigration enforcement regime that leverages the work of state and local criminal justice actors in bringing noncitizens into the deportation pipeline.

CRIMINALIZED SCHOOL DISCIPLINE

This comment cannot fully unpack the complex entwinement of schools and the criminal enforcement system, but it can offer a few key snapshots that help to illustrate the linkage. First, schools are increasingly a site of criminal justice surveillance technologies. "According to the National Center for Education Statistics, 60 percent of high schools conduct random searches using drug sniffing dogs, 84 percent use cameras, and 12 percent use metal detectors to screen students."[13] 68 percent of students ages twelve to eighteen reported that a security guard was assigned to their school.[14] The Supreme Court has given school officials broad leeway to conduct suspicionless drug tests of certain students, as well as intrusive strip searches of students on levels of suspicion that fall far below that which would be required outside of the school setting.[15] These surveillance technologies are concentrated in schools attended by poor and non-White students.[16]

A second, related trend is the increased presence in schools of uniformed police officers. School administrators tend to partner with these officers in ways that reduce the legal rights of the students in their charge and facilitate "the arrest of students whose crimes may otherwise have been considered too minor to warrant calling the police (e.g., involvement in a fistfight)."[17]

A third trend is the adoption of zero-tolerance policies that require swift and relatively severe punishment—often including suspension—for even minor infractions of school rules. As with heightened surveillance methods, it is low-income students and students of color who bear the brunt of the harsher punishment.[18]

A fourth trend, highlighted by the fictionalized case study here, is the rise of anti-gang initiatives tied to criminal enforcement. The US Department of Justice provides funds to local law enforcement to develop community anti-gang initiatives, some of which include schools as partners. This trend also has deleterious effects on students of color. Strong social forces hypercriminalize Black and Latinx youth, and the criminal enforcement system produces and perpetuates gang affiliations and identities for members of communities in heavy contact with that system.[19] Law enforcement and politicians further mischaracterize and manipulate weak and anecdotal evidence of gang affiliations to suit their own goals.[20] Federally funded gang intervention programs thus expand the net of students subject to gang labeling and widen the population subject to the civil, criminal, and immigration consequences of being labeled a gang member.

IMMIGRATION CONSEQUENCES OF HYPERCRIMINALIZATION AND GANG LABELING

For immigrant youth, the short- and long-term consequences of such policies can be much more severe than for their US citizen counterparts—and both they and educators are operating in an unprecedented landscape of immigration enforcement. The federal budget for immigration enforcement has increased more than twenty-fold since the early 1990s. Immigration-related crimes now account for about half of the prosecutions in the federal criminal justice system, up from less than 5 percent in the early 1990s. Most significantly, the federal government has shifted from discouraging or taking a neutral stance toward state and local involvement in immigration enforcement to encouraging or even requiring such cooperation.

Sometimes, state and local cooperation is achieved contractually—as when the federal government signs agreements with state, county, or local law enforcement entities pursuant to section 287(g) of the Immigration and Nationality Act. These agreements allow state or local officials to investigate immigration status and assist with federal immigration enforcement efforts.

Sometimes, state and local cooperation is involuntary. The Secure Communities program requires that all local and state arrest data be run through federal databases to determine the immigration status of offenders; Immigration and Customs Enforcement officers may then initiate immigration enforcement actions against any noncitizen as they see fit. Furthermore, the Trump administration has initiated lawsuits against states and localities that have attempted to shield immigrant residents from immigration enforcement. The power of states and localities to control the participation of their own officials in federal immigration enforcement efforts is thus very much in question.

Finally, some states and localities have decided to actively assist in federal immigration efforts through their own legislation. Arizona's SB 1070 section 2(b) requires officers to inquire into immigration status and communicate with federal officials, for example, while Texas's SB 4 prohibits local governments from limiting their own employees' cooperation with federal enforcement efforts.

All of these developments should send a clear signal to public officials—including school administrators—that both the Trump administration and some state officials are seeking active and uncritical collaboration by all government officials in federal immigration enforcement efforts. What might that mean for programs like the one that the Rosefield County School Board is considering?

At bottom, it means that Juan Ramirez's concerns are not hypothetical. These concerns are real and urgent. For students who lack legal status, any interaction with a criminal enforcement official—whether federal, state, county or local—is a potential gateway to deportation. With its attempted rescission of and refusal to accept new applications for the Deferred Action for Childhood Arrival (DACA) program, the Trump administration has made it quite clear that even childhood arrivals who are in school and on track for graduation should expect no particular solicitude when it comes to federal immigration enforcement.

Those who fall under the broad auspices of gang intervention efforts will certainly be at risk for deportation. They will also be at risk for exclusion from future legalization programs that require findings of "good moral character" or that bar individuals who pose unspecified "threats" to the community. This was a problem for some youth seeking protection under DACA, and would almost certainly be a problem under future immigration reform bills.

Gang intervention programs may also increase the vulnerability of immigrant youth with legal immigration status. Gang labeling jeopardizes an immigrant's ability to establish good moral character—a prerequisite for naturalization to citizenship. Gang labeling also jeopardizes the ability of lawfully present immigrants to travel internationally, since it can pose barriers to their reentry at the border on national security grounds.

School officials who wrestle with a dilemma such as this must do so with the full awareness that they will not be able to insulate students from federal immigration enforcement efforts that may be set in motion by students' contact with criminal enforcement actors. In a political climate that prizes deportation over discretion, educators' choices can sustain or squarely undercut *Plyler*'s promise.

Jennifer M. Chacón is the former Chancellor's Professor of Law and senior associate dean for administration at the University of California, Irvine School of Law, and is currently a professor of law at the UCLA School of Law. Her recent research, which focuses on the intersection of criminal and immigration law enforcement, has been funded by the National Science Foundation and the Russell Sage Foundation.

How to Interrupt Safety for Some and Precarity for Others

LEIGH PATEL

I read and reread this case in early 2018. When I first received it, I tossed and turned over the fact that intertwined violence, surveillance, militarization, and safety for a select few have marked this nation since its inception. I also thought of the many classrooms and schools I have been part of where youth and adults took on the arduous, love-filled work of interrupting the trauma and violence in blighted neighborhoods. They persisted in difficult, complex community accountability circles out of a commitment to refuse enclosure or banishment as solutions to harm. These topics are new neither to me nor to most anyone with the slimmest understanding of the challenges facing schools and society at large.

Gang violence is but one of many deeply distinct yet connected loci of violence and aggression for the protection of some. And yet, gangs are also a symptom of the problematic collectives that form in Black and brown neighborhoods that are overpoliced, and at the same time burdened with underresourced schools, food deserts, and a paucity of public space. The early twenty-first century has seen entire school districts become privatized, urban areas spliced even more distinctly by segregation, and a worrying trend of shuttering public schools. In these contexts, contingent safety for some gang members is provided by virtue of being part of the gang. Law enforcement itself can also be seen as a social force of violence and aggression for the protection of some. This depends largely, sadly, upon how one is racially read by law enforcement. The commonality between gangs and law enforcement—of safety being fickle and coming with a violent price—is hard to miss.

The case also brings to bear the thin, if not invisible, line between law enforcement and deputized immigration enforcement. Through the 287(g) program, law enforcement officers have been able to choose to participate in questioning and detaining people who are suspected to be in this country without documentation from the United States government. Migration is the result of the push and pull forces of global capitalism. The trends of migration into the United States over the past twenty years have been from the global South, meaning that suspecting someone to be an unauthorized immigrant almost always entails racial profiling. This only adds momentum to the unseemly history of law enforcement in this nation that began as the mechanism to pursue enslaved peoples who had slipped from bondage.[21]

On February 14, 2018, these intermingled forces of violence, property, safety for some, and accelerated precarity for others crystallized in a cruel way. That day, a nineteen-year-old entered a high school in Parkland, Florida, and carried out a mass shooting that left seventeen people dead and fourteen more injured. In the aftermath of this mass shooting, there were the predictable prayers from politicians and little action. But then the sitting President of the United States proposed that an answer to mass shootings in schools would be to arm up to 700,000 teachers across the nation, paying them a stipend for their additional sharpshooter skills. By contrast, youth in this community in South Florida, where the median household income is $200,000, confronted their state's senators calling for disarmament in a town hall that was broadcast on prime-time television. Other groups, including the Black Youth Project and the Dreamers, have also called for demilitarization, gun control, and healing over dehumanization. None of these groups have been featured on cable news as headliners unto themselves. This horrific mass shooting and its aftermath also demonstrate the complicated patterns of power and violence in the United States.

This is nation that was built and has maintained a practice of violence. It has been rightly named as a settler colony, a nation which was built through the ongoing and linked practices of land seizure, attempts to remove and erase Indigenous peoples, and enslavement of Black peoples for both property and labor exploitation.[22] This is also a nation which heralds heteropatriarchy. While the #metoo movement of 2018 raised collective consciousness about the widespread violence and abuse that women and men who are not cis and/or hetero experience, it occurred at a time when the nation had as its leader a man who openly and repeatedly objectified women as sexual objects for conquest. Put more simply, this is a nation where racist capitalism and toxic masculinity reign in societal institutions. Schools do not exist outside of these metrics.

There are, in actuality, no barriers between schools and society. Like the thin membranes of the human cell, this society's logic and actions of property, enclosure, and punishment flow in and out of its schools. This nation was formed out of the forced removal of Indigenous peoples from their lands, and through enslaved labor and the attempt to make Black peoples into chattel property. The impulses of racist capitalism, which seeks to erase, replace, and dispossess some people so that others can accumulate wealth and power, still, sadly, persist.

How then should a school, struggling to ensure safety for all its members, contend with these intertwined forces that have centuries-long precedence and yet seem to have reached a next-level articulation of violence? The entanglements are intimidating. School safety officers have become a normalized presence in schools, and young people do build relationships with them, for good and bad. In 2016, school safety officer Ben Fields literally threw a sixteen-year-old Black girl across a classroom while she was seated at her desk. He was suspended, and shortly after his suspension, some students, including Black students at that high school, wore T-shirts that said, "Bring back Fields." How will these students learn about historical and contemporary militarization and enclosure of Black and brown youth while being in close proximity to these officials? What are they learning about themselves as the nation incarcerates roughly 3.2 million people, a major industry profiting from the enclosure of Black and brown people?

Building relationships with law enforcement cannot merely be suggested as a lateral positive gain. These relationships are built within the context of racism, as Ruthie Wilson Gilmore defined it: "the state-sanctioned or extralegal production and exploitation of group-differentiated vulnerability to premature death."[23] Until the nation reckons with its roots, and with its protection of racist capitalism and toxic masculinity, it cannot simplistically embrace police presence in the form of school safety officers, particularly when so many have been deputized to act as de facto immigration enforcement.

In light of this, I recommend that we reach beyond the idea of safety and think instead of community and the deliberate pursuit of freedom. As I thought about the case and the ways in which it so aptly refracts the complexities of a nation that speaks of liberty but acts on behalf of violent stratification, I have come to propose an altogether different set of questions than those the school board considered:

- What community accountability requirements should be set for any adult who is entrusted with youth in this land?
- What unlearning and relearning should law enforcement officers experience to alter their understanding of law enforcement as it began and has been militarized? How might this unlearning and learning help to alter their thinking and associated practices to interrupt racism, toxic masculinity, domination, and surveillance?

- What should students be learning about the origins and purposes of law enforcement? What should they learn from the US Department of Justice's reports on Ferguson, Chicago, and Detroit?
- How can shared governance, without adultism, shape the creation of a community of accountability and answerability?

By refusing the choice as given between more school-based law enforcement and safety as only offered through the state, we are given the purview to ask questions that cut more deeply to the conditions of humanness, safety, and precarity we actively and implicitly create. There is no small amount of racialization in this case study, in who is deemed to be safe and who portends danger. By upending the equivalency between law enforcement and safety, we might better apprehend what it means for a community to create conditions for all its members to be safe. Such a community might draw upon restorative practices rather than enclosure when rules, sometimes arbitrary and often racialized rules, are transgressed. To refuse the choice as given opens up wholly other choices.

Leigh Patel is the associate dean of equity and justice at the University of Pittsburgh's School of Education. Prior to working in the academy, she was a language arts teacher, journalist, and state-level policymaker. Her work addresses the narratives we tell about school and how those narratives create material realities.

Principled Policing

Respecting and Valuing the Community's Voice

KATHLEEN O'TOOLE

The scenario that plays out in this case study is not uncommon. Tasked with confronting an issue, decision makers convene, often as an exclusive cohort, to craft a response. It is only afterward that stakeholder input is sought. As a result, deliberations are rushed and perspectives are left unheard or undervalued. Having spent nearly four decades of my career in policing, I know well the skepticism with which such predetermined solutions are likely to be met. It is a natural and foreseeable consequence of siloed and myopic decision-making, however well intentioned. While certainly not isolated to the field, it is a process that has been pervasive in law enforcement, an occupation rooted in command and control structures.

Still, the answer to the question presented in this case—should Superintendent McMahon recommend the partnership or not?—is an easy, yet qualified, yes. To reject the partnership for fear of what it could become would be to deprive at-risk students of programs and opportunities that have demonstrated potential for success. But, by failing to engage other stakeholders in discussions, those involved in crafting the proposal missed critical opportunities to hear concerns, identify and address barriers to implementation, and build a foundation of legitimacy to support and inform eventual decisions. These concerns could have been substantially mitigated, and greater acceptance attained, by integrating throughout the life of the decision-making process principles of a model I have previously termed "equilibrated governance."[24] As the final vote on the proposal is not scheduled to take place until the next board meeting, time remains to reposition the measure for success.

THE EQUILIBRATED GOVERNANCE MODEL

Principles of governance in both the public and private sectors generally recognize that being accountable to one's purpose and stakeholders is integral to the able functioning of any organization. This is particularly true for law enforcement. Indeed, central tenets of modern policing, paraphrasing from Sir Robert Peel's mandate to the London Metropolitan Police nearly two centuries ago, are to prevent crime and disorder through prevention and deterrence, and to recognize always that the power of the police to fulfill their functions and duties is dependent on the ability to secure and maintain the trust of the public.

My personal experience in police practice on both sides of the Atlantic repeatedly validated Peel's theory. During the Northern Ireland Peace Process, the Independent Commission on Policing—on which I served—received extraordinary input and feedback from more than two thousand written submissions and public testimony at forty community meetings. We built legitimacy and trust by listening respectfully and carefully to those whose lives had been forever impacted by bombs and bullets over the course of thirty years. They certainly had the right to contribute to the process, and they knew best what was required to maintain safety and order in their neighborhoods. As Boston Police Commissioner and Seattle Police Chief, my teams and I engaged constantly with community members to develop multidisciplinary prevention and intervention strategies to address complicated issues around crime, addiction, mental health, and homelessness. We never dictated the agenda—we worked collaboratively. Effective engagement led to successful, nationally recognized programs, productive partnerships, enhanced community trust, and greater police legitimacy.

The model of equilibrated governance is simply a formalization of my decades of experience as a police practitioner. The model supports an organization's ability to meet its commitments to accountability, transparency, and purpose through a balance of agile leadership, authentic engagement, and contextual intelligence. Briefly summarized:

- *Agile leadership* implies in this context a collective approach to decision-making, leveraging the input from and expertise across an organization's members, partners, and stakeholders.[25]
- *Authentic engagement* builds legitimacy with a commitment to active listening; honest, constructive dialogue; and transparency of action and intention, especially in situations (such as presented in this case study) where suspicion or skepticism may be high and ideologies and perspectives at odds.
- *Contextual intelligence* requires learning and understanding a community's history, culture, and capacity in order to recognize and diagnose the dynamic contextual variables at play in a pressing issue; it results in an intentional adjustment of decision-makers' behavior in order to react appropriately in a given context.[26]

Equilibrated governance brings these concepts together to ensure fair representation of stakeholders at all stages of a decision-making process and the agility to bend process as needed or appropriate. It is a model that ensures legitimacy of outcome because it purposefully values and reflects the inputs received.

EQUILIBRATED GOVERNANCE IN ROSEFIELD COUNTY

It is important to remember that the proposed partnership is meant to address an issue over which different stakeholders already share objectives: to confront the rise in gang violence by addressing root causes of gang recruitment through education, awareness, and mentorship. As the discussion in executive session illustrates, the discord centers not on *whether* this public safety goal should be pursued, but rather on *how* such a goal can be achieved without further imperiling fragile communities and straining precarious relationships. Also, given the decision five years ago to remove sheriff's deputies from the schools—a move validated by data showing a dramatic drop in suspensions and rise in graduation rates—how would the schools justify shifting course to welcome deputies back? Taking an equilibrated governance approach can help ensure that the shared objective of community safety can be met while minimizing other risks.

The missed opportunities to this point can be remedied through agile leadership that incorporates and promotes authentic engagement with the community. With apparent flexibility in directing grant funds, school and police leaders should open the program scope to communitywide discussion, so they can identify consensus-based solutions, clear boundaries, and barriers to implementation. Which aspects of the program, for example, raise concerns for community members? Can these concerns be addressed through program modifications or alternatives? How can clear policies be implemented to ensure that deputies assigned to the schools will not engage in 287(g)—immigration—enforcement? Which strategies open up too much risk and should thus be excluded from the program scope? Are there identified needs that remain unmet by the program scope? How have interested stakeholders had opportunities to voice their perspectives on the partnership?

Answering these questions requires early and consistent authentic engagement with diverse stakeholders, including communities affected, existing and potential public- and private-sector partners, subject matter experts, and others. Since so much has already transpired in Rosefield without this engagement, it is imperative that leaders quickly expand discussion beyond the police department and the school district. Officials assume their proposal will lead to success in Rosefield County as it did in Danforth County, but are the two counties sufficiently similar to render that assumption true? Engaging with community organizations in Rosefield will help answer this question, and it will demonstrate a commitment to transparency. Retreating into executive session, by contrast, all but assures that the existing trust between the school district and community will be quickly undermined.

Authentic engagement opens dialogue among all committed stakeholders. Contextual intelligence, in turn, informs perspective. Fair consideration of stakeholder input requires an honest commitment to understanding the experiences that underlie community desires, fears, and concerns. In this case, for example, the sheriff's 287(g) role in enforcement of federal immigration law has clearly fostered suspicion in some communities, bolstered by anecdotal examples of ICE activity. To gloss over this perspective with assurances that these deputies would not be focused on immigration would be to minimize a reasonable concern.

ADAPTING TO COMMUNITIES' NEEDS

This case study may be specific to one program, but it reflects a broader complexity. Just as this program seeks to defeat gang recruitment by addressing deficiencies in other supports, law enforcement often finds itself filling gaps in failed social systems like public health, family support, and treatment of substance abuse disorder. Police should embrace this role as it is philosophically aligned with Peel's principles: if the primary mission of police is to prevent crime and disorder, implementing strategies to interrupt root causes is key.

Moreover, the model reminds us that public institutions should not be afraid to refine or shift course as appropriate. Inherent in the equilibrated governance model is a dynamic, iterative approach to rethinking organizational practices in response to, or anticipation of, evolving circumstances. Just as the decision, five years ago, to remove deputies from the schools reflects a shifted approach, so too can the assignment of deputies as part of this partnership reflect a changed response to changed circumstances. But to get it right, the leaders in this case need to be flexible, authentically engage the communities they serve, and carefully consider the particular context of Rosefield. Doing so would allow the school board to move forward with a transparent, consensus-based program that advances needed interventions and addresses—and hopefully assuages—the community's concerns.

Kathleen O'Toole is a career police officer and lawyer who served as Boston's police commissioner and Seattle's police chief and has contributed to police reform initiatives elsewhere in the United States, the Republic of Ireland, and the United Kingdom. She also holds a PhD from Trinity Business School in Dublin, Ireland.

The Price of Safety in Schools Is Too High When the Most Vulnerable Have to Pay It

Zofia Stemplowska

Schools have to educate children under circumstances that are mostly not of their own making. In this harrowing case, the students and the whole community are subject to gang violence. The scenario invites us to reflect on the fact that as schools strive to address one problem their students face, they may exacerbate another problem. It shows how complicated decision-making is, once circumstances get bad enough. And yet I think that when we take into account the likely consequences and the interests of the most vulnerable children in the community, the superintendent should recommend against the proposed partnership with the sheriff's department.

THE PROBLEM

The most salient facts in this case are as follows. There has been a rise in gang violence affecting schools and the broader community. The gangs recently killed several students. They have also been recruiting students on the school grounds. Significant funds are available for an initiative that will bring sheriff's deputies into schools to teach gang prevention methods to students and staff. Although some question marks are raised in the scenario about the program, it seems that it is sufficiently well-developed to have a real chance of reducing gang recruitment and possibly also gang violence.

However, some of the very students who are vulnerable to recruitment and gang violence are also vulnerable in two further ways, which would be exacerbated by the presence of police on the school grounds should the program be adopted. First, they are vulnerable to a brand of policing that increases their chances of ending up in prison rather than at their high school graduations. Second, a significant number are vulnerable to deportation as undocumented migrants. They may try to reduce the risk by dropping out of school altogether should the program be adopted. The students are thus caught between the power the gangs have over them and the power the state has over them.

THE POWER OF GOOD POLICY DESIGN

All this immediately forces us to think of ways we could try to prevent the worst features of the situation from arising. These ways may not be available in this instance, given the details of the case, but they are worth thinking about because they show the power that societies can enjoy through better policy design.

First, we would avoid some of these problems if the program was not run by the sheriff's office. In the case at hand, it appears that groups other than the police could train and educate the children and the staff. Our funding policies for student support could favor approaches that do not involve law enforcement. Second, even if we suppose that some of the benefits of the program would arise only if police were present in schools (perhaps such a presence sends a more powerful signal to gangs), the officers themselves could be members of the force who are not "trained to enforce the immigration law as part of the 287(g) program."

Third, and relatedly, we can borrow an idea developed by Joseph Carens in the context of addressing the problem of the vulnerability of irregular migrants: namely, there should be a firewall between the deportation force and all other services aimed at securing people's general human rights.[27] Since gang violence threatens the human rights of all students, provision of measures to protect them in the school environment should come with a strict policy that members of the student body cannot be reported to deportation services.

PROTECTING THE MOST VULNERABLE

In the case at hand, these options are not available. If the schools take the money and adopt the program, the following will likely happen. There will be a reduction in gang recruitment and gang violence on the school grounds, but an increase in deportations and in students dropping out of school. The gang activities will then likely shift to target the dropouts and may shift to other districts, as implied by the suggestion in the text that the specific district is being targeted by the gangs; this suggests a different district could be targeted, too. Thus, on the one hand, we have the tangible benefit of reduced gang activity in the school and gang violence against the school population. On the other hand, we have the negative result of deportations and students dropping out.

How bad is deportation? Some of the students will be uprooted from the only place and friends they know. Some will face violence on the journey through the system of detention and deportation, and they may face gang violence and poverty when they arrive. We know that it is not the most vulnerable who become documented or undocumented migrants—the most vulnerable cannot afford to move—but we also know that the push factors have to be powerful to force people to become undocumented migrants. Situations have to be extreme to force parents to send their children away into such precarious situations on their own. All of this means that some students may prefer to drop out than be deported, as Ramirez warns us in this case. Such students will then likely become prey to gang violence outside of the school grounds. They will also face other vulnerabilities that children outside of full-time education face, and their future will be even harder than it was always going to be. If so, we may well have merely shifted the gang activities outside of the school gates while worsening the lives of many.

Even if adopting the program really did lower the chance of gang recruitment to all, the fact that it would render those already most vulnerable even more vulnerable suggests that the program would be rejected by all major theories of justice.[28] Depending on how we fill in the details, sufficientarians (meaning those who want people to have enough for a decent life), egalitarians (who want people to be equally well off) and prioritarians (who tell us to prioritize increases in well-being to the worst-off over increases in well-being to those who are doing better) would likely all agree to offer the protection to the most vulnerable. Utilitarians might disagree, since they call on us to maximize the average or total well-being of all. But if the vulnerable are vulnerable enough, and the benefits to all are small, then utilitarianism, too, may call for us to protect the most vulnerable by not adopting the program.

IMPARTIAL SCHOOLS

Admittedly, no child or family has the personal duty to bear the costs of gang activity on the school grounds in order to protect the most vulnerable members of society. Parents of the less vulnerable children should thus be allowed to lobby for the adoption of the program (I would for my children). But schools can and should act impartially when selecting their policies, even if it would be too demanding to require it of individuals; they should treat all children as mattering equally. Some may argue that schools can and should show partiality to enrolled students; in other words, a school should protect its students, but once they drop out, they are not the school's problem. But a victory for the school on such terms would be its moral failure: it would be bought at the expense of the most vulnerable children. A society fails when it keeps only some children safe. The same dynamic is replicated when we think of the contrast between protecting American children and deported children. The district could buy its own safety at the expense of the children who will thereby end up deported. If a school fails morally when it buys safety for its own students at the expense of others, a nation also fails when it buys the safety of its own children at the expense of other children.

Do the undocumented children have as much of a claim on the school for protection as all the other children? One character in the scenario comes close to implying that they may not. After all, the school did not force the undocumented students to embark on their border-crossing journey. Why not say that such undocumented students now reap what they themselves sowed, and they should bear the price of their own risk taking, and possibly even bear the responsibility for making others subject to greater gang violence?

I think such arguments fail even in relation to undocumented adult migrants, let alone children. Who among us would remain in extreme violence and extreme poverty to avoid committing the "crime" of illegally crossing borders? How can it be a fair price for such an escape that from now on our interests would always count for less? This particular scenario, in any case, makes such arguments irrelevant, because they fail in relation to children: the children are not responsible for becoming undocumented migrants. This raises a further question of how to treat the violent gang members themselves, who operate on the school grounds, and who are also minors, but I will leave this for another occasion.

Zofia Stemplowska is associate professor of political theory and Asa Briggs Fellow of Worcester College, University of Oxford. She writes about the demands of domestic, global, and historic justice.

The Pursuit of Purpose When Fear Holds Power

LAURA BURGOS

Rosefield County, like many US school districts, is struggling to distinguish between the root causes and symptoms of much larger systemic inequities. While the superintendent and school board members are seeking to address gang violence as a problem that warrants action, they are ignoring the deep-seated power imbalance, dictated by race, power, and privilege, that underlies their narrow definition of the problem. Defining the source of the perceived threat as one that is external allows them to absolve themselves of their responsibility for the lack of safety and well-being of the overall community. By defining success by what is *prevented*, rather than by what is *invented*, they neglect the true mission the school should aspire to serve. As community leaders, they should be considering the current stigmatization of immigrant youth through divisive language and stereotypes, and the district's responsibility to combat the racial discrimination it perpetuates. Instead of acknowledging how this context influences their own behavior, this group of decision makers attempts to resolve a much narrower challenge of whether to partner with law enforcement. The question at the heart of this case is not whether the superintendent should recommend the partnership, but how he and the entire school board can gain clarity on the district's mission and purpose as an entity responsible for educating a community during a time where there exists a national agenda fueling the sanctioned exclusion of Brown bodies.

TO PROTECT AND SERVE . . . AND EDUCATE?

The allocation received from the Department of Justice (DOJ) comes with a predetermined agenda. While a portion is expected to support community programming, there is no other local entity identified as playing a leading role in this partnership. With such an investment from a major government agency, there is an opportunity for an interagency approach that extends beyond the school board and DOJ to include local nonprofits, community leaders, activists, and artists. However, the connection between the proposed gang prevention program and the district's larger vision in unclear.

It appears as though the goal is to pull multiple levers, including providing professional development for teachers and creating student job opportunities, in an effort to create a "sense of community." Yet asking deputy officers to teach anti-gang curricula will likely impede any community-building efforts, as it asks students and teachers to trust those who enforce the law, a reactionary measure, to simultaneously employ a proactive approach to teaching the law. I can clearly recall the presence of police in my school as a fifth grade teacher in the East New York section of Brooklyn. On one occasion I unsuccessfully pleaded for an officer not to arrest a student of mine for a minor schoolyard fight. Intent on teaching him a lesson, the officer dismissed my plea and transported him to the local precinct. Understanding the impact of the criminalization of Black and Brown youth, I cannot fathom this officer successfully teaching any type of conflict resolution curricula to our students.

Furthermore, Rosefield County Schools' proposed effort to have officers engage in proactive programming doesn't address the root causes of why gangs form and engage in illegal activity to begin with. The late Tupac Shakur once proclaimed in his song, "Changes," "Instead of a war on poverty, they got a war on drugs so the police can bother me." In the case of Rosefield County Schools, there appears to be a war on gang activity rather than one focused on ensuring access to necessary social support systems and community resources for families new to the community. If Rosefield County was truly committed to ensuring students' and families' well-being, it would prioritize the mobilization of social service agencies and community-based organizations, not law enforcement.

THE POWER OF LANGUAGE

There is also danger in the manner in which school board members sometimes equate immigration status with gang affiliation during the meeting. When Gonzalez asks, "why they've chosen our county and kids," she implies that gang violence is an external force perpetrated by outsiders. In claiming that Central Americans have victimized Rosefield County, a so-called "all-American community with no defenses," Austin similarly blames an entirely separate subcontinent for behavior that has transpired locally, drawing a correlation between citizenship status and gang culture.

Yet the gang violence experienced in Rosefield County is an American issue, constructed and perpetrated locally and across all racial and ethnic groups. Gonzalez and Austin's incomplete analysis of the problem further serves to relieve the community of assuming responsibility for the role it plays in creating and sustaining the drivers of gang activity, including poverty, social isolation, and systemic oppression. The manner in which school board members are labeling and dismissing the very students and families they are supposed to serve raises further questions around the larger district narrative. Who does Rosefield County Schools want to be, and for whom? Furthermore, should an outside agency such as the sheriff's office—or even the US Department of Justice—dictate this?

PERCEPTIONS OF PROTECTION

Based on the context given, one can assume that students do not generally view the presence of law enforcement as academic support. In addition, these officers' identities and qualifications are unclear. Do they live in the local community? What training have they received in areas such as cultural responsiveness, social-emotional learning, and the like? There's irony in how the group that could plausibly be described as the biggest gang in America—that is, law enforcement—is seeking to save others through gang prevention. If that is the goal, the identity of a deputy officer in Rosefield County needs to be redefined. The aspirational goal of officers occupying a dual role, one of enforcer and teacher, will never come to fruition during a time when they are the public face of removing children from schools and families from communities.

Trying to make the distinction between the sheriff's deputies and ICE officials is rooted in a falsehood. The proposed partnership is reminiscent of New York's *Operation Matador*, a collective effort between local and federal law enforcement divisions focused on deporting suspected gang members, regardless of prior criminal history. This initiative is supported by the language in the Criminal Alien Gang Member Removal Act, a bill that calls for the deportation of undocumented individuals suspected of gang activity.[29] While not yet enacted into law, the introduction of the bill represents the expectations that many political leaders have for local law enforcement officers as federal immigration law enforcers. If Superintendent McMahon dismisses this reality, insisting that officers assigned to schools would not play a role in the school-to-deportation pipeline, one must question who he is there to truly serve. As a school district leader, his answer should not depend on children's citizenship status.

COMMUNITY-DESIGNED SOLUTIONS

I can't help but think how the board meeting would have played out if the school community was engaged in designing a cross-sector solution to gang activity, rather than voting on a high-level decision designed by those furthest removed from the everyday threats of violence, disconnection, and deportation. Families' desire for mentorship and internship programs, along with the expressed interest of the local Boys and Girls Club, indicate a current opportunity gap for the area's high school students. With the resources and influence of the Private Industry Council, there is room to reinvent the high school experience for students in a way that evokes innovation rather than fear. Activating student leadership, even engaging students who are formerly or currently gang affiliated, could be the lever that drives change and unity. However, Superintendent McMahon must first articulate a clear mission for the district. Until he does, he will run the risk of allowing an outside agenda rooted in fear to dictate the identity of the schools expected to serve the best interests of children.

The Rosefield County school community does not need protection; they need a shared community vision. This is the only way they will shift their priorities from classifying some community members as threats and others as victims to uniting everyone around the everyday human needs of safety, support, and stability.

Laura Burgos, EdLD '18, is a former New York City public school teacher who has spent over fifteen years leading change efforts in traditional public, nonprofit, and private education settings. She currently serves as a senior director within the University of Virginia's Darden/Curry Partnership for Leaders in Education (PLE).

How to Overcome "Contradictions of Control" in Schools—Hint, Don't Call the Sheriff

José S. Plascencia-Castillo

"José, you will be helping Officer Joe with paperwork. It will be part of your senior project. Do that, and you will graduate," said Mrs. Jones, the vice-principal of Lakeside High School, my alma mater. Inwardly, I groaned. Officer Joe had a negative reputation among the student body. Chicana and Chicano students nicknamed him "Robocop" to highlight his tough demeanor and robot-like posturing. Growing up in one of San Diego's most criminalized neighborhoods, I had also learned a few things about police officers. In the streets, I would often hear police officers refer to Mexicans as "illegals" and "wetbacks." In school, things were no different. In fact, I vividly remember Officer Joe singing "one little wetback, two little wetbacks, and three . . ." as a group of friends and I walked his way during lunch. Needless to say, I was not looking forward to being Robocop's assistant.

But there was another reason why I *feared* that assignment. As an undocumented high school student, I often wondered if the officers in our school could enforce immigration law or detain students based on their immigration status. While Officer Joe never targeted me any more than my US citizen friends, I always felt that such interactions could lead to my deportation. This constant unease reflected a broader paradox of my educational experience. On the one hand, I had to navigate under the radar to avoid deportation. But on the other hand, I also had to take risks to prove myself to my peers and to show I was a worthy individual among friends who were born in the United States. For example, when Officer Joe was tough on my friends and me, we would retaliate by tagging the school's bathroom. My friends who were secure in their citizenship status always seemed to enjoy this moment more than I did. I was not only scared of being caught by Officer Joe, but I also wondered if he could refer me to immigration officers for my behavior.

I tell this story because it is my own high school experience that leads me to argue that Superintendent McMahon should not recommend partnering Rosefield County Schools with the sheriff's department. Like many undocumented high schoolers, I have wondered why school administrators unleash the force of law enforcement on their own students. American courts have made it clear that public schools are required to teach all students—including undocumented students. This reflects the fact that schools are, and should be, safe spaces for undocumented students. However, resource officers have the ability to disrupt the school environment in which undocumented students feel protected. Thus, Superintendent McMahon should not recommend adding more resource officers to Rosefield's schools. Instead, he should consider alternative ways the district might disrupt the allure of gang involvement and recruitment.

THE "CONTRADICTIONS OF CONTROL"

In my research, I work closely with not only undocumented Chicana and Chicano youth, but also youth who are involved with gangs. Stepping back from my own experience, I have begun to see, firsthand, how a complex system of criminalization shapes the experience of these groups of youth. Many of the Chicana and Chicano youth I work with seek refuge from stigmatization in subcultures where they have room to resist the ways in which both the seemingly mundane dimensions of school culture and the sort of daily lived harassment from law enforcement and other authority figures marginalize them and distort their identity development. These subcultures, by no means perfect spaces, allow Chicana and Chicano youth to express and practice the full complexity of their identities.

It is easy to characterize such behavior as the development of an "oppositional stance" or identity.[30] Some sociologists suggest that youth develop oppositional identities when dominant cultural attitudes marginalize or alienate the values, beliefs, and behaviors of a nondominant group. Youth react by defining themselves in contrast to dominant values. Such a view, however, does not fully describe the processes that I see at work among Chicana and Chicano youth.

The sociologist Robert Garot places more emphasis on the interaction between school policies and youth identity development, a process he calls "contradictions of control."[31] According to Garot, preemptive harsh sanctions imposed by school officials on gang-involved students reinforces "tough identities." Consequently, when schools focus their efforts on managing and controlling students, youth disengage from learning, which further facilitates their adoption of a tough identity.

In this view, schools' efforts to control students, especially by criminalizing their behavior, is thus unlikely to work as an effective deterrent. In fact, doing so may actually elicit and entrench the value of "tough" identities in students targeted by control and criminalization efforts. Given the level of responsibility schools possess in the identity formation of students, one must ask: What are the risks of adding resource officers in a high school? Are such policies the best way to mediate gang involvement, recruitment, and proliferation? And how might this impact undocumented students, who face additional risks when schools implement policies that control and criminalize students?

THE RISK OF ADDING RESOURCE OFFICERS IN SCHOOLS

Superintendent McMahon's decision should be guided by what we know about why youth join gangs and about law enforcement's relationship to that process. One theory that explains why youth join gangs suggests that youth seek to resist the racial and economic subordination that leaves their communities vulnerable to exploitation.[32] Others argue that some individuals living in poverty will develop subcultures and engage in deviance as a means to resist and reject the values of a mainstream system that has rejected them.[33] Beyond rejecting their rejecters, researchers observe that even the most disreputable gang-involved youngsters desire acceptance, recognition, and incorporation into conventional society. In fact, when asked, gang-involved youth imagine themselves in a nine-to-five job, with a high school diploma, or even a college degree.[34]

All too often, law enforcement seems to exacerbate rather than disrupt such patterns. Criminologists have found that police academies train officers to practice a rogue and hostile masculinity. As Angela Harris explains, "Police officers in poor minority neighborhoods may come to see themselves as law enforcers in a community of savages, as outposts of the law in a jungle."[35] Such an attitude hardly seems appropriate to even risk connecting to schools—as my experiences with Officer Joe also anecdotally suggest.

Thus, given what we know about why youth join gangs and how law enforcement typically understands its roles in economically and socially marginalized neighborhoods, it seems entirely unlikely that the presence of resource officers in schools will reduce students' involvement in gangs. Instead, they may contribute to the creation of the sort of hostile environment for young people that unfortunately encourages gang *recruitment*. Again, such an environment is doubly dangerous for undocumented youth.

ADDRESSING THE GENESIS OF GANGS

As I read this case, I could not ignore the resonance with my own experience, bringing with it ghosts of the past. I have learned that there is immense value in listening to such ghosts. As sociologist Avery Gordon observes, "if you let them, the ghosts will lead you to what has been missing, which is sometimes everything."[36] This case is no different. If our point of analytical departure is to question a partnership such as the one described in this case and not the genesis of gangs in our communities, we risk failing both documented and undocumented youth. While issues of gang recruitment and gang proliferation are real, they should not be dealt with in ways that may exacerbate the pull of gangs among Latinx youth. And they certainly should not be attempted in ways that put undocumented youth, an already vulnerable population of students, further at risk.

José S. Plascencia-Castillo is a PhD student in the department of sociology at the University of California, Riverside. His research focuses on gangs, adolescent subcultures, and the criminalization of Chicana and Chicano youth.

CHAPTER 5

Eyes in the Back of Their Heads 2.0

Student Surveillance in the Digital Age

MEIRA LEVINSON AND GARRY S. MITCHELL

Students have always been watched while in school. Teachers magically grow "eyes in the back of their heads" to monitor student behavior even when their backs are turned. Whether it's redirecting a daydreamer, intercepting a note, assigning lunch detention for tripping a classmate, or contacting the guidance counselor when a student seems isolated on the playground, high levels of teacher surveillance keep students on task and, often, keep them safe.

As students' lives have increasingly moved from the physical to the digital world, however, distractions and signs of risk have as well, making them more difficult for teachers to spot. Instead of trying to hide their superhero drawings underneath a math worksheet, students using laptops in school can seamlessly switch desktop views from Fortnite to NewsELA as the teacher heads their way. Educators may also have a harder time keeping tabs on students' social and emotional development. Seizing a nasty note surreptitiously passed from desk to desk is one thing; seeing into students' exclusive group texts and cyberbullying on their Instagram feeds is another. Furthermore, students who are thinking of hurting themselves or others can now easily access information about how to binge and purge, commit suicide, join an extremist organization, or plan a school shooting. They may also easily find communities of like-minded adolescents who reinforce their curiosity and urge them on to unsafe, even deadly, practices.[1]

In light of these concerns, lawmakers at the federal, state, and local levels have passed legislation mandating that schools limit and/or monitor students' online activities. In 2000, Congress passed the Children's Internet Protection Act (CIPA), which requires schools receiving federal funds to restrict minors' access to harmful sites, educate students about online safety and cyberbullying, and monitor their online activities. More recently, legislatures in all fifty states have passed anticyberbullying legislation that holds schools legally responsible for student expression both on and off school grounds.[2] Although the details vary state to state, laws generally specify that schools have disciplinary authority and responsibilities whenever students are using school-provided devices (such as an iPad or a Chromebook), even if they are off campus and not engaging in any school-based activity.[3]

Such rules give educators significant *authority* to look after students' well-being, which they may appreciate, but also a breathtaking degree of *responsibility* to protect students "wherever and whenever" they are online.[4] Schools' and districts' responsibilities have been reinforced by a string of lawsuits by parents of children who have committed suicide potentially in response to bullying, including cyberbullying.[5] With school shootings in the United States now approaching an average of one a month, educators may find themselves similarly on the defensive for failing to monitor students' digital activity prior to their bringing a gun to school.[6]

Even when they recognize the benefits of such monitoring, therefore, educators may feel overwhelmed by the magnitude of the task. As one administrator asked, "Where are the people and the resources to do this?"[7]

The answer? There's an app for that. Or, more accurately, there are many apps for that, purveyed by dozens of companies ready to sell digital monitoring services to schools and districts. Thousands of school districts have signed up, many contracting with multiple purveyors to enable more complete surveillance of students' digital lives. Teachers, superintendents, information professionals, and even students themselves attest to the increased confidence and control such services provide. At the same time, however, civil liberties advocates, mental health professionals, and parents have raised warning flags about the ways in which pervasive digital surveillance may violate students' and families' rights, inculcate antidemocratic norms, and interfere with students' socioemotional development. When combined with a drumbeat of revelations about unauthorized data sharing and data security breaches by major companies such as Facebook, districts must wrestle with the question of how much digital surveillance is too much—and what is not enough?

DIGITAL SURVEILLANCE TOOLS: A PRIMER

Digital surveillance companies vary in size and sophistication from mom-and-pop operations serving a single district to global corporations monitoring millions of students across thousands of school districts.[8] Taken together, however, they offer a similar suite of services, including such tools as screen sharing and monitoring, keystroke capture, keyword tracking, automated content analysis of student work, social media monitoring, and video capture of students' online activities.[9]

These tools are reshaping educators' capacities to look after the students in their care. Screen sharing and monitoring software, for example, transforms teachers' abilities to keep students focused on learning when they are working on computers or tablets. Teachers can sit at their own computer and observe every student's screen in real time. They can view thumbnails of all students' screens simultaneously, or zoom in to check out any one student's activities in greater detail. Teachers can also control students' devices directly from their centralized station. They can direct-message individual students, reminding them to stay on task; they can pause or close specific or all students' screens; and they can share their own or a student's screen with an entire class. The learning opportunities that arise from being able to give students in-the-moment feedback on their research and writing, or from screen-sharing a student's novel problem-solving approach with the whole class, are tremendous. So, too, is the power that teachers are gaining to monitor and control students' work and behavior.

As one teacher enthuses in a promotional video by digital surveillance company GoGuardian, "Kids are really good at knowing that exact moment that you're not looking at *their* screen and this way I'm *always* looking at their screen."[10] Furthermore, the knowledge that they are always potentially being monitored by the teacher can influence students to monitor themselves. In the same GoGuardian video, a student explains appreciatively that the software not only improves his focus in real time, but also that it helps students' mindsets be "groomed" to focus on schoolwork throughout "the rest of their academic career."[11]

Teachers themselves may be beside the point. GoGuardian touts its Smart Alerts artificial intelligence (AI) technology as "designed to inspire behavioral self-modification among students as they become more aware of their online behavior. Through sending students [automated] personalized messages while they are browsing, Smart Alerts empowers students to be better digital citizens and modify their behavior appropriately."[12] Impero Software, another global provider of digital surveillance tools to schools, similarly touts that it helps schools "support digital citizenship through real time monitoring"[13] by helping students "develop the skills and perspectives necessary to live a digital lifestyle that is safe, ethical and responsible, as well as inspired, innovative and involved."[14]

Impero aims to accomplish this through the use of keyword detection libraries to flag students who type or access phrases that may signal a need for help. Keyword libraries range from "adult content" to "self-harm" to "weapons and violence."[15] When a student types or accesses one of the thousands of identified keywords, Impero takes a screenshot or real-time video of the student's online activities and sends it to school officials. Educators or network administrators can then analyze the student's digital activity and decide whether the student poses a threat to himself or others.[16] Superintendents are quoted crediting this kind of surveillance technology with preventing suicides, pornography exposure, other forms of self-harm, and even kidnapping by online predators.[17]

Rather than tracking student keystrokes, Gaggle focuses its automated content analysis and warning system on non-public "communication and collaboration tools that schools provide to their students"[18] such as G Suite (also called Google Classroom, currently in use in over 50 percent of schools nationwide[19]), Office 365, and Canvas. Gaggle can scan millions of student files simultaneously, looking for signs of inappropriate or dangerous content. Gaggle may also monitor notifications from students' private social media accounts such as Facebook or Snapchat if students sign up for the accounts using a school-provided email address.[20] This comprehensive level of monitoring, Gaggle claims, helps school districts "stay on top of incidents involving guns, weapons and other threats (including suicide and self harm) found in students' G Suite accounts."[21]

Other providers encourage schools to monitor specific students about whom they are concerned. For instance, Schoolvue offers schools the option of flagging "at-risk" students "so they can be easily identified and safeguarding statistics can be viewed against them."[22] It also provides a "dynamic group" feature enabling "vulnerable students across the school [to] be seen from a single view" of the program.[23] Some companies also invite students themselves to flag their peers for additional monitoring. Impero's Confide button encourages students to report "any concerns they have about another student" through an "anonymous method of disclosure."[24] Impero's website explains, "When it comes to reporting suspicions around radicalisation or extremism, this anonymous communications channel makes it easier for concerns to be raised without a backlash from friends or families which can often serve as a deterrent."[25]

CONCERNS ABOUT DIGITAL SURVEILLANCE OF STUDENTS

Despite many educators' and policy makers' excitement about these tools and their capabilities, other stakeholders have raised a stream of concerns. Most fundamentally, civil liberties advocates worry that school-based digital monitoring normalizes a surveillance state. Since administrators consistently (and correctly) assert they "don't even need a specific reason for remote accessing"[26] students' devices, given their legal responsibilities to monitor students, the Massachusetts ACLU warns, "we are sending the wrong message to young people when we tell them that they should have 'no expectation of privacy,' and that they should simply get used to this."[27] The *fact* that schools, employers, and the state are all monitoring private individuals, in other words, should not be used to justify or normalize such intrusion.

Second, *who* is subjected to surveillance is likely tainted by human bias and outright prejudice. Black and Latinx youth, for instance, are disproportionately seen as threats and hence subject to heightened surveillance and punishment as compared to White and Asian youth.[28] High percentages of Muslim children also report having been bullied by peers *and teachers* on account of their religion—a phenomenon that may be explained by the fact that teachers are "[no] different from the rest of Americans, 61 percent of whom have a negative view of Islam."[29] School officials have for years falsely accused both Arab and Muslim students of posing terrorist threats.[30]

Digital surveillance poses similar risks of discriminatory application. Consider Impero's keyword library for "counter-radicalization (including Arabic script)."[31] The library "consists of more than one thousand trigger terms including 'apostate,' 'jihadi' and 'Islamism,'" as well as 'caliphate' and the names of Muslim pro-democracy and civil liberties activists.[32] Since the library contents are proprietary, we can't be sure how many white nationalist and supremacist terms or names are included. We view it as unlikely, however, that their respective weight matches the overwhelming frequency of white nationalist as compared to Islamic violence and terrorism.[33]

Third, the very tools that aim to increase student protection can inadvertently expose students through surveillance "overreach."[34] For instance, when Gaggle's safety team conducted automated content analysis on twenty million drive files, it found that over 160 thousand were "actionable," requiring them to contact a "school or district emergency contact."[35] However, much of this actionable content resulted from students unknowingly uploading inappropriate content to school-issued accounts when backing up to the cloud.[36] As students mistakenly backed up their personal diaries, text messages, and even nude photos to school servers, they unwittingly exposed themselves before a host of school professionals and private vendors who have contracts with districts to view student data.[37]

Fourth, adolescents may find their normal developmental processes—which appropriately include risk-taking and identity exploration—stymied due to overreactions by untrained staff who are monitoring digital threats.[38] Mental health and counseling professionals have pointed out, for example, that information technology (IT) directors are often responsible for assessing alerts from digital surveillance tools. In light of their total lack of any mental health or counseling training, IT directors may misidentify and over- or under-respond to threat notifications.[39] Students at risk may not get the help they need. Students who are not at risk may be inappropriately questioned or even punished for developmentally healthy expression.

Finally, many people have raised concerns about the compulsory nature of the surveillance, as well as lack of transparency around how student information is accessed, stored, and used.[40] Some districts have told parents that students "may be monitored," for instance, without revealing that monitoring methods allow them to remotely "track a device's location, take screenshots, log keystrokes, and even activate webcams."[41] This led one father to object, "When they are able to come into my household and see what I'm doing at home, that really bothered me . . . They didn't say that once you signed up for this, that they can see what they're actually doing at home."[42]

WHY DISTRICTS EMBRACE DIGITAL SURVEILLANCE OF STUDENTS

Despite these concerns, it is worth remembering that digital surveillance tools accomplish at least some, and perhaps many, of their aims. As we have noted throughout this case study, school and district personnel—even students themselves—readily offer testimonials about the positive effect of these programs on student learning, digital citizenship instruction, and student safety ranging from cyberbullying to suicide prevention. Educators also express appreciation for regaining time to focus on more central aspects of their jobs, such as developing engaging lessons or focusing on whole-school improvement. Furthermore, these programs aid schools in meeting rigorous legal mandates from both federal and state legislatures.

In addition, despite the concerns about bias raised above, automated surveillance is likely far more efficient, effective, and even equitable than the piecemeal surveillance educators and school administrators otherwise attempt. In the absence of digital surveillance tools, educators would still monitor students; student supervision and discipline have been hallmarks of schooling since time immemorial. As racially disparate preschool suspension and expulsion rates demonstrate, student surveillance also perpetuates bias and prejudice from the earliest stages—and that isn't because preschoolers are sharing incendiary memes or posting worrisome reflections on Google Classroom.[43] As with other algorithmic tools used to predict human behavior, digital surveillance software will inevitably *echo* human bias, but it need not *exacerbate* it.[44]

Third, digital surveillance in schools may well prepare students for the widespread monitoring that they will encounter as both workers and citizens. It is well established that employers have the right to collect, store, view, and assess the content of employees' every keystroke on a work-provided device, server, or cloud storage system, whether at work or at home.[45] Furthermore, employers monitor employees' electronic files, communications, and search history for exactly the same reasons as schools do: namely, to limit legal liability and to increase productivity.[46] Given these parallels, Gaggle's reminder to parents that "when your child is using school-provided technology, there should be no expectation of privacy"[47] may simply be realistic career preparation. Similarly, insofar as the National Security Agency alone collects billions of online records per month by accessing the data centers of Yahoo and Google, students may well come of age subject to pervasive government monitoring.[48] In this respect, students who are subject to school-based surveillance arguably benefit from learning how to demonstrate responsible digital citizenship for a new age of state surveillance.

DEBATING THE LIMITS—IF ANY—OF DIGITAL SURVEILLANCE

So, when using digital surveillance tools, what balance *should* school districts strike between protecting students' well-being and preserving their civil liberties? Should schools be subject to any limitations on their ability to monitor students' use of school-provided hardware, software, or cloud-based storage and apps? If so, on what grounds—and who should have the right to make this determination?

Or we might pose the question the other way around, and ask: How could the state possibly have the right to compel children's school attendance, require their use of electronic tools such as Google Classroom or iPads, and then surveil them via those very same tools? Should students really have to give up their (and their families') rights to privacy simply in order to receive an education?

Finally, might district and school administrators, educators, parents, and students find ways to agree on digital surveillance practices even in the absence of reaching broader philosophical agreement on the value of safety versus liberty? Should in-class surveillance tools such as screen monitoring be welcomed, but out-of-school tools be banned? Might automated content analysis be allowed, but only if those who field the alerts are trained in mental health and counseling? Could the debate over districts' adoption of surveillance technology itself educate the public about digital citizenship learning in the twenty-first century?

Monitoring Students in British Schools

The Prevent Duty

GEMMA GRONLAND

Although school shootings and similar threats are nearly unheard of in the UK, British teachers will readily empathize with US teachers as they try to fulfill their legal and moral responsibilities to keep students safe. With the introduction of a "Prevent duty" in schools in 2015, teachers in Britain are required to have "due regard to the need to prevent people from being drawn into terrorism."[49] As part of their safeguarding duties, teachers must identify those who might be vulnerable to extremist narratives, or who express extremist views through word or deed. If a teacher has a concern, they are to report it to their designated "safeguarding lead," who is tasked with the decision of whether to report the concern to law enforcement for assessment. However, the guidance also notes that teachers are free to raise concerns directly with the Department for Education's extremism hotline, or indeed, directly to local police.[50] As I discuss below, educators as well as scholars are strongly divided about the premise, design, and impact of Prevent on students and on society. The lessons we are learning in the UK may be useful in guiding debate in the United States about surveillance of students in schools.

WHY DO WE HAVE PREVENT?

Prevent was introduced in 2007 as a response to the rising terrorist threat after the 7/7 bombings in London in 2005. It was conceived as a way for law enforcement to prevent terrorism by tackling extremist narratives. Some scholars have seen Prevent as divided into two chapters: Prevent 1 (2007–11) and Prevent 2 (2011–today). The former was largely structured around projects intended to build community cohesion, while the latter marked a move to policing communities deemed at risk of fostering or succumbing to extremism.[51] Prevent 2 also saw the introduction of the Channel Programme (a counselling program run by the police for those vulnerable to radicalization) and WRAP (Workshop to Raise Awareness of Prevent) training for frontline public sector workers.

Many have argued that the Prevent duty moved into schools following two high-profile cases of extremism within schools. In 2014, Ofsted (a nonministerial department of the UK government) investigated twenty-one schools in Birmingham amid claims of a creeping "Islamification" of state schools.[52] The Park View Educational Trust, which ran schools in the area, was accused of placing ultraconservative Muslims in teaching posts in order to indoctrinate students. The case collapsed in May 2017 after it was revealed that government officials failed to disclose exculpatory evidence, and the claims were agreed to be falsified, or "dishonest."[53] Additionally, in February 2015, three schoolgirls from a diverse borough in London fled to Syria to join ISIS.[54] Much of the press coverage pointed the finger at their school for not noticing signs that might have hinted at the girls' extremist allegiances.

While professionals in the field claimed that radicalization was not happening on school property, Parliament nonetheless passed Prevent legislation that explicitly made schools responsible for both preventing and reporting extremism. On the prevention side, Prevent requires schools proactively to teach "fundamental British values." The guidance literature defines extremism as "vocal" or "active" opposition to fundamental British values "including democracy, the rule of law, individual liberty and mutual respect and tolerance of different faiths and beliefs."[55] Teaching such values is intended to safeguard students against extremist views. On the reactive side, all teachers are now required to report concerning behavior to their safeguarding lead. This person decides whether the report needs to be passed on to a Prevent Officer (in high-profile areas where there is a perceived terrorist threat) or to Channel directly. From there, the Channel panel determines whether the pupil requires intervention.

RESPONSES TO PREVENT

Educators, community leaders, and researchers are internally divided about Prevent, raising both significant concerns and pointing to possibly reassuring data in assessing Prevent's impact on students, schools, and communities. These discussions are likely relevant to those assessing the expansion of student surveillance in the US, as well.

Education professionals express distaste for the part of Prevent which mandates that they teach "fundamental British values." They are generally happy to teach values like mutual respect and tolerance, but they express strong opposition to claiming that such values are uniquely British, which they fear opens their classrooms up to a creeping nationalism. After all, what is fundamentally British about respect for democracy, rule of law, or individual liberty? While Britain does not insist we pledge allegiance to the flag, why not call these fundamental *human* values instead?

Researchers have also criticized Prevent in schools for misappropriating the language and norms of child protection in service of patently political ends, providing a flimsy definition of *radicalization*, and mandating teachers to monitor students in a pre-crime space where "vocal dissent" is enough to shorten the pipeline between school and law enforcement.[56] Less direct in their criticism, some academics have used literature on human rights education to suggest we are over-securitizing schools and taking an exclusionary approach to citizenship education that does not do enough to fight off extremism.[57] They argue that politically controversial issues should be debated in schools to help children be critical of extremist ideologies. Yet with Prevent, we risk shutting this down. Finally, many critics claim Prevent is discriminatory, operating on a Muslim-threat logic that serves to perpetuate Islamophobia.[58]

At the same time, actions are being taken that may reduce anti-Muslim bias, and at least some schools seem to be implementing Prevent in ways that could actually support their antiracism work. The policy now includes guidance on preventing right-wing extremism, for instance, which suggests a move to make it less Muslim-biased. Much of the guidance literature and training also stresses that Prevent should not be a "burden" and schools are free to decide on their own needs.[59]

A highly publicized study, "What Prevent Duty Means for Schools and Colleges," captures the disparity between the policy on paper and in practice.[60] Few educators in the study criticized Prevent (although criticism was higher among Black and minority ethnic teachers), and most expressed a need for something like Prevent to be in place as an extension of schools' safeguarding duties. Some schools were using Prevent to strengthen work around racism and inequality, supporting one researcher's claim that "frontline education and welfare institutions" are alert to discrimination and hence not acting as "willing tools of state Islamophobia and surveillance."[61] While teachers did seem to voice worries over societal discrimination, they did not see this as operating at the institutional level of their schools.

Recent statistics reinforce both supporters and critics of Prevent. Between 2015 and 2016, a total of 7,631 people were reported under Prevent, with 33 percent of those reports coming from the education sector. Only 381 people, or 5 percent of the total reported, were screened as requiring Channel support.[62] On the one hand, this might suggest that Prevent is working to identify vulnerable students and get them the help they need without subjecting the vast majority of students to law enforcement intervention. On the other hand, critics raise concerns about the high percentage of referrals from the education sector, as well as whether the data-haul from law-abiding children and long-term impact on society are at all "evidence-driven."[63]

AN ONGOING DILEMMA IN THE UK

Research into Prevent in schools is very much in its infancy, and we do not have a full grasp on the myriad ways teachers are enacting it. Prevent advocates rightly point out that terrorism poses a real threat, teachers are not blindly reporting to law enforcement, and there are procedures in place to mitigate against schools' sleepwalking into discrimination. Yet, the securitized nature of the policy—it was a Home Office (law enforcement) policy before it moved into schools—and the ways in which it is conducted on the ground by education professionals, is under-studied. With regard to the case of digital monitoring in the US, we might approach it with similar caution: the long-term effects of monitoring will not yet be clear. The ways in which teachers manage their duty might be very different to how we ethically problematize the policy on paper.

Gemma Gronland taught English to ages eleven to eighteen in London's diverse boroughs. She completed her masters in education at Harvard Graduate School of Education in 2016 and is currently completing a PhD at University College London, examining Prevent policy in schools.

The Limitations of Social Media Surveillance

Rachel Levinson-Waldman

Between the growing prominence of social media, dwindling funding for counselors and other resources, and schools' expanding responsibilities for student safety on and off campus, school administrators are understandably tempted by software programs that promise to alert educators to possible threats. Some of these products may even periodically make good on their promises, providing warnings about potentially worrisome postings before school officials would have become aware and allowing concerned adults to intervene.

These programs are not, however, the silver bullet they seem to be. Any educator or administrator considering purchasing one of these programs needs to take serious account of the downsides and involve parents and students in an honest discussion of their practical impacts. And where these programs are rolled out, transparency is a must.

ACCURACY

As an initial matter, automated social media monitoring systems often simply are not accurate enough to justify their cost or intrusiveness.[64] Predictive tools require clear, consistent definitions of problematic content in order to operate effectively. Many of the threats that these tools are designed to find, by contrast, are not susceptible to clear definition. For example, tools searching for signs of online extremism or radicalization are likely to be stymied by the fact that there is no agreed-upon meaning of those terms, and no consensus about whether particular behaviors reliably indicate that an individual is vulnerable to radicalization.[65] Instead, they may end up relying on imprecise (and often biased) proxies, such as a faulty assumption that Arabic-language posts are more likely to reflect extremist content.[66]

Social media is also highly contextual. Scholar danah boyd has documented teens' use of online *steganography*, or hiding messages in plain sight, as a way to navigate the different audiences reading their online posts. Teens post song lyrics that look innocuous to a parent, for instance, while signaling something else entirely to peers.[67] This kind of confusion played out during the trial of Boston Marathon bomber Dzhokhar Tsarnaev, when it emerged that the quotes the FBI had been relying on as evidence of Tsarnaev's extremism and desire for martyrdom came instead from a Russian rap song, Jay-Z lyrics, and a Comedy Central show.[68] How could a machine-driven tool parse the layers of meaning in a post that is designed to confuse, and who is likely to have more incentive, time, and creative ways to mislead the program than a teen?

Even when a poster isn't actively trying to mislead an algorithm, the technology can still stumble. Automated algorithms are notoriously poor at assessing unfamiliar lingo. One tool, faced with the slang *af*, concluded that the entire post was written in Danish.[69] These programs can also have difficulty distinguishing among different uses for the same word, as a police department discovered when it tried to filter social media for the word *bomb* and mostly got posts about "bomb" (that is, "excellent") pizza.[70]

DISPARATE IMPACT

Social media monitoring will inevitably have a disproportionate impact on students of color. The programs themselves may have built-in racial bias, focusing on search terms that are more likely to affect communities of color. The ACLU revealed, for example, that the Boston Police Department's social media monitoring efforts focused primarily on terminology relating to Islam and African-American activism—among them Ferguson, #blacklivesmatter, and #muslimlivesmatter—despite wide agreement by law enforcement agencies that antigovernment extremists posed a far greater threat than Islamic radicalism.[71] Schools can mitigate such bias by paying close attention to the terms programs monitor and demanding regular oversight and audits.

However, even where the tools themselves strive to be neutral, the impact is not likely to be. The unequal treatment of students of color is well-documented: research demonstrates that black children at every level of schooling are punished more harshly than their white peers, even when they break the same rules.[72] This history suggests that regardless of how the tools themselves are built, decision makers will impose stricter penalties on students of color for their online expression. This is not strictly hypothetical. One Alabama school district that paid an ex-FBI agent to comb through students' social media accounts on the basis of anonymous tips ultimately expelled over a dozen students for their online transgressions; although the district's student body was only 40 percent black, 86 percent of the students expelled were African-American.[73]

IMPACT OF FALSE POSITIVES

Where students are wrongly flagged as dangerous, that identification carries a real risk of further alienating already marginalized students. One reporter in Oregon spent months profiling a family whose son had been identified as a potential threat, noting that the factors that had brought him to the attention of authorities—his black trench coat, his awkward social skills, even his interest in weapons—likely emerged from his place on the autism spectrum rather than signaling an incipient threat to his fellow classmates.[74] Not only did the scrutiny from the school fail to turn up any damaging information, it ultimately drove him out of the high school, creating—in his parents' words—"a dropout."[75] While social media wasn't at issue in his case, it is not hard to imagine a similar situation playing out based on online information. Not every case will be a false positive, but the real-life consequences of those that are should give decision makers pause.

PERVERSE INCENTIVES

These services also often boast a built-in conflict of interest. A company seeking to distinguish itself on the grounds that it spots unique problems will be inclined to find more problems, whether or not they actually warrant attention. As the saying goes, "if all you have is a hammer, everything looks like a nail." At the same time, few social media monitoring companies have metrics in place to measure the effectiveness of their services.[76] The combination of the two—vendors with an incentive to be profligate and few resources directed toward assessing the success of their efforts—is a recipe for overreach.

LACK OF TRANSPARENCY

Despite the high stakes, students and their parents likely know little about the scope of these tools. Research shows that while monitoring companies may assume that students are effectively assenting to being tracked by virtue of posting on public sites, students more often believe (in error) that companies are prohibited by their privacy policies from sharing personal information with third parties.[77] And even if they do understand the reach of the monitoring technologies in general terms, it is likely to mean little as a practical matter—few will know what posts a company is actually sweeping up, or what information is being shared with school administrators or even law enforcement. Notably, at least one outfit, Geo Listening, allows students to request a copy of all information the company has collected about them. Other firms should consider following this policy, and perhaps more critically, schools could insist on this kind of transparency as a condition for contracting with a monitoring company.

ANTIDEMOCRATIC NATURE

One element of American education is (or should be!) to teach students to operate in and contribute to a democracy whose values include freedom of speech and dissent. Monitoring students' every expression on social media instills a lesson that is distinctly at odds with these values, teaching them instead to predict and accommodate an authority figure's opinion before they even put virtual pen to paper. Historian Timothy Snyder has termed this "anticipatory obedience," and cautioned against it as a step toward authoritarianism.[78] While it may seem hyperbolic to describe looking for signals of suicidal ideation online as a sign of authoritarian creep, the message it sends to students is that they are always under observation. Schools may see short-term benefits from this monitoring, but the longer-term impacts could be far more detrimental.

NOT THE ONLY OPTION

Finally, deciding not to use one of these tools does not mean going dark. Social media is, by its terms, social—any post that could be picked up by a monitoring tool will be seen by other users as well. After it emerged that Nikolas Cruz, the perpetrator of the shooting at Marjory Stoneman Douglas High School in Parkland, Florida, had littered social media with threatening posts, there was an explosion of calls for increased social media monitoring. Failure to see his posts was hardly the problem, though; multiple individuals had reported his statements to local police and the FBI.[79] In other circumstances, a peer, parent, or community member might reach out to a friend or trusted adult to flag a post that appears to be of concern. While social media will undoubtedly hold revealing information, schools and districts do not need to spend tens or hundreds of thousands of dollars to tease it out. And if they decide that these tools will add sufficient value to direct precious resources their way, they must take the time and effort to carefully oversee their use and their impact on the school community.

Rachel Levinson-Waldman is Senior Counsel to the Liberty and National Security Program at the Brennan Center for Justice at the New York University School of Law. She writes regularly on issues relating to surveillance, privacy, policing, and technology, including providing commentary on law enforcement access to social media, predictive policing, body cameras, license plate readers, and other types of surveillance technologies deployed in public.

Seeing Eye to Eye with Students

A Case for Collaborative, App-Enabled Approaches to Supporting Safety and Well-Being

Carrie James and Emily Weinstein

The issue of school surveillance of students' digital activities is timely and polarizing. As part of our research on digital dilemmas, we surveyed more than three thousand educators and parents from all fifty US states and more than two dozen other countries during the 2017–18 school year. We investigated perspectives on a breadth of issues related to digital life, as well as on dilemmas related to supporting and preparing youth for a networked era. On the question of whether schools should monitor students' social media accounts, 50 percent of educators agreed schools should monitor, 33 percent disagreed, and 17 percent were undecided. Similarly, 49 percent of parents agreed, 36 percent disagreed, and 15 percent were undecided.[80]

In post-survey interviews with educators, we asked participants to elaborate on their thinking. Repeatedly, we heard their initial, strongly stated *agree* or *disagree* reactions shift into more complexity and discomfort. Alongside concerns about free speech and privacy, educators began to grapple with other dimensions of the issue: What does *monitoring* really mean and when is it warranted? Even if some degree of surveillance is deemed appropriate, is it feasible? What should actually be monitored and by whom—and, crucially, how will schools decide whether, when, and how to act on the information revealed through their surveillance efforts?

TO MONITOR OR NOT? THREE BASELINE CONSIDERATIONS

We turn first to the question of *when* it is appropriate to monitor at all. We note at least three important baseline considerations that should inform decisions about digital surveillance and monitoring in schools: Who owns the device? Where is the device being used? And how is it being used—that is, for what purposes?

A growing number of schools have one-to-one laptop or tablet programs, whereby each student is given access to a device in school and, sometimes, to take home. These devices are typically provided with guidelines dictating "acceptable use." When devices are owned by a school, being used on its grounds, and provided to students with clear rules, surveillance can simply be perceived as a reasonable approach to ensuring compliance with policies to which students have presumably already agreed. Further, as the case discusses, schools may be legally obligated to ensure that student conduct on these devices is monitored to ensure student safety and well-being. Yet while surveillance is often warranted in these instances, we believe schools have a responsibility to ensure that students remain cognizant of the full extent of monitoring activities even if they can't opt out.

When school-provided devices are permitted to be taken home or otherwise used off school grounds, monitoring may also be appropriate. In such cases, the school has provided students with tools that can be used for a range of purposes, including social interactions and content browsing. Ethically, if not legally, schools may be obligated to ensure devices are used for their intended purposes and not in potentially detrimental ways—especially on school-based platforms (such as Google Classroom) and email accounts. Yet, when students use their personal, password-protected social media accounts on school-provided devices, monitoring their activities raises more significant puzzles related to student privacy.

Even deeper tensions surface around scenarios regarding school surveillance of students' activities—school-related or personal—on student-owned devices. Here, considerations around the "where" and "how" of use are again relevant. School oversight may feel more appropriate in cases where a student makes a threatening comment to another student within an app in the school's Google Classroom space as opposed to on their personal Instagram or Snapchat accounts. Both scenarios can result in student-to-student antagonism, outright conflict, and possibly a diminished sense of safety and community in the school. Whether the threatening comment was posted while students were on school grounds or off—or on a school platform or personal social media account—may be irrelevant when there is undeniable spillover into school spaces.

TRIMMING THE LEAVES VERSUS GETTING TO THE ROOTS

For some educators, the desire to keep students safe from physical harm is sufficient justification for nearly any degree of oversight. School shootings are now front of mind and revealing social media posts offer the possibility of just-in-time intervention. But do schools need apps such as Gaggle to detect these posts when large audiences of classmates are already witnesses to their peers' posts? Or do schools instead need better processes to facilitate student reporting and school response?

Opening the doors to monitoring students' posts also inevitably raises dilemmas about posts other than those that indicate violence or threats to physical safety, like sexually explicit messages and inappropriate forms of teasing among friends. Monitoring students' online posts also places educators in an inherently reactive position. As one administrator explained, "It doesn't go to roots of it. It goes to the top leaves, and then you just try to cut down what you don't like. But we need to get at it from the roots instead." The roots, in her view, are decision-making, empathy, and communication skills, supported intentionally by school curricula, culture, and policies.

In the abstract, questions about monitoring students' posts are also devoid of the complicated reality of *decoding* their messages. In the service of violence prevention, Desmond Patton and colleagues have spent years studying social media posts of gang-affiliated youth. Their methods to identify aggression, grief, and threats in teens' posts require multiple steps, careful review, and—critically—rich contextual knowledge. For example, consider how Patton and colleagues unpack the meaning of a tweet that youth shared following the killing of seventeen-year-old Gakirah Barnes:

> SHIT #KRAZY Man ! #BIP AY #HITTA & AY MF #STL #EBT LEGEND K.I & HBD #BOSSTRELL @TyquanAssassin @Stl_trell #GaNgGaNG pic.twitter.com/ifvVTZKVZP
>
> This tweet is translated up to the @ handles as, "Things are crazy, man! Ball in paradise all you killers and all you motherfucking St. Lawrence and Eberhart legends, K.I and, honored by death, Boss Trell."
>
> "Ball in paradise" is slang for "rest in peace." St. Lawrence and Eberhart refer to gang neighborhoods. "K.I" was one of Gakirah's nicknames, and Rodney "Boss Trell" Stewart is a deceased gang member.[81]

Effectively decoding youths' digital messages is a complex endeavor. Gaining access to posts is merely a first step; effective prevention and intervention hinge on understanding students' intentions and the backstory. Even in less distressing cases, youths' uses of emojis, memes, and abbreviations may result in the most concerning posts evading recognition.

This interpretive challenge furthers the case for building systems and cultures that empower peers to take action when they see concerning posts. Youth are often best equipped to understand peers' intended meanings and to detect concerning posts that evade algorithmic detection; they are also less likely to misconstrue innocuous posts. Yet whether or not youth will actually turn to adults to share what they see depends on trust rather than on the availability of features like Impero's Confide button. Do youth perceive school administrators as likely to respond with swift and punitive action or to begin by listening and trying to understand students' perspectives?

AN "APP-ENABLING" APPROACH

This is not to say that there are no helpful roles for apps to play. Apps are, in general, neither good nor bad. Rather it is in how educators leverage digital tools that will give rise to both potentialities in the case of monitoring. In their book *The App Generation*, Howard Gardner and Katie Davis differentiate between app dependence and app enablement.[82] Being app-dependent means allowing technologies to determine and constrain the realm of possibilities and actions; being app-enabled means using technology to expand and enrich one's endeavors.

As educators consider whether and how to use apps to monitor students, they should deliberately and carefully consider the role apps play in the *process* of supporting student development and safety. Optimally, an app-generated alert—whether it be to a conflict between students, threats of violence, or possible signs of suicidal ideation—triggers a robust intervention process. This process should be supportive of students' well-being, build their sense of agency as stakeholders in keeping their communities safe, and enhance their trust in the adults in their lives. We caution against app-dependent approaches to surveillance, which are likely both ineffective and prone to undercut these outcomes.

If schools want to leverage revealing social media posts to keep their students safe, they will benefit from students' buy-in and investment. Our survey data suggest that parents and teachers, although somewhat divided on the topic, are more likely than not to favor school monitoring of students' social media accounts. Perhaps not surprisingly, emerging data from a similar survey of youth suggest that they are instead inclined to oppose such practices. One knee-jerk reaction to this finding might be that youth merely want to avoid getting into trouble with adults for inappropriate online activities. But starting with that assumption only derails the start of productive and open cross-generational conversations about online life. If schools wish to protect their students, they must start by listening and trying to understand their students' media experiences.

Carrie James is a research associate and principal investigator at Project Zero, a research center at the Harvard Graduate School of Education (HGSE), and a lecturer on education at HGSE. A sociologist by training, her research explores young people's digital, moral, and civic lives.

Emily Weinstein is a postdoctoral fellow at Project Zero. Her research examines how social technologies shape and reshape the social, emotional, and civic experiences of contemporary adolescents and young adults.

Middle and High School Student Responses

Students Are Smarter Than Any Blocking Software

ALEXANDER KOSYAKOV

If I were to name one constant that has defined my time in high school, it would be *.io*: online multiplayer videogames that bear a URL ending with the domain .io. During my freshman year everybody played Agar.io. Sophomore year, it was Narwhal.io. The most recent plague is Surviv.io.

Surviv.io games require teams to collaborate with one another; they cannot be played alone. Students would therefore send out surreptitious invite emails using their school devices in class with clever subject lines like "Review Materials." Students played Surviv.io in learning centers, during free periods, and everywhere in between—but almost always under a guise of feigned hard work.

When the administration finally found out about Surviv.io and realized it was a shooting game, they blocked the site on the school Wi-Fi. But here's the thing: students continued to play the game. They found redirect URLs, alternate URLs, and all sorts of other ways to circumvent what the school believed to be an impenetrable barrier.

Students are only going to be encouraged to find more work-arounds if schools try to restrict their digital participation. I've seen it happen too many times. For example, Reddit is blocked by our school, but kids in my calculus class are still able to access it through some sort of black magic that they call a "VPN."

I understand why surveillance makes sense from a liability standpoint, but this is a fight that schools will never win. We are the generation best integrated with digital technology. Underestimate us at your peril.

Alexander Kosyakov is a junior at Greenwich High School in Greenwich, Connecticut. He is a member of the school's We the People: The Citizen and the Constitution team and serves as student body president.

Monitor Us Because We're Mischievous, but Don't Treat Us Like Criminals

McKenna Dixon

As a rising eighth grader, I am excited about using school-provided iPads and computers. I know that my use of these devices will be monitored, as they all have an app called "Securly" that allows the school to restrict certain websites and keywords and to receive notifications if we try to access those websites. I have frequently heard students complain about these restrictions, and about their lack of privacy. They made good points, but I also believe that digital surveillance is necessary in moderation.

Digital surveillance programs such as Gaggle go too far when they allow administrators to monitor students' private lives and social media, view all their online activities, and take control of what students do online. Such programs teach young kids that they are not entitled to any privacy and also that others can totally control what they do on the internet and in real life. These are not good lessons for students to learn. I also worry that apps that allow teachers to choose who to monitor will harm students' long-term opportunities. Will having a reputation as "the bad kid" or "the one who needs to be watched" affect how their peers treat them, how they behave in school, or whether they are admitted to high school or college?

On the other hand, things risk getting out of control if we have no surveillance. Trust has to be earned, and at the end of the day kids are still kids. We do mischievous things. We need the opportunity to learn from our mistakes, which the surveillance software can help us do, so long as it's gentle like GoGuardian or Impero. The school gives us devices to use, and it should monitor us in some way because we are still kids who have a lot to learn.

McKenna Dixon is an eighth-grade student at the Berkeley Carroll School. Technology plays a huge role in her generation's life, and she wants to make sure that kids are safe on the internet because sometimes the internet can be dangerous, and every kid should learn how to use it wisely.

Increased Monitoring Will Increase Discrimination

Adriana Alvarado

Although more advanced methods of monitoring students may help prevent violence, self-harm, and bullying, they also risk significantly exacerbating discriminatory surveillance. Especially given the current political atmosphere of the United States, with school shootings seemingly ever more common, and hate crime rates rising higher than they have been in a decade, school surveillance will only make schools more dangerous for students of color.[83]

As a Latinx student in a California public high school with a wide racial achievement gap, I have both experienced and witnessed discrimination from various teachers in my school. I have seen Latinx students get suspended and even expelled for minor offenses like truancy or the possession of marijuana, while White students have been given little to no punishment for the possession of more dangerous drugs, like alcohol and cocaine. Even though this area is considered liberal, discrimination is highly prevalent. Nor is my experience unusual. Nationwide, students of color are almost four times more likely to get suspended or expelled than White students.[84]

My high school currently has cameras blanketing the campus. If the school upgraded their surveillance, then the likelihood of students of color being punished for minor infractions would rise. I would like to believe that these biased practices would disappear with staff training before more invasive technology is put in place. But I cannot put my faith in such training because of the countless times that administrators and teachers have simply brushed aside evidence of discipline discrimination. The bias that students of color have to currently face make school an uncomfortable learning environment where they cannot thrive. Expanded surveillance systems will lead school staff to engage in even more unnecessary questioning of students of color, which will in turn ultimately distract students from their learning.

Adriana Alvarado is a queer Latina activist with a passion for social justice issues and the dream of diversifying STEM. She graduated from Terra Linda High School (San Rafael, CA) in June 2018 and will enter the University of Redlands in the fall of 2018.

Monitoring Requires a Personal Touch

VAISHALI SHAH

I attended Greenwich Country Day School (GCDS), a small private school, before matriculating my sophomore year at Greenwich High School (GHS), a large public high school. I have thus watched two very different school administrations cope with the dangers of the rapidly evolving digital age.

At GCDS, I benefited from administrators who applied a personal touch to digital monitoring. In eighth grade, for example, I emailed a friend, "I want to do the bomb," for my history thesis—but neglected to reference the Manhattan Project or even our history class. I also conducted extensive research on purchasing firearms for a paper on gun control reforms. Fortunately, a real person, Mr. Martinez, was the one monitoring my digital behavior. He stopped me in the hallway to confirm that my potentially incriminating research was purely for academic purposes. As soon as I reassured him, we went on with our days. The experience proved that surveillance technology used in conjunction with in-person dialogue can help students feel both protected and encouraged to use the internet as an academic resource. Had I been attacked, or flagged as a risk, I might have been deterred from pursuing similar topics in the future.

At a large public school like GHS, students are more likely to be formally investigated for similar misunderstandings. My junior year (2017–18) was filled with fear of school shootings and gun violence. After our school was threatened, the armed policemen who guarded the doors made my classmates and me feel like criminals. Had I continued to research gun purchases at GHS, I, too, might have been flagged as an enemy to the community I am so grateful to be a part of.

School administrators who rely solely on mechanized precautions create a culture of fear and intimidation that stymies student inquiry. Students can feel truly safe only when caring, human adults act as checks on automated surveillance.

Vaishali Shah is a rising senior at Greenwich High School who recently graduated from the competitive constitutional law program, We the People: The Citizen and the Constitution. She is a facilitator on the NAMES diversity team, a member of the varsity dance team, and a tutor through AVID, a college-preparatory program for students from underrepresented socioeconomic groups.

What Big Brother Never Saw

Nithyani Anandakugan

While teaching *1984*, my English teacher facetiously cautioned that "Big Brother is watching." Although I had noticed the school cameras before, I understood the extent of school surveillance only after her remark. Still, I felt no safer. Schools ostensibly protect students by tracking their online behavior and even monitoring them indiscriminately using programs like Gaggle and Impero. But what value do these systems have when student safety itself is increasingly elusive?

Before the Parkland shooting, Nikolas Cruz crowed about attacking Marjory Stoneman Douglas High School in three cellphone videos and a YouTube comment.[85] Though the former student posted on forums outside school jurisdiction, school leaders knew about his plans, yet they failed to respond appropriately. Police and FBI officials also overlooked tips because Cruz's threats fell below the legal standard for authorities to respond. Thus, officials took no meaningful action despite having access to otherwise informative digital surveillance data.

I fear this failure will necessarily remain common. Adults at large suburban public schools like Stoneman Douglas and the one I attend must screen thousands of students' online activity for inappropriate or dangerous content every day. This is no simple task. Realistically, how likely is it that they will notice one student's subtle signs among the thousands of data points that bombard their screens?

Furthermore, many students will offer no digital clues at all. Although suicide remains the second leading cause of death for individuals between the ages of ten and twenty-four, students with depression rarely post their symptoms online.[86] Despite heightened surveillance, students remain at risk; meanwhile, adults fixate on student search histories rather than engage with students themselves.

After noticing the hallway cameras, I didn't change my behavior: school surveillance felt inconsequential to me. This may be how digital surveillance plays out, too. Big Brother is watching, but he seems not to care.

Nithyani Anandakugan lives in Acton, Massachusetts, and will graduate from the Acton-Boxborough Regional High School in the spring of 2019. She is interested in the meaning of democracy, the meaning of identity, and the meaning of that new Beyoncé song.

Digital Monitoring Prepares Students for the Real World

NATALIE PARKER

Schools' primary purposes are to promote education and prepare students for the harsh realities of the working world. Given that our society also tasks already underfunded school systems with responsibility for keeping students safe, schools should be able to use digital surveillance to meet these demands.

As a high school student and the daughter of a math teacher, I have some sense of the difficulties educators encounter when balancing their many responsibilities. Students' increasing dependence on the digital world further complicates educators' jobs. The case clearly shows how students face multiple risks, including cyberbullying and being constantly distracted from school. Teachers who use digital surveillance to monitor screens can minimize negative outcomes while increasing student productivity. This allows educators to fulfill their responsibilities to promote education and ensure students' safety, while also preparing students for the surveillance that is prevalent in today's work culture.

This is not to say that schools may exercise *carte blanche* surveillance. Students and families must be able to engage with technology in ways that are comfortable for them. For instance, students at my school can place sticky notes over the cameras on the school-provided Chromebooks if they aren't comfortable with the school watching them continuously.

In the end, however, schools are right to provide students with monitored devices, as this prepares students for surveillance in the workplace as well. Digital surveillance is simply another way that school systems fulfill their responsibilities of protecting and educating students.

Natalie Parker is currently a student at Michigan City High School and aspires to be a neurologist in the future.

Schools Should Reaffirm Privacy While Protecting Students

Bryan R. Warnick

Student privacy in schools is an important ethical concern given both the harm students can suffer if confidential information is inappropriately revealed, and their right to develop the capacity for autonomy. There are also powerful ethical reasons to surveil students—namely, to keep them safe and to protect equality of educational opportunity. While privacy and surveillance appear to compete with one another, schools can draw on what I call the "educational criterion" to surveil students in a limited fashion while reaffirming the value of privacy and respect for students' rights. Appropriately designed policies and civic education can reestablish the proper balance between privacy and digital surveillance in the context of American schools.

WHY PRIVACY IS IMPORTANT IN SCHOOLS

One reason to protect students' informational privacy is that unwanted exposure of personal information can cause students serious harm.[87] The obvious example is when students' explicit pictures become public. The humiliation and psychological trauma associated with this disclosure is as real for students as it would be for adults. Medical or educational information might also be inappropriately disclosed through digital surveillance technologies, which could harm students in the future.

Another reason to protect student privacy has to do with the "developmental rights" of students to acquire capacities for freedom, responsibility, and autonomy.[88] In order to develop these capacities, students need to learn to make decisions based on their own well-considered reasons. Like adults, however, students often do not act on their own reasons when they know they are being surveilled; rather, surveillance exerts an external force, pushing them to act as we would want them to act. It does so in particular by impeding their "expressive privacy," as students may well self-censor in response to the knowledge that they are being watched. School surveillance thus impedes students' opportunities to practice making decisions based on their own reasons within an unconstrained expressive space. In so doing, school surveillance may stymie essential pathways for developing autonomy.

WHY SURVEILLANCE IS IMPORTANT IN SCHOOLS

At the same time, students arguably also have the right to have their privacy *restricted* in online domains. Students' use of social media can provide powerful insight into their social and mental health. By keeping an eye on students' digital lives, educators can identify and serve those who need help, whether by providing them with resources or implementing interventions. Equality of educational opportunity requires that students receive such services—and hence may require that educators keep careful watch over students online. This becomes particularly important when students are contemplating violence. The example of Stoneman Douglas High School shooter Nikolas Cruz shows how students do post clues about their intentions online.[89] This fact highlights an uncomfortable question: Are the general benefits of privacy mentioned in the first section worth the loss of a human life, particularly the life of a child? This is a central dilemma of the modern surveillance state.

It is undoubtedly true that concerns about student safety are often exaggerated, particularly when it comes to concerns about loss of life. When it comes to murder, for example, school is one of safest places for students to be. In 2013–14, children and youth were eighty-seven times more likely to be killed outside of school than inside of it.[90] Still, there do seem to be real issues with lower-level forms of violence, bullying, and intimidation.[91] And, while instances are still rare, it is undeniable that American schools are sometimes deliberately chosen as places to enact targeted mass shootings. The trauma of these high-profile, mass school shootings cannot be overestimated.

If even a small handful of such horrific incidents can be prevented by monitoring students' technology use, as surveillance advocates plausibly suggest, is that not something that makes surveillance not only allowable, but morally required? If so, should we simply give up on privacy for students?

THE PROPER BALANCE: THE EDUCATIONAL CRITERION

In this conflict between student privacy and students' safety in schools, I have argued elsewhere that educators need to think in terms of an "educational criterion."[92] According to this criterion, *how* student rights are limited really matters. If rights are to be limited because of legitimate needs of schools, they must be limited in an educational way, a way that simultaneously attempts to reaffirm the value of those liberties. These reaffirmations can take many forms, including (1) counter-programming that emphasizes the general values of rights, (2) explanations to students about what rights they should normally expect and why those rights are limited in the case of schools, (3) carving out appropriate spaces for the continued expression of rights, and (4) public scrutiny of school policies that limit rights. Let us grant that schools have good reason to monitor online activity for the sake of student safety. How should the requirements of the educational criterion be implemented in the case of student digital surveillance?

The first requirement is curricular programming that emphasizes the existence of a right to privacy and explains the positive role of privacy in human life, both in protecting interests and in allowing for autonomous action. If we are to monitor student online activity, then we should also provide an equally robust civic education that reaffirms the importance of the rights that have been limited in the school context. This project should be undertaken in tandem with the second requirement, that students are owed an explanation of why schools have compromised their rights to privacy by engaging in online surveillance. Such an explanation would include a description of the nature and purposes of schools, and why schools have a special obligation to keep students safe.

How might schools continue to carve out spaces for privacy (the third requirement)? First, they should limit surveillance to *school-provided devices and networks*, and explain why surveillance occurs in those spaces but not elsewhere. Students do need to learn that the expectation of privacy is legitimately reduced when they use resources provided by a third party like a school or employer. Understanding the distinction between school devices and private devices is an important part of their civic education. By highlighting the distinction, schools can also affirm the positive message: We respect and honor student privacy in domains that are not provided by the schools.

What about blanket searches of student social media accounts, which may be completely maintained and updated by students' private devices? At times, it would indeed be appropriate for educators to view such accounts to find out if a student is troubled or in need of help. The principle of maintaining a space for privacy, however, suggests that this should only be done in cases of an already documented problem: a situation of bullying or of a threatening student. Blanket sweeps of all students' social media do not allow students expressive privacy, a space where they can act on their own reasons.

The second way schools can limit the reach of surveillance, and carve out a domain of privacy, is to limit the *types of content* that they monitor or respond to. It is true that student safety is critical, and that educators have an important responsibility to protect students from physical and emotional harm. This means that schools need to protect students from active threats. This does not mean, however, that schools have an obligation to monitor student web searches into, for example, sexuality, marijuana, vaping, or pornography, since these activities do not pose an immediate, direct, and undisputed threat to student safety. Thus, these risks can and should be handled differently from actual threats and bullying.

Finally, both students and the local community should have some input into school surveillance policies. Students should understand how privacy rights can be protected with transparency and scrutiny of public policies. The larger public should know what information educators have access to and be able to debate the limits of such access. This is particularly important because of how surveillance can be inappropriately targeted toward minority students. The community can and should demand policies that forbid unfair racial targeting.

In the end, there are real reasons for schools to take privacy seriously, but also reasons to monitor student online activity. In the US context, the threat of violence and bullying serves as a reason for significant monitoring of online activities. At the same time, this does not mean that schools need to slouch toward endorsing a surveillance state. Educators can take steps to reaffirm the value of privacy even while carefully watching out for students.

Bryan R. Warnick is professor of philosophy of education and associate dean in the College of Education and Human Ecology, Ohio State University. His areas of interest include the ethical dimensions of educational policy and practice.

Everyone Should Be Involved in Designing, Implementing, and Evaluating Digital Surveillance Technology

Erhardt Graeff

Although digital surveillance technologies may seem to be purely *technical* innovations, how technology is designed always also involves *political* choices. Technology design embodies the values of its designers and those who commission the design, as well as the values embedded in the underlying structures it often abstracts and amplifies. When digital surveillance technologies are used in schools without being subject to appropriate political discussion and contestation, they threaten democratic education in several ways. First, they impose a set of policies that affect the rights of students and parents without consulting them in their design and implementation. Second, they may chill legitimate student inquiry or even criminalize students who are researching topics or personal questions deemed taboo or dangerous according to administrators. Building on participatory design and "popular technology" principles, I thus recommend that schools involve students, parents, teachers, and administrators in collective deliberation about the design, scope, and use of digital surveillance technologies.

TECHNOLOGIES HAVE POLITICS

Technologies have political agenda, intended or not; they codify certain values and amplify the power structures that create and apply them.[93] While people often recognize this fact with regard to classroom tools like textbooks, digital surveillance tools are a more recent innovation and lack any meaningful form of democratic representation in their design.[94] Unlike with textbook adoption, there are no state committees deciding what a digital surveillance tool should or should not do, just blanket laws requiring that state schools monitor their students. Furthermore, whereas teachers can supplement textbooks that contain or omit certain topics because of a bias in their design, teachers and school districts likely have substantially less discretion over the way a digital surveillance system operates. Moreover, they may feel they need to monitor everything they can just to help protect the school from some potential liability. When schools lack discretion over technologies, they are making a political decision to value a data-driven sense of safety over the liberty of their students.

The consequences of omitting community discussion and deliberation around digital surveillance are also severe, because such technology has a clear power to reshape community norms through what social theorist Michel Foucault termed "discipline."[95] For example, there is clear evidence that people self-censor when they are aware they may be subject to mass surveillance. Legal academic Jon Penney has found that Wikipedia users were less willing to visit pages related to terrorism after the 2013 Edward Snowden/National Security Agency revelations; furthermore, "younger people and women are more negatively chilled in certain circumstances and are less likely to take steps to defend themselves from regulatory actions and threats."[96]

Monitoring every search on a school device for potentially problematic content may thus push youth to use less reliable or safe forms of technology or sources of information. Youth who might otherwise search for information about safe sex could start censoring themselves because the school is monitoring those searches. Or, if they do conduct the search, they may be flagged based on the biases of the officials reviewing the content. In such cases, students who are trying to protect themselves from sexually transmitted diseases or an unwanted pregnancy could be forced to discuss their concerns with a disciplinary figure at their school rather than a health professional. This could compromise their privacy, exposing personal information and concerns to administrators, teachers, or peers.

DEMOCRATIC EDUCATION AND PARTICIPATORY DESIGN

If we are serious about democratic education and engagement, therefore, students, parents, teachers, and administrators should be actively engaged in deliberating about and negotiating the values embodied in digital surveillance technologies. Then, once school communities arrive at an idea of what digital surveillance should or should not do, they should be empowered to communicate these ideas as a set of specifications back to the technology companies building the software. School communities could create a market for specific features, including enhanced configuration options and measures for data privacy.

These ideas may seem outlandish on the grounds that most people don't understand (or care to learn) highly technical specifications for digital technologies. But there are precedents that illustrate non-elites can and should play a significant role in this area. Virginia Eubanks' Popular Technology approach, for example, shows how even the most marginalized have both the right and also the relevant expertise to contribute to technology design and implementation.[97] She further argues that this is especially important when it comes to government service systems—like schools—that subject people to "low rights environments where there are few expectations of political accountability and transparency."[98] Popular Technology is an explicit response to this political injustice, following the traditions of Popular Education inspired by "Jane Addams and the Settlement House movement, Myles Horton and the Highlander Folk School tradition, and the South and Central American work of Paulo Freire."[99] These traditions "trust in the oppressed" and insist "that democracy be the method and practice, and not merely a goal, of education."[100] Following Eubanks, I argue that school administrators (as well as state lawmakers) should recognize that democratic education extends to decisions about technology use in schools.

In addition to returning political power to the people rather than the technology designers, the resulting conversation would also serve to make students aware about what is and is not being collected about them. School policies around the use of the surveillance platforms could be summarized in simple language and communicated to students on a yearly basis. Students should know their rights and how their data is being used.[101] The United States has enhanced regulations around the collection and use of all personal information about internet users under the age of thirteen (COPPA). Why should a school be responsible to digitally monitor students but not also responsible for protecting their privacy when making them use systems built and serviced by a private company?

Including students in decision-making at school in ways that give them a sense of agency also offers them critical opportunities to practice democratic citizenship. As the case shows, a decision to implement technologies that surveil students without their input strips students of their agency and normalizes surveillance. The alternative offers students an opportunity to debate the value of digital surveillance and to arrive at what best serves the school community's interests—enhancing the students' civic education and increasing a sense of trust and stewardship in the school. In this respect, these discussions can function as an extension of what Diana Hess and Paula McAvoy call the "political classroom." Just as "[w]hen teachers engage students in discussions about what rules ought to be adopted by a class, they are teaching them to think politically," the school can promote students' civic learning by engaging them in conversations about the proper scope of digital surveillance.[102]

These are principles found in approaches to technology design that purposely center community's needs and interests and empower users as co-designers. Participatory design and "feminist human-computer interaction" honor the expertise of individuals and communities in determining how best to solve technical problems in ways that will serve their specific interests, culture, and context.[103] Community members should be involved from the very beginning in framing the problems being addressed and helping to make design and implementation decisions throughout the project's lifecycle.[104] Such approaches to design help realize a vision of democracy and civic education that involves citizens in "world-building" and taking on roles as "co-creators" of democracy.[105] Unfortunately, citizens, especially youth, are rarely included so deeply in the development of policy and community improvement or in the design of technologies that transform their communities through new rules and norms forged by their structure, implementation, and use.

DEMOCRATIZING DIGITAL SURVEILLANCE

Although these ideas may seem daunting, there are some clear, concrete practices that schools adopting digital surveillance tools can put into effect to address issues of rights and representation:

1. Before purchase and implementation, create opportunities for students, parents, teachers, and administrators to converse together about why this system is being considered and how it will be used. Encourage student governments to discuss the issue of surveillance technologies, and civics and government teachers to develop lesson plans and case studies about surveillance technologies for their classes.
2. If a system is going to be purchased or is already in place, find out which features of the student surveillance system are optional and/or configurable. Promote dialog among students, parents, teachers, and administrators about which pieces of data the community is comfortable collecting and how those should be monitored.
3. Establish a strict code of conduct, informed by community discussion, for teachers and administrators who access the personal data of students; have a zero-tolerance policy for misuse and infringements of privacy; and evaluate and update the code and policy on a yearly basis, as well as after any major incident, to ensure that it represents the values of the school community in practice.

By adopting these practices, schools can educate all community members about their capacities and rights as technology co-designers and promote a defensible and even empowering conception of participatory digital citizenship.

Erhardt Graeff is an assistant professor of social and computer science at Olin College of Engineering.

CHAPTER 6

Particular Schools for Particular Students

Are Charter Schools New Democratic Spaces, or Simply Segregated Ones?

TERRI S. WILSON

BARI ACADEMY

In many ways, Bari Academy looks like other elementary schools in Minnesota. Students are taught many of the same things as students in other schools, including reading, mathematics, and science. They take the same state tests every March. They eat lunch in a noisy and cheerful lunchroom, and bundle up to play outside in the same winter weather. But Bari, a public charter school, is also different from other elementary schools. Founded to meet the needs of Minnesota's large Somali immigrant community, the school purposefully nurtures the culture, language, and identity of its Somali American students, who make up 100 percent of its student body.

Parents are greeted in both Somali and English when they enter the school's front office. Licensed teachers—several bilingual in Somali and English—work alongside many support staff members with Somali backgrounds. In addition to welcoming Somali-language families, the school has expanded its standards-based curriculum to teach students how to read and write in Somali, and to include other aspects of Somalia's culture and history. While Bari does not teach religion, it does create a supportive space for Muslim students to observe their faith. Most girls, and all women staff with Somali backgrounds, wear the hijab; boys wear pants, not shorts. Girls and boys split into separate groups for certain activities, including swimming. The school's cafeteria also contracts with vendors from the local Somali immigrant community and only serves halal food. In ways both large and small, Bari Academy aims to create a supportive and empowering community for its many immigrant families.

While distinctive, Bari Academy is by no means unique. This school is one of a growing number of charter schools in the Minneapolis–St. Paul metropolitan area that focus on a specific immigrant or cultural community. In the central metropolitan area, a third of all students enrolled in public schools—over twenty-six thousand students—now attend charter schools. Sometimes termed "niche," "ethnocentric," or "haven" charters,[1] at least thirty schools in the central metro area focus on culturally specific missions organized around the needs and interests of Hmong, Somali, East African, and Latino immigrant families. Other charter schools are organized around an Afrocentric curriculum, while still others offer immersion in languages including Russian, Arabic, German, and Chinese. A growing network of charters known as classical academies also offer Latin and a character-driven educational approach.[2]

Such distinctive schools have been linked to patterns of segregation nationally.[3] These patterns are even more apparent in Minneapolis and St. Paul. While both city school systems enroll a range of different racial and ethnic groups, charter schools have intensified patterns of segregation by grouping particular groups of students into particular schools, often along lines of race, class, ethnicity, and language.[4] In 2016–17, for example, 55 percent of charter schools in the central Twin Cities metropolitan area had student populations that were over 90 percent non-White; 38 percent of district schools were similarly hypersegregated.[5] Moreover, many charter schools focused on particular groups of immigrant students or other students of color. These charter schools were thus more likely to enroll a *single* racial or ethnic student group.

CONTESTED MEANINGS OF SEGREGATION

The rapid growth of these segregated charter schools has raised difficult questions for education leaders and policy makers in Minnesota. For proponents of school choice, such schools represent some of the democratic promise of the charter school movement. As advocates note, charter schools were designed—at least in part—to provide opportunities for students, parents, and community groups to start culturally responsive and anti-oppressive schools, ones that might recognize the values and assets of particular communities. Moreover, choice is not just about increasing the number of new schools; any choice system presupposes at least some variation in the *kinds* of schools that families could choose. It is also reasonable that students with shared characteristics may cluster in different schools. Charter schools designed to serve families' distinct cultural, racial, ethnic, and linguistic identities will almost inevitably attract large percentages of families from these communities, particularly in cases where families have experienced marginalization or discrimination in other schools. Such schools, while potentially being empowering spaces for these communities, are also likely to be highly segregated by race, class, and particular languages.

Proponents of choice note that voluntary (or *de facto*) segregation—when parents choose particular schools relevant to their identities, needs, values, and communities—is quite different than legally enforced (or *de jure*) segregation. Former Minneapolis school board member and education advocate Chris Stewart's reflections are worth quoting at length:

> We have Somali schools, we have Hmong schools, we have schools for Native American kids. And those communities don't really see their schools as segregated or as isolated, they see them as kind of culturally affirming environments for kids that they can't get in a very white state like Minnesota . . . When the government assigns you by race to inferior schools, that is traditionally what we have considered to be segregation. When parents pick a culturally affirming program for their child and they are from a historically marginalized population . . . that is so far from the traditional understanding of segregation that it's almost insulting to call it that.[6]

From this perspective, such charter schools may realize the civic goods of equitable and inclusive cultural affirmation, rather than the civic ills of inequitable race-based segregation into inferior schools.

CONSEQUENCES OF SEGREGATED SCHOOLS

While there are important legal and expressive differences between these different notions of segregation, the harmful consequences often remain the same. Segregation exacerbates existing inequalities between students, as low-income students are increasingly cut off from the opportunities, experiences, and networks of integrated school environments. Indeed, Bari's segregated nature—in particular, its hyperconcentration of low-income English language learners (ELLs)—may bring harm to the very students it was designed to help. While a few schools serving immigrant and nondominant students have posted larger than expected academic gains, Bari (like many other culturally focused charters) has never made adequate yearly progress (AYP) and posts lower average achievement data than both local district and state averages. In 2017, for instance, only 14 percent of Bari's students were classified as "proficient" on the state reading assessments; a mere 8 percent were proficient on the math assessments. These scores are not only dismal in and of themselves, but also compare poorly to aggregate results in the two central districts, where approximately 35–44 percent of students met standards of proficiency in reading and/or math.[7]

Bari leaders contend that precisely because their students face the twin challenges of poverty and English language learning, the school should not be judged by students' academic scores alone—and that in any case, their scores are more-or-less comparable to those of equivalent students across the district and state. They have a point. Test scores for low-income African American or Black students who are also ELLs are abysmally low in both Minneapolis and St. Paul Public Schools and across the state.[8]

These aggregate numbers, however, may obscure the negative impact of hypersegregation and the positive potential of integrated schools. At a nearby district school, Mississippi Elementary, for example, Somali students do better than both Bari and the district, scoring 14 percent proficient in reading and 19 percent in math—perhaps in part because they attend a school in which only 40 percent of students are ELLs, and 66 percent of students qualify for free and reduced lunch.[9] Insofar as academic disadvantage is often exacerbated by policies that concentrate low-income students of color and ELLs in segregated settings, Bari's challenges may be inseparable from its very design.[10] Racially isolated charter schools—what the University of Minnesota's Institute on Metropolitan Opportunity has termed "highly segregated poverty academies"—may be unable to address the academic needs of their students, no matter how hard they try.[11]

Furthermore, research suggests other long-term benefits for both White students and students of color who attend more integrated schools. These include more positive intergroup attitudes, cultural flexibility, increased civic engagement, greater access to informal networks, and improved critical thinking skills.[12] Integration thus enhances *civic* outcomes, in addition to academic ones. Racially isolated charter schools, such as Bari, might potentially cause civic harms, albeit unintentionally, as young people are isolated from opportunities to engage with one another across lines of difference. Here we can ask the question: How will students learn how to interact across lines of difference (race, class, culture, ideology, family background) if they never have the opportunity to do so? Absent such interactions, how should schools prepare students for democratic citizenship in an increasingly diverse country?

As compelling as integration may be, many students and parents at Bari recalled experiences of marginalization and discrimination in their previous schools. Their experiences echoed those of other immigrant families who have found themselves mistreated and misunderstood by schools that are designed to serve predominantly White, middle-class families. Amina, a teacher at Bari, shared an experience that illustrated the systemic bias she faced in other schools. She had previously enrolled her child in Franklin Heights, a suburban school district near her home; in her estimation, the district was considered to be a good one, with academically rigorous schools.[13] However, her son, though fluent in English, was quickly tracked into ELL and remedial classrooms. As Amina recalled, the school saw her Somali American son and immediately assumed that he needed remedial assistance. She asked for him to be tested. While his results showed that he was not only fluent, but actually advanced in English-language reading, Franklin Heights Elementary still resisted putting him in mainstream classes. Even though Amina was eventually successful in getting her son out of ELL classes, he remained tracked into classrooms with academically struggling students. Even with Amina's expertise and advocacy—and against both her explicit requests and the evidence of his reading ability—the school continued to place her son in less academically rigorous settings.

For Amina, this well-regarded suburban school understood her son solely in terms of his Somali identity—and held a deficit view of this identity. She ended up transferring her son to Bari, where she reported that "he was challenged . . . I realized that the teachers, when they're here, they don't look at color or—they don't judge people by income or the color. It's just like how well am I engaging the students." Amina's story reflects and captures what many parents valued about Bari. In effect, the cultural focus and demographic homogeneity of Bari enabled individual children to not be labeled as Somalis, as immigrants, as Black; and therefore to be seen more clearly for who they are.

Yet, spending time only with other Somali American students might still pose concerns. When might students at Bari have the opportunity to interact with students who were different from them: to learn from others, and to expose others to Somali American life? Will girls who wish to challenge cultural practices (by not wearing the hijab, for example) feel supported or even able to express their preferences? How will Somali Americans learn the knowledge and skills they need to succeed in a majority-White state like Minnesota? What are the possible consequences—civic, social, academic—of such separate and disparate schools?[14]

HOW—IF AT ALL—SHOULD CHOICE BE LIMITED?

These questions have grown sharp and uncomfortable for school leaders and policy makers in Minnesota. The number of charter schools focused on marginalized, immigrant communities has continued to grow, raising questions about how to weigh the value of these spaces for particular communities against the potential costs of segregation. Policy makers are also being asked to confront another challenge: the development of other charter schools focusing on more historically privileged communities. These schools—including ones that emphasize STEM education, Montessori curriculum, individualized learning, German immersion, and classical education—enroll more White and advantaged students than their surrounding districts. Athens Classical Academy, for example, which attracts a student population that is 80 percent White and almost 90 percent middle-class (in a city whose public school population is nearly 80 percent *non*-White and 70 percent low-income),[15] is one of the highest ranked schools in the state—likely thanks in part to its socioeconomically advantaged student body.

For some proponents, this is simply how choice works: it provides opportunities for schools to serve the different interests and needs of different groups of children and families. According to this logic, policy makers should not be in the position of evaluating if a Somali-language school is better or worse than a classical academy focused on Latin. For others, it comes down to academic achievement: high performing charters should be able to flourish, and low performing ones should close. But it seems unfair to condemn charters like Bari because they appeal to a historically disadvantaged community (and hence struggle academically) while celebrating other charters that appeal to an already advantaged community (and hence succeed academically).

Schools such as Bari, Athens, and even Franklin Heights challenge us to consider the role and place of integration in American public education. Among other cases, *Brown v. Board of Education* (1954) underscored the importance of equal educational opportunity as an ideal, and the crucial role played by desegregation efforts in achieving this ideal. Yet, many decades later—after widespread resistance and reform—public schools are now *more* segregated than they were at the height of desegregation efforts.

For many school reformers, the resegregation of schools is regrettable, but less important than the academic achievement of students from nondominant communities, no matter what school they attend. Still others see separate schools (when voluntarily chosen) as a better strategy for meeting the needs of students of color and families from culturally marginalized populations. Since public schools are already so segregated, why not encourage schools to segregate in ways that might be beneficial for marginalized students? Yet this assessment—while perhaps realistic—also seems like a defeat. If schools are charged with preparing students for democratic citizenship, shouldn't we expect them to include and exemplify a diverse student body? Finally, even if there are real and immediate advantages of Bari as a culturally protective space, how do we evaluate those benefits against the other possible costs, both educational and civic? In effect: how should policy makers understand and evaluate separate schools like Bari?

Public Education, School "Choice," and Somali Refugee Children

Cawo M. Abdi

This case rightly situates Bari Academy and the Somali students it serves in the enduring, complex challenge segregation poses to American education. Wilson invites us to view Bari—and other Minnesota charter schools—through the familiar yet unfortunate structures of residential and educational segregation that drive concerns about educational inequality. Yet Bari serves Somali *refugees*, a fact that this case does not fully grapple with. To fully understand the questions of inclusion, inequality, and democracy at the heart of this dilemma, it is important to anchor the case within the larger history of Somali refugee educational experiences in pre-migration settings, while also situating Somali students as refugees within debates about school choice and educational inequality in the United States. Doing so, I argue, can further inform how we understand the place of schools like Bari in American public education.

THE SOMALI REFUGEE EXPERIENCE

Most Somali refugees in Minnesota have spent years—perhaps even a decade or more—in refugee camps in Kenya and Ethiopia before arriving in the United States. The majority of the Somali parents now educating their children in the United States originate from a country where the language only achieved its written form in 1973. As is often the case, literacy and access to education were entwined in Somalia. While limited colonial-established education was available to a small number of mostly boys and young men in Somalia before 1973, the official writing of the Somali language created more accessible public education to those in urban areas with sufficient resources to forego the labor of their children.[16] This was only minimally successful, however; nearly twenty years after establishing a written form of Somali, UNESCO reported that only 24 percent of the Somali population (36 percent of males and 14 percent of females) were literate.[17]

Somali literacy and public educational access were also two of the only positive legacies associated with a dictatorial regime that held power in Somalia from 1969 to 1991. Following this regime's demise, all state institutions collapsed. Shockingly, "Somalia has been a country without any level of organized systems of learning" since 1991.[18] The political collapse also sparked an exodus of Somali citizens, who initially sought refuge in the neighboring countries (Kenya, Ethiopia, and Djibouti) while those fortunate enough for resettlement to the Western world moved further afield. The latter, however, are the minority, as close to two million Somalis now remain in refugee camps or are stuck in camps within Somalia for Internally Displaced Persons. The protracted political turmoil in Somalia remains the primary force behind these refugees' flight and for their ongoing exile. In a world where sovereign states are assumed to be centrally responsible for providing law and order, Somali citizens experience ongoing global marginalization and vulnerability, since the current fractured Somali nation has been unable to provide even these basic guarantees to its citizens for the last three decades.

The educational opportunities in refugee camps, and in the low-income countries where the majority of global refugees find first asylum as they wait to be resettled, are similarly dire. For example, a UNHCR report indicates that less than 50 percent of refugee children in poor countries have access to elementary schools, and only 9 percent have access to high schools.[19] This means that the majority of Somali children and even parents coming to the US are often far behind in the number of years of schooling achieved prior to migration. Moreover, this translates to thousands of Somali refugee children with very limited formal schooling joining their age cohort unprepared to master grade-level materials.

UNDERSTANDING REFUGEES' EDUCATIONAL CHOICES

The above historical overview of the education sector in Somalia and the refugee education gap allows us to make sense of the potential choices and challenges that Somali refugee parents in the United States face in educating their children. Given their history, nothing prepares these parents for the highly complex, racialized, and classed American educational landscape. For example, Minnesota's public educational institutions are paradoxically at the top of both achievement scores and the racial achievement gap in the United States. The governor's office thus hails headlines like "Minnesota Students Earn Best ACT Test Scores in the Nation," while simultaneously decrying others like "Minnesota's Failure to Graduate its High School Students of Color is Among the Worst in the Nation."[20]

It should be no surprise that newcomers struggle to navigate such a complex system. Due to the economic constraints that refugees with low human and social capital (such as language, education, skills, networks) inevitably face in a highly developed and highly industrialized society, most of these parents end up settling their families in areas with either low rent or public housing.[21] Unbeknownst to Somali families, the schools in these neighborhoods are often struggling schools that fail to meet state standards. Somali refugees are typically unaware of the link between "better schools" and "better neighborhoods" that the majority of middle-class Americans have internalized—and that is itself racialized.[22] They thus find themselves sending their children to schools that typically inspire headlines of the sort the governor's office frets over rather than the sort it cheers.

Furthermore, my extensive work with Somali refugees shows how their settlement and incorporation in their new American home is shaped by post–September 11 policies and practices characterized by heightened scrutiny of American Muslims.[23] For example, Somali families are highly aware and even stressed out by the fact that Minnesota is one of a very few states where the Department of Homeland Security's Countering Violent Extremism effort is focused. Both Islamophobia, which many American Muslims view as anchoring the recent banning of refugees from mostly Muslim nations, and the apprehension that parents have about their children's linguistic and religious identity inform the choices Somali refugee parents make about schools. As such, it is not surprising that charter schools—especially those that cater to Somali families like Bari—might be identified as a positive and protective resource by these families.

As highlighted earlier, however, the majority of these parents might not have access to resources or even have the basic linguistic ability to evaluate the academic performance and thus the educational outcomes of the various school options open to them. The heated academic and theoretical policy debates on school segregation are distant and inaccessible to the majority of poor immigrant and refugee parents entering into the American educational landscape. Those debates are embedded in the specific racial, political, social, and economic history of the US, including slavery, Jim Crow laws, and court cases such as *Brown vs. Board of Education.* For most socioeconomically marginalized newcomers finding their footing in their new home, the fact that their children simply have access to public education is the priority. The content of that education and its quality—often the flashpoint in debates about segregation and educational inequality—may be more difficult for such families to discern. This is not to dismiss the importance of access to quality education for all, but it does call into question the need to look more holistically at the educational choices Somali families (and other immigrant and refugee groups) make for their children.

In other words, the questions surrounding Bari Academy in this case can only be understood with the dual lenses of what it means to be a refugee from a country where access to education is limited, and how such children—especially Black and brown refugee children—are situated within not only the discourse but the material reality of struggling urban schools. From a researcher's perspective, more insight into how refugee children's cultural, legal, racial, religious, and socioeconomic status informs educational decisions is urgently needed. We know very little about most of these areas, and our challenge as researchers and as policy makers is to produce more scholarship to better meet the educational needs of new immigrants and refugees and to propose policy interventions that can ameliorate the future of these children, their families, and ultimately our nation. It is also this sort of insight that will help us understand whether schools like Bari are, as the case title asks, new democratic spaces or simply segregated ones.

Cawo M. Abdi is an associate professor of sociology at the University of Minnesota and a research associate at the University of Pretoria, South Africa. Her research on migration, family and gender relations, education, and development in Africa and the Middle East has been published in various journals and in her book, Elusive Jannah: The Somali Diaspora and a Borderless Muslim Identity *(University of Minnesota Press, 2015).*

Why Are We Worried About Students at Bari?

Reva Jaffe-Walter

The case study of Bari, a school in the United States that exclusively serves Somali students who are predominantly Muslim, raises a number of concerns related to the civic, social, and academic costs of immigrant-only schools. The idea of a school where students are taught Somali language and culture, where the majority of girls wear the hijab, and where boys and girls are segregated for some activities strikes many as undermining the aim of integrating new immigrants into American democracy and culture. European policy makers have responded to similar concerns. In Switzerland, courts mandated that a Muslim couple enroll their daughter in coeducational swimming classes. Laws in Denmark require preschools to serve pork meatballs, and France has long banned wearing the hijab in public schools.

However, these decisions and policies reveal more about national anxieties and the politicians who exploit them than about the educational needs of young people. They reveal a flawed logic, that swimming with Swiss boys, exposing one's hair, or eating pork meatballs promotes the social and educational incorporation of immigrant students. Rather, my research shows that immigrant students are more likely to identify as full members of their host countries if schools affirm their extant identities and provide them with high-quality learning experiences—even if they do so in putatively segregated settings like Bari.

CHALLENGING FALSE RACIALIZED NARRATIVES ABOUT MUSLIM ISOLATION AND LACK OF ASSIMILATION

In my own research in a public Danish secondary school serving a large population of Muslim immigrant students, teachers described Muslim girls' commitments to their faith as out of place in a nation committed to gender equality and openness. Taking up political discourses of the putative integration crisis in Denmark, teachers encouraged the girls to embrace Danish values of dating and premarital sex and expressed disapproval of their choice to wear hijab.[24]

Teachers thought that they were promoting the civic and national integration of Muslim students in the school; however, the students' stories revealed that the teachers' comments were actually having the opposite effect. The Muslim youth in my study described keeping a low profile in school, holding back during class discussions to avoid questions about their home life, and hesitating to ask teachers for help. (I found similar dynamics in the United States, where immigrant students told me they would "stay silent" to avoid criticism from peers.) Their frustration about being judged in school was exacerbated by daily experiences of surveillance and scrutiny of their identities outside of school as well. These experiences made them feel they would never belong in Denmark. As a male student explained, "If they don't accept me, I don't want to be one of them." Thus, assimilationist attempts by educators to urge immigrant students to "fit in" with national norms might actually encourage their alienation.

We see similar reproductions of nationalist anxieties and racialized conceptions of Muslim students in the Bari case, especially in the concerns the case conveys about "racially isolated" public schools. If this is truly a problem, shouldn't we be equally concerned about the racial isolation of White students in predominantly White public schools? Do Americans ask whether these students are equipped to operate in the multilingual, multicultural mainstream?[25] The motivation behind questions about Muslim students' lack of exposure to American values, particularly the question posed in the case, "Will girls who wish to challenge cultural practices (by not wearing the hijab, for example) feel supported?" draws more from stereotypes about Muslim Americans that linger in the air than from the realities of young peoples' lives. It perpetuates a racialized trope of the oppressed Muslim woman, perceived to be confined by her retrograde culture and community.

The teachers in my Danish study conjured similarly racialized images of immigrant parents who enforced Muslim traditions, preventing girls from becoming self-actualized individuals. In contrast, the girls described their parents as wanting what almost all parents want for their children: safety, access to higher education, and stable and fulfilling employment. Furthermore, the Muslim youth in my study tended to be more adept at navigating across different communities than their native-born peers, given their dynamic life experiences crossing borders between homelands and hostlands. A scan of the Facebook page of one of my Muslim Somali participants reveals images of her with her family in Denmark and Ethiopia, with groups of Danish friends and Somali friends, images of European rock bands, and an image of a bloodstained Somali flag that reads, "Justice for Somalia in

South Africa." This is a reminder that young people don't travel in hermetically sealed bubbles from their homes to schools "cut off" from culture.

EXAMINING THE UNIQUE AFFORDANCES OF SEPARATE SCHOOLS

As a researcher who studies schools that exclusively serve predominantly low-income, recently arrived immigrant students who are English language learners, I am frequently asked about the harm these schools supposedly cause. People are concerned in particular about depriving immigrant students of exposure to native English speakers and American culture. However, rather than focusing exclusively on the putative problems of schools serving recently arrived immigrant students, we should also examine these schools' unique affordances.

The story of Amina's son, who was tracked into remedial courses despite his high test scores, reflects the ways immigrant students can be positioned as less capable in many integrated schools. Research reveals that many immigrant students report feelings of exclusion and marginalization in school that can lead to lower levels of school achievement and an increased risk of dropping out.[26] In my own research, many students described attending middle and high schools in the United States where they experienced discrimination when they used their emerging English language skills. "If I go to a regular American school where lots of other American kids go, and if I have an accent, they will be making fun of me and laughing at me," a student from Sierra Leone commented, explaining why she preferred attending a small school serving only immigrant youth. "But here, we all have an accent."

Whether in Denmark or in the United States, immigrant students need to feel that their identities are accepted and recognized in order to thrive and to fully engage in the life of their schools and in their communities in new home countries. Schools that serve recently arrived immigrants often do this better than more integrated schools do. As a student from Bangladesh explained appreciatively, "I want to thank the school for giving us the feeling that our culture is not bad . . . [M]ost of the time in American schools they want you to forget about your culture. It's really helping me to trust in myself."

Since most immigrant students will not have the opportunity to attend schools that exclusively serve immigrant students, it is critical to ask: How can we get past the assumption that exposure to native-born, English-speaking peers guarantees more equitable educational opportunities, and instead help more students benefit from the kind of safety and belonging that they experience at Bari and at some of the schools in my study? During this period of heightened discrimination and racialization of Muslim students in the West, students are in need of schools that offer safety and welcome their multiple selves in a process of sustaining connections to homelands and host-lands.[27] One important step is for schools to embrace students' cultural and religious affiliations with their home countries, rather than assuming students have to shed these affiliations in order to belong in their host countries.

RECOGNITION AND BELONGING ARE NOT ENOUGH

While it is critical for students to experience safety and cultural recognition in schools, this cannot come at the expense of the rich educational opportunities that students require to access higher education and social mobility. English language learners are frequently denied access to rigorous curriculum and supports. However, the US public schools serving immigrant students where I conducted my research have outcomes that significantly exceed other local schools that serve this same population of students.[28] These schools challenge the idea that schools that exclusively serve immigrant students inevitably provide fewer educational opportunities to their students. In these schools, teachers and leaders collaborate in instructional teams to ensure that students are able to access the academic skills, social capital, and linguistic skills they will need to be successful in college.

In conclusion, when asking the question about whether Bari is extending or limiting opportunity for its students, one must critically examine the nature of the motivating concern. Is this concern about Muslim immigrant students' integration concealing national anxieties, or is it related to the opportunities available to students? Rather than being preoccupied with young people's cultural and religious identities, perhaps we should turn the lens to examine how racialized hierarchies inform the underprovisioning of resources in schools serving immigrant students.

Reva Jaffe-Walter, an assistant professor of educational leadership at Montclair State University, is an educational anthropologist who focuses her research on nationalism, immigration, and schooling. Her book, Coercive Concern: Nationalism, Liberalism and the Schooling of Muslim Youth, *was published by Stanford University Press in 2016.*

Reframing the Ethical Dilemma

White Americans Are Uninterested in the Costs of True Integration

JARVIS R. GIVENS

The ideal of integration in American schools is an important aim to strive for if education is to be a truly democratic project. Yet, many factors continue to impede the realization of this goal. Namely, the heavy reliance on a dominant ideology and curricula that privilege White, protestant, English-speaking, and middle-class experiences in the learning culture. But more than this, there has been a lack of interest on the part of the dominant group to attend racially mixed schools, particularly racially mixed schools that have more than a marginal number of Black students. This fact often hides in plain sight.

White students are the most hypersegregated group of learners in American schools. White families have been resistant to anything more than marginal diversity in schools that their children attend. For instance, the average White student attends a school that is more than 77 percent White. Similarly, the vast majority of White children attend schools where less than half of the student body is poor, compared to only 37 percent of Blacks and 36 percent of Latinos.[29] This trend is consistent with patterns of segregation in Minneapolis schools as well, the context in which the Somali families that choose the Bari charter school (over the culturally unresponsive and highly segregated district schools) find themselves.

In January of 2018, the superintendent of schools for Minneapolis shared that local trends indicated White families left schools when 30 percent or more of the students were of color. These trends are particularly exacerbated when the students are Black and poor.[30] Some scholars have come to call this phenomenon a racial "tipping point;"[31] noting a set of anxieties that occur when Black students come to represent a sizable percentage of the student population. Furthermore, while some White parents express an interest in their children attending "diverse" schools, they also emphasize their interest in sending their children to "the best" schools, which usually translates to schools that are overwhelmingly White.[32] In other moments they are flat-out resistant when even minimal desegregation efforts are proposed.[33]

Therefore, while integrated schooling is certainly an ideal worth striving for, the burden of this goal should not be so firmly placed on the backs of students who have been historically and systemically underserved over generations. How might the lack of interest on the part of White Americans to achieve the promise of the *Brown* decision (that being a full and equitable desegregation program) be addressed as a first effort toward democratic education? The hypersegregation of White students in schools is a result of the fact that White Americans, who have historically been most privileged in American schools, are invested in maintaining it. This is a dilemma that policy makers should engage head on.

Furthermore, Black and immigrant families' engagement with schools like Bari via school-choice options reflecting market-based reforms should not be read as a wholesale dismissal of the fundamental ideals of democratic education. To do so would fail to recognize the vexing dilemmas in which these families find themselves. These are more often than not pragmatic decisions made by parents seeking the best opportunities for their children that will cause the least amount of harm. One scholar of race and educational policy has referred to this tactic as "acting neoliberal" as a means to describe the conundrum of Black parents who take advantage of (or endorse) educational reforms that seemingly compromise the promise of past civil rights struggles for equality and justice in public education.[34] That is to say, a decision to send one's child to Bari does not necessarily mean parents believe in market-based reforms like charter schools over desegregated public education. They are choosing what they see as the pragmatic, single best option at the time, even as this means appropriating conservative school-choice options.

Black parents' choice of schools for their children is often times motivated not only by rigor or cultural alignment, but also by their assessment of which option is going to do the least amount of (racial or psychological) harm to their child. This is a tortured, invisible, and often unaccounted for choice, to sacrifice possible academic outcomes in order for their children to be whole.[35]

Minority parents are making decisions on a terrain that they did not choose. The reality is that the color line reflected in school demographics and the politics of choosing is inextricably linked to the dominant group's long-held resistance to sincere efforts to desegregate. To truly integrate would include transforming curricula to upset the mythologies and power of whiteness, while altering teaching demographics to better reflect student populations. It would also require White students to attend schools that are beyond their racialized comfort zones, the same way this has been required of non-White students in desegregation efforts of the past. It cannot be a one-way street.

At first glance the academic assessments for Bari are abysmal. But the reality is that the scores for the district schools are also far from impressive, in particular for Black and immigrant students. Furthermore, we should expand the aperture for thinking about the range of student developmental outcomes at Bari and across the district. Math and reading scores are not the only important indicators of whether or not a school is effective in the lives of children. These are limited measures of students' intelligences, abilities, and development. Yet our society mistakenly continues to look toward these statistics to determine what educational success looks like, or to make decisions about what schools are "good" or "bad." This is especially unfortunate given the unique circumstances surrounding the ethnic and racial particularity of the Bari school.

The concern about civic education being compromised, given Bari students' racially and ethnically insulated school community, is an important one. Yet, the relationship between civic education and desegregation is complicated by historical context. It is unclear that students being educated in environments that are homogeneous in ethnic, religious, class, or racial demographics stunts the development of civic engagement. For example, civic education was a strong component of many segregated Black schools during the pre-*Brown* era, which certainly had some impact on the Civil Rights Movement overall.[36] Civic education was arguably more engaging in these contexts than in the schools that Black students were required to attend after desegregation took place. In other words, there are effective ways to prepare students in schools like Bari to be civically engaged, even if students are not in close proximity to others (namely White students). This is especially true if citizens from the dominant group are unwilling to respect them and treat them with dignity.

In 1955, the African American writer and cultural anthropologist Zora Neale Hurston critiqued the ruling of *Brown v. Board of Education* in plain language—her critique was not aimed at the ideal it represented, but called attention to the sheer reality that a "court order can't make the races mix." She followed this with the question of: "How much satisfaction can I get from a court order for somebody to associate with me who does not wish me near them?"[37] Hurston articulated a perennial challenge to efforts focused on achieving justice and equity in schools through desegregation efforts. While it is important to uproot any and all forms of discrimination in policies and laws, the reality is that you cannot legislate public sentiment, as the legal history of desegregation efforts painfully suggests.[38] This reality has caused a number of scholars across time to question the costs of forced desegregation efforts, particularly for Black students who find themselves in unwelcoming learning environments with unsympathetic educators.[39] These students are perpetually recognized as *the others* being invited in on probationary and contingent terms.

The largest impediment to desegregation in American schools has historically been, and continues to be, a lack of investment on the part of the dominant White society. The schooling context in St. Paul and Minneapolis seems to be no different. The level of scrutiny and concern applied to the students and families of the Bari school might serve better if it were turned toward the demographics of students who are the *most* privileged and the *most* segregated. The burden of realizing the promise of education for democracy needs to be placed on more than the backs of students from historically underserved communities. Just because these students seem to be "the most in need"—itself a status that is due to generational practices (nationally and globally) that have structured the hoarded privilege of White, middle- to upper-class communities while underdeveloping others—does not mean they should bear the brunt of the costs. To the extent that it is a zero-sum game, let the privileged students pay the cost for once.[40]

Jarvis Givens is an assistant professor at the Harvard Graduate School of Education, having earned his PhD in African diaspora studies from the University of California, Berkeley. His research takes an interdisciplinary historical approach to explore the interior lives of African American teachers and students during Jim Crow, with a particular focus on their classroom experiences.

The Civic Costs of Charter Schools and the Need for Systemic Reform

COURTNEY HUMM

Although people have always contested what it means to be "educated," and hence what public schools should aim to achieve, Americans generally expect schools to prepare children socially, academically, and civically for adulthood in a democratic society. The case study about Bari Academy forces us to ask: what should happen when these expectations collide, when some children, parents, and communities are forced to prioritize one of these values above others? Must we accept these tradeoffs as sometimes inevitable, or could we create public schools that can truly help all children achieve all three of these goals? I believe that Twin Cities public schools *can* serve all children well, but to do so, they need to learn from Bari how to create socially and culturally affirming spaces while establishing high expectations for immigrant, low-income, and English language learner students.

CHARTER SCHOOLS STEP IN WHERE PUBLIC SCHOOLS FAIL

The rise of charter schools in Minnesota, and across the nation, is evidence of a public school system that fails to align with the values of all learners and their families. The Minnesota charter statute, the oldest in the country, states, "The primary purpose of charter schools is to improve all pupil learning and all student achievement."[41] Over twenty-six thousand students in the Minneapolis–St. Paul metro area are enrolled in charter schools. This suggests that a third of the students in the metro area have felt their needs would be inadequately met in traditional public schools and have turned to charters instead.

Charter schools are not held to the same social, academic, and civic expectations as traditional public schools because, once established, they have the freedom to hone their mission to fit the needs of the students who self-select into the school. The educational values promoted, then, are dependent on the mission and vision of the school. Since charter schools serve particular subgroups of the population, they are held most accountable to those groups' needs.

The Bari Academy case touches upon the ways in which families, faced with inhospitable treatment at neighborhood public schools, choose to leave the system in favor of a school that welcomes, affirms, and empowers their social and cultural identities. Insofar as Bari's achievement data is lower than both the local and state averages, families have been forced to prioritize social and cultural needs over academic needs.[42] This case makes clear that there is an imperative to reform traditional public schools to prepare children socially, academically, and civically to ensure that families need not sacrifice one for the other.

THE CIVIC COSTS OF BARI ACADEMY

Educators in a democratic society are responsible for providing students with the character, knowledge, and skills necessary to become active citizens in a democracy.[43] The students at Bari, while socially and culturally supported, are not prepared civically or academically to participate fully in a state that is over 80 percent white.[44] Schools must foster a democratic character in students by promoting a sense of self-understanding, individual efficacy, and a respect for differences. To accomplish that goal, students of diverse backgrounds must be given opportunities to interact with one another in meaningful ways, both academically and socially. Since many of us live in communities segregated by class, race, or ethnicity, schools serve an essential civic mission to give students the opportunity to interact with those different from themselves. Students need to mix across demographic lines in school and in the classroom in order to learn about one another's practices, beliefs, and communities, so that they can take each other's interests appropriately into account when contributing to the democratic processes later in their lives.[45] Research also shows that the more meaningful, face-to-face contact people have with other racial groups, the less likely they are to be prejudiced.[46] Developing empathy for those different from themselves, as well as the skills to respect difference, would be difficult to institute in a school as segregated as Bari Academy.

ALL ARE WELCOME HERE

At the same time, we cannot assume that public schools are currently doing what it takes to meet the needs of the Somali students who have chosen Bari Academy. The case reports that many students and parents in the Bari community recalled experiences of marginalization and discrimination in their previous schools. The systemic bias evidenced through Amina's fight to get her son out of both ELL and "classrooms with academically struggling students," for example, pushed her away from the district school. Immigrant families' experiences described in the case of being "mistreated and misunderstood by schools that are designed to serve predominantly white, middle-class families" must serve as a call to action to reform our schools. The Metropolitan Council reports that people of color have accounted for 92 percent of all population growth in the Twin Cities metro region since 2000.[47] It is imperative that schools reform to meet the needs of these learners and their families.

I recommend, therefore, that district schools adopt some best practices from Bari in order to make our public education system more hospitable for all families. Charter schools are often described as "laboratories of reform" that can help spur public school innovation more broadly. Bari Academy serves as such a laboratory, as it gets a lot right in its service to the Somali community. Families feel welcomed and affirmed, students feel their culture is respected in school, and the teachers and staff reflect the background of students. How can the best practices of Bari Academy be applied to larger district schools where students from Bari will be more academically challenged and civically prepared for membership in a diverse, and predominantly white, Minnesota community?

First, schools must place parents and teachers on the same team by ensuring that all families, including newcomers, feel welcomed and are treated equally. Classroom studies document the fact that underserved English learners, poor students, and students of color routinely receive less instruction in higher-order skills development than other students.[48] Culturally and linguistically diverse students and students of color must not be relegated to the lowest-track classes. Decreasing the use of tracking, and integrating classes within district schools, is an important step toward ensuring that children do not feel labeled based on their race or ethnicity.

Bari Academy also ensures that students feel their culture is respected in school. Students are taught to read and write in Somali, the curriculum includes aspects of Somalia's culture and history, and halal options are offered in the cafeteria. Cultural respect for all learners must be a cornerstone for reimagining public schools. As the Twin Cities and other metropolitan areas become more racially and ethnically diverse, there is a "need for curriculum to function both as window and mirror, in order to reflect and reveal most accurately both a multicultural world and the student herself or himself."[49] At the schoolwide level, districts must ensure that teachers are educated about the cultural backgrounds of their students and can serve their unique needs.

Finally, the case mentioned that Bari Academy has support staff members with Somali backgrounds and teachers who are bilingual in Somali and English. Attracting, recruiting, and retaining teachers of color and from culturally diverse backgrounds is essential in welcoming all families to public schools. Students of color now make up almost a third of Minnesota's school population. Only 4 percent of teachers, however, are people of color.[50] Recruiting and retaining teachers of color serves students of color and white students alike, as "minority teachers have higher expectations of minority students, provide culturally relevant teaching, develop trusting relationships with students, confront issues of racism through teaching, and become advocates and cultural brokers."[51]

Making schools more hospitable for learners like those who have chosen Bari won't just benefit Somali students. White students attending traditional public schools will benefit, as well. The test scores of white students won't drop, the diverse environment may compel them to work harder, and they may become more empathetic and less prejudiced because of the personal relationships they will build with students from different backgrounds.[52] In a state where the percentage of people of color is projected to grow from 13 percent to 25 percent by 2035, we would all do better to learn to interact, live, and work together.

WE ALL DO BETTER WHEN WE ALL DO BETTER[53]

The civic health of our democracy necessitates that public schools are hospitable for all students. Drawing best practices from Bari and applying them to all public schools would ensure the civic good of integrated education without forcing families to choose among cultural, academic, and civic educational aims. That families and educators felt the need to create Bari Academy is itself a signal that public schools require immediate reform. Pushing these families to opt out of the traditional public system has an academic and civic cost too high to bear. It's not incumbent, though, on these populations to demand systemic change in our public education system. The burden lies on practitioners, policy makers, and administrators already working within the system. Our democracy depends on it.

Courtney Humm is an instructor of education at St. Olaf College in Northfield, Minnesota. She taught high school social studies for the past ten years at a charter school in St. Paul, Minnesota, and at an international school in India. *She thanks Ben Paulson and John Welckle for providing extensive feedback on earlier drafts of this commentary.*

Black Charter Schools and White Liberal Ambivalence

MICHAEL S. MERRY

"Particular Schools for Particular Students" describes many of the positive features of Bari Academy, a public charter school in Minneapolis–St. Paul, that serves its Somali Muslim population.[54] It acknowledges that schools like Bari serve as a haven for families who have experienced "marginalization and discrimination in other schools," and concurs that schools like Bari are especially good at recognizing "values and assets of particular communities."[55] To her credit, Wilson includes the stories of Somali families who have left noncharter public schools—many of them integrated and high achieving—where both the parents and the children are mistreated and misunderstood, where there is systemic bias in terms of how children's abilities are assessed, and where their children generally receive an inferior education in part owing to the racist stigmas they must continually endure.[56]

Yet while the case conveys admiration about the school's mission, Bari emerges in this portrait as a failure, both in literal and symbolic terms. To demonstrate its *literal* failure, Wilson cites Annual Yearly Progress (AYP) data, an unusual move given that progressive scholars have long argued that AYP is sanction driven; that it uses a mean proficiency standard regardless of the population a school serves; that it unfairly holds teachers and administrators accountable for variables outside of their control, such as mobility rates and homelessness; and that it fails to capture the educational value that a school contributes (that is, the value added by the school community), something not reflected in a standardized test score.

So would Bari Academy be portrayed in a different light if—say, within a decade—it became a top performing school, one that matches or even surpasses the city average? Better still, would Bari be viewed as a success if it were to combine academic excellence with its aim to offer "a supporting and empowering community," one that includes in a non-tokenistic way the cultural and linguistic features of its pupils and their families? Something tells me that the verdict would be the same. Even when Bari's core mission includes combating racism and structural oppression—core progressive values—charter publics that serve minority pupils elicit ambivalence, at best, from White liberals. So what is going on here?

Well, a charitable reading might be that there is cognitive dissonance, where one espouses two or more contradictory beliefs at the same time. The case details that Somalis suffer routine incidents of racism and anti-Muslim discrimination, both inside and outside of school, and it underscores studies that consistently show that racialized minorities in Minneapolis–St. Paul are losers in a system designed to favor the dominant White population in a state ranked second worst in the country—behind Wisconsin—in terms of racial inequality.[57] Wilson therefore sincerely believes in the important work of Bari, which exists to better serve a minority group that has suffered a great deal of violence, discrimination, and exclusion. Indeed, she concedes that Bari is an "anti-oppressive" and "culturally responsive" school serving a stigmatized and disadvantaged community.

Yet because there is cognitive dissonance, there is a competing belief. And the belief that must prevail in this struggle of ideas is that we should always favor *integrated* schools; homogenous (charter) schools have no place in this script.[58] Hence, notwithstanding her obvious sympathy for Bari's mission, accommodating this more dominant belief requires that Wilson compare Bari to a single integrated school in order to illustrate why the latter is preferable to the former. But in doing so, she downplays the mistreatment and marginalization of Somalis in mainstream schools in order to illustrate her point, not unlike several of the scholars whom she approvingly cites do. And so in order to mitigate the tension of espousing conflicting beliefs, Wilson can acknowledge Bari's valuable contribution and, at the same time, suggest that the school represents "defeat." Whatever the school's real and potential merits, Bari must also be a *symbolic* failure.

The clearest indication of this symbolic failure is the case's repeated invocation of the term *segregation*, an emotionally charged label in the American context that appears no fewer than twenty-six times. We thus read, in rather tendentious prose, that charter schools like Bari "have been linked to patterns of segregation nationally," that they have "intensified patterns of segregation," that they are "racially isolated," and finally, that they are "hypersegregated." Even the very title of the case reinforces this reading. Framed in this way, many readers no doubt will share Wilson's concern about the opportunities and citizenship of Bari's pupils.

Yet behind the case's framing lie a number of problematic assumptions: Is it true that integrated schools will improve educational opportunities for stigmatized minorities? The evidence offered in the case says otherwise. Or is it the case that attending mixed schools will result in the kinds of democratic citizenship that Wilson would like us to imagine? Here the case offers little evidence, and Wilson instead leans heavily on modal auxiliary verbs like *could* and *might*, implying that only integration can lift all boats, rather than, say, other enabling conditions likely present in the school.[59]

For members of the Somali community—visibly Black and Muslim in a largely White and Protestant state with a long history of institutional racism—being portrayed as self-segregating is a caricature that diminishes both the school's purpose and value to the Somali community.[60]And thus when the case raises the worry about whether Somalis, by virtue of their hypersegregation, will "have the opportunity to interact with" pupils who are different from themselves, the irony is not lost on Somalis, nor on the Twin Cities' many other minority communities for that matter. Indeed the same integrationist logic would mean that there is little hope for democratic citizenship in Minnesota's hypersegregated *White* schools, which after all comprise the vast majority of schools in the state (and the Midwest), including those one finds in urban White liberal neighborhoods. (You know the ones: look for the dog parks, brewpubs, organic co-ops, compost gardens, and ubiquitous yard signs saying things like "Here all people are equal, Black Lives Matter, and diversity is celebrated.") Indeed, however much White liberals may decry segregation, they are no less inclined than their more conservative counterparts in the suburbs to prefer White-majority neighborhoods and to avoid majority-minority schools.[61] In the case, however, we find these concerns relegated to a footnote.

So the real problem in this case is not charter publics like Bari, which after all represents a paradigmatic case of a reasonable and pragmatic response to segregation and institutional discrimination. Nor is the problem that Somalis are exercising their voluntary right—like everyone else—to associate with others like themselves if they want to. The problem is also not that Somali parents wish to take the education of their children into their own hands, and moreover, on their own terms. Other parents do this as a matter of routine, albeit some of the time—as other examples in the case suggest—with far more questionable motives. Nor is the problem that Somali Muslims are dupes of conservative propaganda; Black Muslims in Minnesota know that Republicans are not their natural allies. And though daunting, the problem is not even poverty; after all, poverty is rife in Minnesota's White farming communities and small towns. No dire predictions about educational failure here.

To my mind the problem is twofold. First is an integrationist bias, a corollary of which is to view schools serving brown and Black children as always imposed, always unfortunate, and always inferior. Second is an ideological opposition to pragmatic alternatives to the standard public school, no matter what the evidence says, no matter what the realistic options for integration are, and no matter how often parents demand alternatives for their children—alternatives that more privileged parents unfailingly have at their disposal. To Bari's supporters, it is sometimes difficult to distinguish these biases from deficit thinking, or implicit racism.[62] But of course it is the institutional manifestation of racism in the school system, including discrimination in integrated schools, that the folks at Bari are repudiating.

Bari undoubtedly has many challenges ahead, just like all schools serving poor students do. But with the right kinds of resources in place, Bari—still relatively young compared to non-charter public schools—stands a reasonably good chance of making good on its aim to deliver higher expectations for pupils; fewer special education diagnoses; fewer school suspensions; higher graduation rates; more recognition of cultural, linguistic, and religious differences; fewer incidents of bullying and racist violence; and generally a more positive space in which to learn. And precisely because these goals are both feasible and just, Bari deserves better than White liberal ambivalence, or worse, disapproval; it deserves our support, even when it may have a long way to go.

Michael S. Merry is professor of philosophy in the Department of Childhood and Development Studies at the University of Amsterdam, the Netherlands. He is the author of Culture, Identity and Islamic Schooling *(2007),* Equality, Citizenship and Segregation *(2013), and the forthcoming* Educational Justice *(2019).*

Charters of Freedom or Fracture?

ROGERS M. SMITH

As this compelling case of Minnesota charter schools makes clear, diversity and equal citizenship can be deeply in tension. Minnesota is home to charters that range from Bari Academy, which primarily serves poor Somali immigrants, to Athens Classical Academy, which primarily serves affluent White Americans. Despite other virtues, neither school does much to close the differences, the gaps, or the inequalities so evident between them. Does their diversity represent an inspiring realization of American freedom to pursue many forms of happiness, or a set of barriers to meaningfully equal citizenship? As the title of the case puts it, are these charter schools new democratic spaces or simply segregated ones?

CONFLICTING IDEALS OF EQUAL CITIZENSHIP

Although, as our now-reflexive revulsion at the term *segregated* shows, the tensions between embracing diversity and realizing equal citizenship are far from new in America, they have come much more to the fore in recent decades. For the first two-thirds of the twentieth century, struggles for equal citizenship in the US put forward the ideal of equal citizenship as a uniform, unitary status—with an identical set of rights and duties for, at least, all adults. Advancing that ideal seemed to many the best way to counter the many forms of racial, ethnic, and gendered second-class citizenship then still explicitly embodied in American laws and practices. But in the last third of the twentieth century, in the wake of the civil rights movement, the women's movement, and kindred liberation movements, there was a shift. A range of activists and thinkers, including proponents of Black power like Angela Davis and feminist theorists like Iris Young, argued that uniform, unitary citizenship often worked against meaningful civic equality for, especially, various subordinated communities. They contended that certain kinds of differentiated citizenship, like some forms of affirmative action, or self-governing rights for indigenous peoples, better served egalitarian goals.

Those views were and remain controversial. Many claim that all institutions of differentiated citizenship, including very different and unequal charter schools like Bari and Athens Classical, are always balkanizing, divisive, and unjust. Yet sweeping dismissals of the legitimacy of all forms of civic differentiation reveal only ignorance or insincerity. In truth, there always have been and always will be many kinds of differentiated citizenship. A vast array of widely valued legal and political institutions—federalism, age qualifications, religious exemptions, accommodations for disabilities, opportunities for naturalization and dual citizenship, limited jurisdictional forms of corporate citizenship, and many more—all mean that citizenship will never be a fully uniform, unitary status. But the many kinds of differentiated citizenship arise for many different reasons. Some can be traced to continuing struggles against unjust forms of subordination, some to desires to recognize and accommodate distinct cultures or religions or geographic communities; some stem from efforts to adjust rights and duties appropriately for differing physical and mental capacities, some from efforts to foster productive forms of corporate powers and responsibilities. Sadly, many are best explained by other motives, including efforts to legitimate and institutionalize systems of domination over groups labeled as inferior and exploitable.

FORMS OF DIFFERENTIATED CITIZENSHIP

Though differentiated forms of citizenship are ubiquitous, people disagree deeply over *which* forms are desirable, empowering, and egalitarian, and which are instead unjust forms of subordination and oppression. Along with the rise of movements seeking distinctive forms of recognition, representation, and often redistribution for long-disadvantaged groups, those disagreements have proliferated and intensified. They are now basic, inescapable features of political life in every modern democracy. As a result, for modern democratic theory and theories of equal citizenship, and perhaps even more for architects of modern public policies, the fundamental questions must be, not whether we will have uniform or differentiated citizenship, but rather what forms of civic differentiation *undermine* meaningful civic equality? What forms are reasonably *consistent* with it? What forms are in fact *necessary* to achieve it?

These questions are made usefully concrete by this case study. Charter schools often represent rejection of the ideal of uniform universal democratic education in favor of education that promotes the development of distinctive talents, interests, and identities, including tech schools and music schools, but also schools with distinctive ethnic, linguistic, and religious identities. This shows that they are very much institutions of differentiated and differentiating citizenship. And so they are charged with contributing to segregation, balkanization, and destruction of common and shared public commitments and engagement. Yet they are also praised as a means to promote egalitarian diversity and multiple forms of personal and group self-realization.

Which are they "really"? Though the case raises the question, it does not insist on any final answer because the evidence shows that they are both. Bari Academy is enabling many Somali immigrant families in Minneapolis–St. Paul to sustain their distinct ethnocultural identities and to fend off stereotyping and marginalization, while also providing an education that seeks to prepare members of the community for more effective participation in American society as a whole. But not only do its students score abysmally on standardized tests, they score more poorly than Somali children who attend a nearby conventional public school. Students at Athens Classical Academy are learning to sustain some of the West's most valuable cultural resources, and they do extremely well on all measures of academic success, further strengthening their already excellent prospects for success in later life. But arguably, this only means that this charter school helps the rich not just stay rich but get richer. It also seems unlikely that their charter educations lead either Bari students or Athens Classical students to see their counterparts at the other school as fellow citizens with whom they identify, or whom they see as civic equals. It is more likely that they do not see those students at all.

But don't we Americans want our Somali citizens, including new immigrants, to be able not just to retain but to celebrate their cultural heritage, just as we want to maintain and celebrate our classical cultural heritage? Doesn't freedom for diversity mean that we must not only allow, but also assist both endeavors? But don't we care about the fragmentation and inequalities that accompany those endeavors? Shouldn't we have schools that encourage senses of shared civic identity, and that provide strong ladders of opportunity for all, on a roughly equal basis?

PARTICULAR, NOT GENERAL ANSWERS

The answers, of course, are yes to all of the above. Pitched at the most general level, those *yes* answers contradict one another. So, we should not seek answers at the most general level. In deciding just how "particular" particular schools for particular students can and should be, we must recognize that the answers will vary in particular contexts. We need not and should not judge all forms of differentiated civic education, all charter schools, as intrinsically good or bad. We should instead ask whether, in their contexts, they are or are not contributing on balance to meaningful civic equality, as well as serving other goals, such as the preservation and enjoyment of enriching cultural traditions and identities. In some contexts, like my adopted home of Philadelphia, we must especially worry about the impact of the proliferation of charter schools on traditional public education and on race and class segregation and inequalities. Yet in confronting those dangers, we must be careful not to foment so much discord and distrust that we foster disenchantment with teachers and education in general.

In the field of education, then, we must resist the temptation either of monocropping, planting everywhere the same seeds of whatever variety appears most marketable now, or of letting a thousand plants bloom unattended. Here, as in many other spaces, democratic self-governance must include ongoing efforts to let the greatest possible variety of fruits and flowers flourish, by seeking to meet the particular needs of each now, by rotating them as conditions change, and by pulling the weeds. To be less metaphorical, we must seek to insure that Bari Academy students have the added resources, in terms of teachers, facilities, nutrition, health care, and supplies, that they need in order to make greater academic progress despite barriers of poverty, language, and culture. We must also seek to provide for Athens Classical Academy students the kinds of additional experiences, including programs of civic engagement and service learning, that they need to grasp the nature and extent of their privileges, and the costs that providing those privileges involves, for others and even for themselves. Finally, we must sit back periodically and ask, is this whole current array of charter schools, traditional public schools, and private schools really the best we can do for all—or do we need to do some rotating, strengthening one sector, limiting another, so that the students we have now will on balance be better served? To do that work well, we will need to keep constantly in view the kinds of examples, and the kinds of questions, that this case raises. But in societies chartered as democracies, the responsibility for finding the right answers for our time and place must always rest with ourselves.

Rogers M. Smith is the Christopher H. Browne Distinguished Professor of Political Science at the University of Pennsylvania, with a secondary appointment in the Graduate School of Education.

CHAPTER 7

Politics, Partisanship, and Pedagogy

What Should Be Controversial in K–12 Classrooms?

ELLIS REID, HEATHER JOHNSON, AND MEIRA LEVINSON

Timothy Eiger bounded into the history department office and flopped into the waiting chair, panting as he swung his overloaded briefcase onto the floor. "Sorry I'm late," Tim apologized. "It took forever to sign off on the new football uniforms, and then Mr. B had a zillion questions about the districtwide midterms next week. Anyway, what have I missed?"

"We're just trying to figure out our final PoP topics," Patricia Perry responded. She was standing at a whiteboard covered in stickies, which her colleagues Jack Beale and Melissa Mendoza were attempting to organize into coherent groups. "As you know, we have two more for this semester, and we need to finalize them before break. You arrived at a good time to help us think through the topics we've brainstormed. They're kind of all over the place, and we're not sure which ones to choose."

The "Power of Persuasion" curriculum, better known as PoP, had been a core element of Northern High School's tenth grade social studies curriculum for the past six years. PoP challenged students to research and critically evaluate a controversial issue, take a position, and present their argument to classmates. Each social studies class then selected the strongest "pro" and "con" position papers to go to the schoolwide PoP-Off, which took place during the ninth- and tenth-grade morning assembly. Before the assembly started, students would complete an anonymous poll about where they stood on the issue. The winning representatives from each class then had ninety seconds each to present their PoP-Talk to convince their peers about the desirability of their position. The baton passed back and forth between "pro" and "con" presenters; students in the audience had T-charts to keep track of the evidence for and against. A second poll was taken at the end of the assembly; whichever side managed to convert the largest number of people was declared the PoP-Off Powerhouse for that topic, and the students' names were announced over the loudspeaker at the end of the day. PoP was popular among students, teachers, and parents—but it depended on teachers' selecting the right controversial issue to focus on each time.

"Yeah, there's a lot here," Tim affirmed. "Do you have any top contenders?"

"I really think trade with China should be top of the list," Patricia said. "It's been all over the news lately, and I think it'll be a great way for our students to begin investigating US-China relations. They can learn about protectionism and free markets, get some macroeconomic theory; it's a good prep for my AP Econ course, too."

"Well, that's certainly leading the news cycle. But do you really think that our students will be excited about a trade war with China?" Melissa sounded dubious. "Don't you all say that PoPs work best when the students are really engaged in the topic?" Melissa was new at Northern High, having just graduated from college with her teaching certification the year before. Although she often deferred to her more veteran colleagues in these planning meetings, she was starting to gain confidence in speaking up, especially when she felt she could represent a more youth-oriented perspective.

"Well, it might not be at the top of their list. But it's important, and probably even more important than we realize," challenged Patricia.

Jack jumped in. "I totally agree trade is an important and relevant topic, just not for this setting. I'm with Melissa on this. Do I need to remind you about when we tried the Iran Nuclear Deal PoP? They were so disengaged. It was awful. Let's try to pick something closer to home, something that affects their everyday lives."

"You're probably right," Patricia conceded. "I'll just weave it into my classes when we study trade. So can we cross that one off the list?" Melissa, Jack, and Tim all nodded their heads in assent as Patricia put a line through "trade with China" on the board and pulled off the relevant stickies. "Which one should we discuss next?"

Melissa surprised herself by speaking up again. "What about free speech on college campuses? There's been a lot going on at the U this year; I know the Black Student Alliance was occupying the Provost's office earlier this semester after those emails came out mocking safe spaces, and FIRE always has a booth going in the Quad to mobilize students against speech codes. Not to mention all the protests and debates that have been going on at campuses around the country. It seems like every week a new challenge comes up."

"This seems like a perfect topic for PoP," Tim responded enthusiastically. "There are strong, evidence-based arguments on both sides, multiple stakeholders, and several relevant and important issues: freedom of speech, diversity and inclusion, the role of higher education in a democracy . . ."

"It's also a really interesting context to learn about political protest and organizing," Jack added. "I'd love for Northern students to get involved themselves—head over to the U to talk to some of the student organizers there. This could be a great opportunity to build some college connections, and for our kids to see people of color advocating for their rights!"

Melissa was bolstered by the enthusiasm but was not convinced that it was unanimous. "Patricia, you look hesitant."

"Well, I guess I'm worried there's just not that much to say," Patricia explained. "Aren't academic freedom and open debate the bedrock values of higher education?"

"Those are absolutely important values," Melissa responded. "But there's an argument to be made that speech can have a real psychological toll that isn't shared equally across the student body. I think a lot of campus activists are arguing that there's a tension between supporting free speech and fostering a community that is welcoming to students of all backgrounds."

"I don't get how that overturns academic freedom," Patricia replied, "but I guess that's the point of these PoP topics, that there are strong views on both sides of the debate. And it sounds like you can help advise students on the 'safe spaces' arguments?" Patricia queried Jack, who nodded in enthusiastic affirmation. "OK, I'm willing to try it."

Tim immediately jumped on the agreement. "Great! One topic down. Maybe this won't be as difficult as we thought. What's next?"

The four teachers pondered the remaining groups of sticky notes. "What do you all think about including the debate about transgender students' access to bathrooms?" Jack ventured. "That's big in the news right now, but I don't know . . .," he trailed off.

"I think it's a great idea," replied Tim. "At least a handful of states have considered legislation on exactly this issue, and I know our district office has had more than a few meetings about our bathroom policies. Like it or not, these questions are something I think we need to prepare our kids to think about. What makes you sound so hesitant, Jack?"

"Well, I guess I'm wondering if we should be treating transgender bathroom rights as a controversial question. Yes, it's being debated here and around the country, but that doesn't mean it *should* be."

Jack paused for a second, trying to collect his thoughts. "I mean, I can't imagine supporting PoPs in favor of the legislation being considered in some of these state courthouses. How can we treat gender discrimination as something that is controversial, not just wrong?"

"I've got to say, I'm a bit surprised, Jack," Tim said, crossing his arms over his chest. "You're not usually the one in the room advocating to take an issue off the table."

Tim was right. Jack wouldn't normally shy away from discussing controversial issues. He certainly didn't when the district pushed back on the department for letting students debate Black Lives Matter. But he wasn't so sure this time. "It feels different now," Jack replied. "The tone of the political rhetoric, the partisan rancor—it's a lot less clear to me what's considered out of bounds anymore."

"It may feel different," Tim responded, "but our job is the same. It is our responsibility—and, frankly, our privilege—to prepare our students to be informed and engaged citizens. Regardless of what we personally believe, this is a topic being debated on a national stage."

Patricia chimed in. "Tim's exactly right. Folks are talking about transgender issues—from CNN to our families' dining room tables. I mean, we've already received two different sets of federal guidelines about who should use which bathroom. You don't have to like it, but these questions are out there, and we need to prepare our students to think about them critically."

"Hold on. I get that this is empirically controversial. People are definitely arguing about transgender rights. That doesn't mean it's a legitimate topic for debate," said Melissa. "I mean, look at the Japanese internment camps. Those were empirically controversial in 1941, but we'd never treat them as open for debate today, and I don't think anyone should have treated them as open for debate back then either."

Tim spoke. "I think we would all agree that we have to be careful here. Political debate is more polarized and partisan than I've ever seen it in my lifetime. But our focus ought to be on how to facilitate this conversation—or any difficult conversation—in the classroom, not to prevent the conversation from happening in the first place. Frankly, I would argue that our inability to engage with both sides is part of why we are in this mess in the first place."

Patricia added, "And a good citizen needs to be a critical consumer of media, especially today. We must create a learning environment that fosters critical thinking and sound reasoning, not censor or limit students' academic investigations. Weren't those our goals when we started PoP?"

"I hear you," Jack conceded. "Inquiry, critical thinking, and persuasive writing and speaking are incredibly important to me. But I just don't think that debating what are effectively human rights questions is ethically reasonable. And I don't think as a school we should be encouraging students to treat this as having multiple reasonable perspectives."

"So you would impose your own judgment on everyone else?" Patricia responded incredulously. "That's a total violation of our duties as teachers! It is our professional responsibility to remain neutral."

"Is it professionally responsible to condone discrimination on the basis of someone's gender identity? I call that hate," Melissa shot back.

Patricia looked shocked. "Hate? Really? When I was in school I was taught that sex was biological, and I bet the same is true for many of our parents as well. I know some folks may have different ideas today, but we can't just force these new values down people's throats—nor should we."

In a different tone, Patricia continued, "Look, these are emotional issues. I get that. But censorship of mainstream political issues is not the answer. That's partisanship masquerading as protecting our students."

Tim agreed. "I think that's right, Patricia. There are arguments to be made on both sides. I think a lot of folks—some of our families included—sincerely believe that allowing people to choose which bathroom to use presents a real safety issue. Plus, I know for a fact that at least some of the traditionalists are arguing for schools to make single-person bathrooms available to any student who wants to use them. That doesn't like an attack on human rights to me."

"Exactly!" affirmed Patricia. "Melissa, I appreciate your concern for the young people of Northern, but I don't think you're giving them or ourselves enough credit; I think we can handle it. Also, deciding these issues are somehow off the table here at Northern is not in line with our mission, our duty as educators to prepare the next generation of citizens."

"It's also our responsibility to ensure that we are upholding basic democratic principles like tolerance, equality, and human rights," Jack countered. He looked physically pained as he tried to imagine how an open, balanced debate on transgender rights squared with his commitment to helping students become empathetic, engaged citizens. "Debating a person's right to be themselves is not in line with the democratic values that we as educators are tasked with instilling in our students as future citizens. I'm happy to talk about gender identity in class. In fact, I think we should talk about it, but I can't present the two sides of the debate with balance."

"And let's not forget, there may very well be transgender students at Northern," reminded Melissa. "What do we say to them?"

Although no student had publicly identified as transgender at Northern, the neighboring school district had two transgender students. The district didn't have any policies in place for how to support transgender students when they first came out, and the debate about what the district should do raged in the local newspapers for weeks.

"That's exactly why we should be addressing these issues in our classrooms! *Especially* for students who are questioning, we should create a safe space to discuss the arguments and counterarguments they'll need to discuss these issues out in the world," answered Tim.

"Yes, I agree we should discuss transgender issues, to equip our students to respond to the hate," Jack affirmed. "But with PoP, we can't do that since students could take either side. And I can't imagine that any of our questioning or potentially trans students would experience the PoP-Off assembly as a safe space! Three hundred kids all voting on their bathroom rights and hooting for the anti-trans side? I don't think so."

"Jack's absolutely right," Melissa said. "We can talk about transgender rights in class, including the right to use the bathroom for the gender with which you identify. But we can't make this a PoP topic."

"So we pick a side for them? I feel like I'm starting to sound like a broken record here, but that's so partisan!" Patricia countered. "The best way to show respect for our students—all our students—and to prepare them as democratic citizens is to recognize they can handle adult questions. Transgenderism is a controversial issue that affects our students. I think it's a perfect PoP topic," Patricia concluded.

"This disagreement is starting to seem bigger than just this topic," Tim remarked. "I guess I'm starting to wonder: what *are* our guiding principles in picking PoP topics? Should we treat anything as off the table, or is everything fair game if it's in the news and people are taking different sides? What weight, if any, should we give to our own political and ethical beliefs, versus our general obligations as professionals? How should we be preparing our students for democratic citizenship in what feels like an increasingly uncivil world?"

Moving Beyond the Echo Chamber

NEEMA AVASHIA

The day after the 2016 presidential election, I sat in a restorative circle with my students. We began to process our feelings around the election by taking turns answering simple restorative questions: What happened? What were you thinking and feeling when it happened? What can we do to make things right for each other? What emerged from these conversations—their general disbelief in the outcome, and their inability to understand the almost sixty-three million voters who supported Trump in the presidential election—gave me pause. As their civics teacher, what was my role in this? In my efforts to affirm my students' identities, had I failed to effectively teach them about the significant fissures in our national landscape?

I teach in a public middle school in the heart of Dorchester, the most densely populated of Boston's neighborhoods. My school, like schools in so many cities across the US, is profoundly segregated when it comes to race and socioeconomic status. It is largely segregated by political view, too. My students grow up in school environments that are largely echo chambers—spaces where their peers share similar viewpoints to their own, and where adults often work very hard to counter negative messaging about our young people that arises in the media or on the political stage. If anything, I think that my students often assume that because people in our community are in agreement on an issue—like the DREAM Act—that issue is not controversial in our society at large.

But many of the issues my students assume to be settled are not settled in American society. As such, the question remains whether or not we should frame them as controversial in school environments. The issue in this case is thus broader than transgender rights; it asks teachers like me to reflect on our role as educators in bridging the very vast divides in opinion that exist among communities across the country. To do so, educators need to simultaneously make three pedagogical moves: 1) affirm students' identities; 2) provide significant historical and political context for the debate; and 3) unpack the different perspectives on the debate. What concerns me about the current format of PoP is that teachers emphasize the third goal, but pay less attention to the first or second, which are equally—if not more—important.

CREATING SAFE SPACES

As the educators' discussion in the case makes clear, the PoP curriculum seeks to engage students in encountering, and hopefully starting to understand, different perspectives on controversial issues. However, it is less clear whether educators at Northern High have created the conditions under which students can safely do so. Have they established norms around respect for different identities in their school? In order for students to feel confident in expressing their point of view, or in taking risks and exploring alternate views, they need to have spent time reflecting on their own identities and on understanding the identities of their peers. And they need to have done this in a school environment that clearly messages support and acceptance for students of all backgrounds and beliefs. To engage in a debate about transgender rights without having established in the school community that transgender students are safe and accepted is extremely dangerous.

That said, to pretend that there is no national debate about transgender rights is also dangerous. Without paying attention to the reality of national disagreement, students may end up thinking that they are safer than they really are. Sometimes, in our efforts to create safe spaces in schools, we forget that safe does not just mean *affirmed*, it also means *aware*.

While affirmation communicates to students that we support them, and that they are safe within the walls of our school building, awareness involves actually equipping students with the knowledge and skills needed to dissect injustice when they encounter it, understand its roots, and advocate for a more just society. For example, my school is one where you will see teachers and students alike wearing shirts with slogans like "Black Lives Matter" and "Immigrants Make America Great" on a regular basis. Our hallways are filled with posters expressing that people of all backgrounds are welcome within our community. Our school administration and staff are ethnically and linguistically diverse, and we work hard to make clear to students that our diversity is a source of tremendous pride. In these ways, we affirm. But this year, I also started my first day of school by having students analyze an image of the White supremacists rallying at Charlottesville. We defined White supremacy and examined the historical foundations of White supremacy in our country. I did this because I knew my students had been struggling all of August to understand the *why* behind Charlottesville. Yes, the image was scary. Yes, the words, "You will not replace us," chanted by those protesters were frightening to my students. But the fear was there whether I taught the content or not. My students' social media feeds had been replete with images and videos from Charlottesville. By providing them with the language and tools to identify White supremacy, I sought to ensure that they understood the root causes behind the rally. By understanding the roots, they were able to see the depth of the issue, and begin to think about ways to address it.

PRIORITIES OF PEDAGOGY

It is also less clear how the PoP format supports deepening students' understandings of the topic. Context—historical and political—is important. For example, exploring the national conversation and social conditions that made Japanese internment a reality in 1941 can provide powerful insight into the treatment of Muslims in America after 9/11. Both cases can even be tied together by an essential question like, "How has America's definition of who belongs, and who is an enemy, changed in moments where our nation's safety has been threatened?" But absent student's engagement with that essential question, a *debate* about either Japanese internment or Muslim registries will likely lack nuance.

PoP places a premium on persuasiveness, rather than on contextualization or deep understanding. This is risky with any topic, because it can lead the debaters to make the most polarizing arguments in an effort to pull audience members to their sides. In the context of an issue like transgender rights, this pedagogical strategy is especially concerning because some of the most polarizing arguments about transgender bathroom access are rooted in ugly, unfounded rhetoric. Furthermore, the structure also replicates the very issue we are having in society more broadly, where people are so entrenched in their viewpoint that they are unable to find the points of agreement that could lead us away from disagreement and toward consensus.

Northern High teachers do have an alternative. They could embed PoP debates within a larger framework of essential questions and enduring understandings that contextualize the issue. Housing each debate under a thematic umbrella enables students to both gain specific knowledge about the debate topic and build broader knowledge of the issue in context. For example, teachers could help students discover the similarities and differences between the fight for transgender rights now and the civil rights battles of previous movements. And most importantly, instead of the quick poll of seeing how students' minds changed from the beginning to end of the debate, the school could score the debaters on a series of indicators, persuasiveness being one, but contextualization and consensus building being others, in order to determine the PoP Powerhouse. By emphasizing not simply the debate, but the debate in context, as well as using a multifaceted evaluation of the debate rather than a binary one, Northern High teachers would better model the kind of discourse that our country so desperately needs at the national level.

BEYOND THE ECHO CHAMBER

National conversations in our country are becoming increasingly shaped by echo chambers. Similarly, our young people are being constantly bombarded with videos and posts on social media that are rooted in a particular perspective, and sometimes not even supported by actual facts. As educators, the challenges such a context presents are profound: How do we teach young people to parse the information overload, understand the beliefs and experiences that inform different perspectives on an issue, and come to conclusions that are rooted in sound facts? How do we ensure that they understand, or are equipped with the tools to understand, alternative perspectives even when they don't agree with them? I don't think educators can meet these challenges by simply rehearsing the national debates in their classrooms, but they also do little to help by presenting issues as though they are not controversial. Instead, I believe our only option is to develop structures in our schools that allow students to safely and carefully wade through controversy, understand its complexity, and come out of the experience with a better understanding of who they are, what they believe, and how they can work to build consensus with others who believe differently.

Neema Avashia is an eighth grade civics teacher in the Boston Public Schools, where she has been teaching since 2003. She is a 2013 Boston Educator of the Year.

Cultivating Judgment

Walter C. Parker

We see in this case a group of teachers exercising judgment and trying to make a good choice. As the philosopher William Talbott writes, "There is no theoretically neutral account of good judgment."[1] True enough; good judgment will always rest on some set of values. Talbot continues, "I believe that we must have it and exercise it in order to say what it is and to determine how best to cultivate it." I concur. Practicing good judgment is essential to knowing what good judgment is.

In order for teachers to cultivate good judgment in students, they need to have developed this power, to some extent, in themselves. They then need to exercise it, which should not only further develop it, but also help them figure out how to cultivate good judgment in their students. When it comes to teaching controversial issues I believe it is best, therefore, for teachers to develop their own and their students' judgment and not waste precious time telling students what to believe. So, I agree with Patricia that we should respect our students enough to cultivate *their* thinking and not use school time to propagate our own views. However, this does not mean that transgender rights is an appropriate PoP topic—I suggest that for reasons of student safety, it is not.

CULTIVATING JUDGMENT VERSUS INDOCTRINATION

At the core of many controversies in education is disagreement about the relationship between education and society: should schools serve the status quo or work to transform it? There are roughly three responses to this question, and they fall on the political right, left, and center. On both the right and left are rather clear visions of the good society, and schools are technologies for realizing them. In other words, educators on both the right and left have an end in view—a political goal, a vision—and education is a means to this end. On the right, students are to be taught to succeed in and serve the current social order. On the left, students are to be taught to change the status quo in order to create a more just and vibrant democracy, one that would include the economy rather than leaving it in the hands of the market, and one that would actively combat racism.

In the center is the progressive position of John Dewey: Educators should help students acquire knowledge through "intelligent study of historical and existing forces and conditions," but they also should teach students to use their minds well—to think critically, to examine competing perspectives and accounts, and to value and use democratic deliberation and scientific inquiry to sort them out and reach decisions.[2] But educators should not tell students to what end they should use these competencies; students are not to be indoctrinated but left free to use their minds as they see fit. It is up to them—intelligent, democratic citizens—to engage in the ongoing work of government of, by, and for the people. It is up to them to think the not-yet-thought.

A little history will help illustrate the differences between these views. This anti-indoctrination stance was developed in a later phase of the Progressive Era.[3] In the years between the two World Wars, educators like George Counts and Charles Beard embraced indoctrination as an inevitable component of social reform and encouraged their fellow educators to get on board with it. According to historian Robert Westbrook, Counts argued that "capitalism could not be reconstructed into a more humane social order unless the conservative indoctrination to which students were subjected was challenged by radical counterindoctrination." Westbrook suggests that Dewey took a more nuanced position:

> Dewey agreed that much of the education in American schools was little more than indoctrination, "especially with reference to narrow nationalism under the name of patriotism, and with reference to the dominant economic regime." But these threats to democracy, Dewey argued in 1935, did not justify counterindoctrination as a means to promote democratic ends.[4]

Dewey scolded Counts and other indoctrination advocates on the left for doubting the power of scientific reasoning and democracy in their students' hands when it had been so effective for themselves. "If the method of intelligence has worked in our own case," he asked them, "how can we assume that the method will not work with our students?"[5]

The cataclysms to come changed this debate. The rise of the Nazis and the Soviets—both ideologically doctrinaire, both totalitarian and murderous, both ethnonationalist and intent on making youth, through "education," into good fascists or communists—spurred a reaction. That reaction was a nonideological movement in education that opposed ideological extremism per se. It has lasted, for the most part, until today (although not without plenty of competition).

Importantly, Dewey's middle way prevailed. That it is a middle or centrist way does not mean that it is neutral; it does have an end in sight—continuation and consolidation of the democratic experiment. It rests on values such as tolerance, freedom of conscience and expression, justice, inquiry, evidence, and open-mindedness, not toeing a party line or forcing one's own beliefs onto others. But it avoids telling students what the ends of the democratic experiment should be. It attempts, as best it can, to leave that up to them.

People living in societies that are attempting to create or maintain democratic ways of living together are obliged to weigh evidence and grapple with competing accounts. They are required not to jump to conclusions but to be patient and evenhanded, to sort things out, to listen and read, to think and observe, and to exercise judgment. Everything from jury duty to voting and deciding on public policy depends on "we, the people" being able to pull this off. It is democratic work and intellectual work all at once, and it is not easy and certainly not natural (people are not born this way). Education is needed, for it sponsors intelligence in operation. This is the evidence- and logic-based way to apply the mind to problems. It is a values-rich way, too, for it unabashedly values critical thinking and experimentation, revision in light of evidence, regard for multiple perspectives, and an open future. It values, in other words, a political culture that favors science (evidence, transparency, refutation) over folklore or dogma, and democracy (freedom, justice, popular sovereignty) over tyranny and oppression. Importantly, it does not prescribe where students should end up. It does not propagandize them but, instead, respects their budding autonomy and, with it, their growing capacity to make uncoerced decisions.

DEBATING TRANSGENDER RIGHTS

If we value this middle way, then Patricia offers good advice: "We can't just force these new values down people's throats—nor should we." In other words, we should not tell our students what to think as this risks indoctrination and abandons the middle way. To fellow teachers, I say: generally, don't bother students with your opinion. Why? This is not about you; it's about them. Sharpen *their* thinking and cultivate *their* judgment by giving *them* plenty of opportunities to exercise both. Don't waste time telling them your beliefs, although *do* promote the values and methods of science and democracy through both your curriculum and instruction.

But Patricia is mistaken, I believe, when it comes to the suitability of this particular issue for a school debate. Teachers should avoid debates on issues that could endanger students—in this case transgender students, who have a suicide rate much higher than the general population.[6] They should stick to issues that teach powerful subject matter alongside critical judgment but without threatening vulnerable students. There are plenty of these, from historical issues to current policy disputes, and students will still be developing their capacities to think, to listen, to weigh alternatives, and to be fair. They can, on their own and in other settings, use these capacities on issues that may be inappropriate for debate in a school assembly.

Finally, when teachers do share their beliefs, Talbott's advice is sound: Do it strategically. Share to show. That is, when teachers do tell students their own positions on controversial issues, they should do so in order to demonstrate how they reached their judgment. Most important, they should show students what respectful disagreement looks and sounds like, displaying especially the attitude they have toward those with whom they disagree and the care with which they consider opposing views. Modeling is a powerful form of instruction and can help students grow their own powers of critical judgment.

Walter C. Parker is professor of social studies education and political science at the University of Washington, Seattle. He is a member of the National Academy of Education and conducts research on the high school government course.

Trans*+ and Gender Identity Diverse Students' Right to Use a Bathroom

Debating Human Dignity

SJ MILLER

While reading this case, a quote stuck out: "But I just don't think that debating what are effectively human rights questions is ethically reasonable." I wish this were a common belief. Ever-present for me is, why debate peoples' rights to be treated fairly and with decency? Why treat them as commodities? In this case, how is it even a question that a student's right to use a bathroom in a public school (any school for that matter) that comports with their gender identity is contestable, let alone debatable? This question, however, is only one of many facing trans*+ and gender identity diverse (T*+GID) people, and it cannot be taken out of the current political context. Many fear that treating bathroom rights as contestable contributes to a political culture that seeks to legalize, sanction, legitimate, foster, and condone structural and widespread discriminatory practices against T*+GID people. Bathrooms now; what's next?

PUTTING THE DEBATE IN A LARGER CONTEXT

The current political climate has created a maelstrom of social, economic, psychological, and academic concerns for T*+GID students. In the bumpy wake of President Trump's election (who from here out will be referred to as #45, the forty-fifth president, because of my discomfort in writing or speaking his name), the many successes put into place during the Obama administration either face repeal or have already been repealed.[7]

For T*+GID students, these changes are already well underway. There has been an increase in bathroom bills that will force trans*+, and those perceived to not have a gender identity that comports with apparent gender, to use restrooms or locker rooms that do not match their gender identity. For T*+GID students in particular, fourteen states have introduced legislation that would forbid them to use bathrooms or locker rooms.[8]

Paving the way for these changes in bathroom policy was the rollback of Obama-era guidelines that clarified that Title IX's sex-based discrimination extends to gender identity. Religious conservatives—who view both sex and gender as divinely dichotomous—were particularly outraged.[9] Twelve state attorneys general from southern states immediately began federal litigation to overturn these suggestions. In August 2016, Judge Reed O'Connor, of the Federal District Court for the Northern District of Texas, issued a sweeping stay, barring the implementation of the suggestions in any state.[10] The Trump administration's public hostility to trans equity and civil rights led the retraction of the Obama-era suggestions in February 2017.[11]

THE GUIDELINES

Otherwise known as the *Federal Guidance*, they encouraged any schools receiving federal funds under Title IX to protect the rights of transgender and gender-nonconforming students. These protections included the rights to:

- use a bathroom and locker room that matches their gender identity
- have their names, pronouns, and student records addressed by how they self-identify
- dress in ways that match how they self-identify
- be respected and treated according to their gender identity
- be protected for identifying as nonbinary or genderqueer
- have all personal information held confidential under the Family Educational Rights and Privacy Act (FERPA)
- access student health plans under the Affordable Care Act
- be protected from anti-trans state laws under Title IX.

If schools failed to comply with the *Guidance*, they could be sued by the Department of Civil Rights and Education.

The unconscionable happened on February 22, 2017, only thirty-three days after #45 was sworn into office. The Department of Justice (DOJ) rolled back its support for the *Guidance*, withdrawing federal protections for transgender students to use a bathroom that confirms their gender identity.[12] The DOJ's stance was possible because the *Guidance* is not a set of federal regulations, but merely strongly worded suggestions. Without regulations, the fear is that T*+GID youth will continue to be vulnerable to the shifting political and legal reviews.

However, there are other mechanisms in place that offer some protection. For example, eighteen states, plus Washington, DC, have public-school bathroom protections in place. In addition, local ordinances in roughly two hundred cities and appellate court rulings under Title IX in the First, Fourth,

Sixth, Seventh, and Ninth Districts confer some level of protection.[13] T*+GID youth in private schools, however, remain terribly exposed and vulnerable because decisions are often left to the discretion of stakeholders who are often exempt from particular regulations.

Even with these protections, there are still significant obstacles to overcome. Consider the case of Gavin Grimm. Gavin, who was initially allowed to use the male bathroom at Gloucester High School, was later denied bathroom use by the local school board. The ACLU took his case to the Fourth Circuit and won. Then, the school board petitioned for a Writ of Certiorari to the Supreme Court of the United States. The case would have been the first ever heard on transgender rights, but the Supreme Court sent the case back to the Fourth Circuit—precisely because #45's administration rescinded the *Guidance*—and it is now in a state of indeterminacy. With the delay, states without protections have the opportunity to impose discriminatory practices. In fact, as I write this comment, the US Department of Education confirmed to BuzzFeed that it will reject bathroom complaints from transgender students and refuse to investigate claims of antitransgender discrimination.[14] This is an aggressive departure from the legal consensus that the federal Title IX law protects transgender students.[15] Any defense now must be heard in state courts.

DEBATING T*+GID BATHROOM RIGHTS

As the Northern High teachers debate whether to include bathroom rights as a PoP topic, Patricia notes that educators should "foster critical thinking and sound reasoning, not censor or limit students' academic investigations." However, Jack counters Patricia's concern with the worry that animates my response: "But I just don't think that debating what are effectively human rights questions is ethically reasonable. And I don't think as a school we should be encouraging students to treat this as having multiple reasonable perspectives." Contrasting Patricia and Jack illuminates a difficult values trade-off: to not debate is harmful censorship, and to debate is an abuse of human dignity. But, put into the broader political context we now live in, the trade-off seems easy to solve: Bathrooms now; what's next?

Jack's concern underscores the fact that restricting bathroom rights is a form of institutionalized violence. A 2016 UNESCO report observes that countries cannot ensure equitable quality education and lifelong learning opportunities if students are discriminated against because of their actual or perceived sexual orientation and gender identity.[16] Evidence shows that for T*+GID students, the impacts of inequities manifest in disproportionate rates of lowered academic gains, mental health issues, suicidal ideation, homelessness, presence in foster care and/or group homes, substance abuse, bullying and/or being bullied, truancy, expulsion, and sometimes, pushout into the crime processing system.

Relief during the day is something everyone needs. The psychic toll on one's emotional and psychological well-being when denied bathroom privileges given to others is not just cruel, it is reprehensible. In other words, to put such a topic up for debate—to leave it as an open question—for an at-risk group of students in a hostile political climate likely amplifies the risk for a cascade of material, physical, social, academic, emotional, and psychological harm. It is also morally irresponsible to even consider.

SCHOOLS NEED TO LEARN ABOUT GENDER IDENTITY

Understanding the social, historical, and current and past political context about T*+GID students is much larger than the topic at hand. While bathroom rights are one of the most controversial issues facing these communities, it cannot be parceled out. Unless we all invest in these individuals' human rights—and divest from structures that perpetuate injustices—we contribute to the institutional pressures that negatively impact these student's lives. As an example, one teacher in the case used word *transgenderism*. This term is pejorative, as if it is something happening to someone: a person is transgender. *Transgender* is a noun, just as *man* and *woman* are, which identify gender as a state of existence. When it comes to understanding gender identity, teachers, who have influence over students' well-being and development, can foreclose, minimize, and alienate students when they use inaccurate terminology. I believe that change is not just probable, but possible, as we commit to staying active in this lifelong work.

sj Miller, PhD, is a trans+-disciplinary scholar whose research emphasis is on policy and schooling practices about gender identity. sj is the director of the joint MA programs in English education and ELL teacher certification at the University of Wisconsin–Madison.*

Framing and Structuring Discussions of Controversial Issues

PAULA MCAVOY

As I read about the disagreement among the teachers at Northern High, it was clear that the teachers have some criteria guiding their selection of PoP topics. At different points in the conversation, they agree that a good topic:

- has "strong, evidence-based arguments on both sides"
- is interesting and accessible to tenth graders
- has multiple and conflicting reasonable views
- is an issue for which legislation has been proposed or a policy is being discussed locally, regionally, or nationally
- has evidence of public disagreement.

At first glance, the topic of transgender bathrooms in public schools looks to tick all of the boxes. But Jack raises a concern. He asserts that this topic does not meet criteria number three: competing *reasonable* views. He argues that denying transgender youth the right to use the bathroom of their choosing is a denial of their identity and is thus discriminatory. He is happy to teach about gender identity, but he is uncomfortable inviting students to persuade their classmates to endorse discrimination.

Patricia pushes back on Jack's framing. "How can it be," she seems to be wondering, "that nearly all schools in the US are designed with two sets of restrooms and there is no reasonable defense of that system?"

These teachers are struggling because public recognition of transgender identities is an issue that is "tipping" in US society.[17] That is, traditionally US society has treated gender identity as a settled issue—there is widespread agreement that that there are two genders and those genders align with one's sex organs. However, transgender men, women, and children have been advocating for public recognition, and granting that recognition is to accept that a) gender identity is not necessarily determined by biological sex, and b) our social arrangements ought to be reconsidered in light of this understanding of gender. This advocacy has pushed gender identity toward being an open issue, one in which the traditional relationship between gender and biology has become unsettled. While there are strong indications that recognizing transgender identities looks to be the direction that society is going, we are living in a moment in which people disagree about the relationship between biology and gender. That disagreement is challenging many taken-for-granted policies.

In these "tipping" moments, many will often find themselves struggling in the way that these teachers are. Some, like Jack, want to argue that change is coming, so let's just get on board and teach young people to be on the right side of history. Others, like Patricia, see value in letting young people work through the issue. First, because that might be more democratic—everybody's side gets heard. And second, because open discussion could be a more effective way of creating change in society; students are invited to re-examine their previous beliefs about gender and not simply told they are wrong.

I see merit in both Jack and Patricia's views. While I find myself wanting to side with Patricia, because I believe schools are places in which young people should learn to discuss difficult issues of the day, I argue that the PoP activity is not the right venue for this topic.

PROFESSIONAL JUDGMENT AND CONTROVERSIAL ISSUES

The teachers in this case are deliberating about the *topic* of a potential discussion (that is, transgender bathrooms), but when teachers decide to ask students to discuss a controversial issue, there are many more moments in need of professional judgment. A teacher will need to make decisions about the following:

- framing the question
- preparing the students
- designing the discussion format
- facilitating the discussion
- debriefing the discussion

Each of these moments is ethically complex. For example, when preparing the students for a discussion, the teacher will need to decide which materials will be assigned to the class to help them formulate their views, and this might mean that some resources will be deemed inappropriate for the classroom. This decision might be made for concerns about accessibility or for academic reasons. For example, a teacher might reject a reading or video for citing bad evidence, being based on faulty arguments, or presenting an otherwise reasonable view in a way that is offensive or in bad taste. Additionally, for a topic like transgender identities, the teacher will need to be ready to explain the relationship between biological sex and gender and provide students with the vocabulary they will need to use—and not use—in order to have a respectful discussion. All of this requires the teacher to make many professional judgments that rest on particular educational aims, the needs of students, disciplinary standards, and the context of her school.

For a PoP-Off, there are two fixed constraints on the teachers' judgments: first, the question needs to be framed so that there is a pro side and a con side; and second, the discussion format must follow the established PoP protocol, which includes an anonymous poll, public debate, a second poll, and announcement of the winner. These two constraints lead me to conclude that debate about what bathroom transgender students should use is not the right topic for the next PoP-Off.

THE POP PROBLEM

Forcing the question into a pro/con format exacerbates Jack's concern that the activity invites an attack on identity and a defense of discrimination. For one thing, the questions such a format requires are problematic. Consider the following framing for a PoP debate: "Should students be required to use the restroom that aligns with their biological sex?" This framing leaves open the question of whether transgender is a real identity, and consequentially it invites the argument that there is no such thing as a transgender person. This could turn the debate into a disagreement about gender identity and not bathroom policy. If there are transgender students in the audience, or students with a transgender parent or family member, this makes them the topic of the discussion, and it carries with it an attack on their identities.

To avoid this, the teachers could frame the question this way: "Should transgender students be allowed to choose the bathroom that aligns with their gender identity?" This question grants that transgender is a legitimate identity, but it still does not avoid concerns about discrimination. Given that the overwhelming majority of the school is not transgender, the question sets up a situation in which cisgender teens are discussing whether to grant or withhold transgender teens' access to the restrooms in which they feel most comfortable. In a pluralistic democracy, using a marginalized or minority identity as a criterion to limit access to a public good is again an issue of discrimination.

A third question framing could be, "Should our school have a private use bathroom for anyone who chooses to use it?" This, as Patricia notes, is the direction many schools have gone. But this framing of the question is hardly controversial. Beyond a debate about whether it is worth spending school resources for a private bathroom option for all students, there is little interesting to debate.

My other reason for deciding against this issue is that the PoP format rewards the team that convinces the most people to change their minds post-debate, and consequentially the tone of the activity is winner-take-all with "hooting" for the victors. While this competitive format is likely what makes the activity engaging and pushes the participants to strengthen their arguments, I agree with Jack that this is not the right venue to discuss gender identity. My main concern is that the most appealing view on the anti-trans side would be to argue that bathrooms are more dangerous when they become more inclusive. I suspect that in many communities that might have some wide appeal, but it is nevertheless specious. Not only is there little evidence for this view, but within this debate, transgender persons are viewed as dangerous outsiders, perhaps motivated by criminal impulses. The framing is far from one that accepts transgender youth and teachers as legitimate members of the school community.

ALTERNATIVE FORMATS

My recommendation against using this issue for PoP does not mean that bathroom policies should not be discussed at school. If we take the issue out of the PoP format, then a classroom teacher could ask a deliberative question that is more open to various possibilities. For example, a teacher might offer the following question for discussion: "Given the concerns of transgender teens, if we were to design a new school building, how should the bathrooms be configured?" Alternatively, the teacher might ask, "Given the concerns of the transgender community, what guidelines should the Department of Education issue regarding bathroom policies in public schools?" By removing the pro/con framing, deliberative questions allow students to consider more possibilities, the issue becomes more complex, and the discussion is less combative. Further, as an educator, I would feel better about a student sharing in a deliberation that she feels uncomfortable with the idea of using a public bathroom with a transgender student who had been born with male sex organs. Within a classroom deliberation, I can facilitate that discussion without it being a winner-take-all competition.

Paula McAvoy is an assistant professor in the Department of Teacher Education and Learning Sciences at North Carolina State University. She is the coauthor, with Diana Hess, of The Political Classroom: Evidence and Ethics in Democratic Education *(Routledge), winner of the 2016 Outstanding Book Award for the American Educational Research Association and the 2017 Grawemeyer Award.*

Bathroom Access for All

How to Educate Without Indoctrinating

Tetyana Kloubert

Like the teachers at Northern High School, teachers across Germany struggle with teaching controversial issues. Unlike the United States, however, Germany has established guidelines for *how* such issues should be taught in the classroom. These guidelines emerged from discussions in postwar Germany about how to make the historical experience of the totalitarian regime with its "educational" (that is, propagandistic) strategies impossible in the future, and how to prevent the exploitation of civic education for ideological partisanship. After thorough, long-lasting discussions, pedagogues and political scientists agreed on what has been named the "Beutelsbacher Consensus." It has three main guidelines:

- *Prohibition Against Overwhelming the Student.* It is not permissible to entrap students intellectually, by whatever means, for the sake of imparting desirable opinions and hindering them from "forming an independent judgment."
- *Treating Controversial Subjects as Controversial.* Matters that are controversial in intellectual and political affairs must also be taught as controversial in schools. This demand is closely linked with the first point above. If educators treat differing or alternative points of view as forgotten, suppressed, or ignored, they lay a path to indoctrination.
- *Giving Weight to the Personal Interests of Students.* Students must be put in a position to analyze a political situation and to assess how their own personal interests are affected while also seeking ways to influence the political situation they have identified.

These are useful guides for *how* to teach a particular topic, but as the case of Northern High School makes clear, the question of how to teach controversial topics may be superseded by concerns about *what* topics should be taught in the first place. This is not an easy task, and here the Beutelsbacher Consensus guidelines offer little help. In fact, because of the second principle's mandate that topics that are politically controversial should be taught as controversial, choosing what topics to teach takes special importance. I suggest that the Northern teachers should take two considerations into account as they decide whether to include transgender students' bathroom access in the PoP curriculum. First, are there nondiscriminatory perspectives on either side of the issue? Second, will treating the topic as a controversial issue enable all students within the school community to participate as equals in the discussion?

NONDISCRIMINATORY PERSPECTIVES

The demand for nondiscrimination remains a central issue when deciding how to discuss controversial matters in schools. An issue should not be debated if one of the positions suggests that members of certain groups are generally considered to be less valuable and thus not full and equal members of society. Treating such views as defensible openly contradicts the basic values of liberal democracy. Schools in a liberal democracy thus cannot tolerate such utterances, even if they might develop critical thinking skills among students or emphasize freedom of expression.

However, let us look closely at the given example and ask the concrete question: would putting the topic of transgender students' access to bathrooms into the PoP curriculum mean (automatically) that one of the perspectives in the discussion is discriminatory? I would argue that this is not a necessary conclusion.

If this topic were to be included in the PoP curriculum, the teachers do not have to focus the discussion on the question of supporting or denying the basic rights of transgender people (as such denial is obviously discriminatory). The PoP discussion could, for example, focus on the conflict of values in an ideologically diverse society. The shape of the debate would then be different. On the one hand, the establishment of gender-nonspecific bathrooms can be considered a sign of society's recognition of the rights and sensibilities of transgender people, and can therefore be interpreted as enhancing values such as diversity and tolerance. On the other, the gender-nonspecific bathrooms could be interpreted as a sign of disrespect or insensitivity vis-à-vis other cultural or religious groups, thereby potentially misrecognizing the rights and sensibilities of those groups. Transgender bathroom policy, in other words, becomes a means to engage students in thinking about the challenge of reconciling diverse, often conflicting, points of view in a democracy.

Although this shifts the locus of the debate, including the topic in the PoP discussion is important. Preemptively excluding sensitive topics from discussion undermines the pedagogical goals of the PoP format; namely, to analyze a controversial issue, to evaluate the different positions, and to judge for oneself whether a position is acceptable or not. An automatic exclusion of such topics, justified by the argument that dealing with a difficult topic could possibly hurt someone, undermines the opportunity for students to make decisions on the basis of reasonable arguments, regardless of whether the discussion concerns a wrong and reprehensible perspective or only those perspectives that deserve attention.

Thus, it would be helpful for the teachers to return to the pedagogical goals of the PoP curriculum. If the goal is to focus on developing the capacity for discussion and judgment—and should therefore prioritize weighing different, even ethically ambiguous positions—then including transgender bathroom rights makes sense. But if the goal is instead to focus on topics that are of a more ethical and nondiscriminatory nature, the curriculum should only consist of topics defined by ethically justifiable points of view. Or, using the words of German scholars, the limit of controversy lies in the "ethical rationality" and "in the demand to represent only those cultural positions as legitimate in educational offerings, which in turn are willing to recognize others as legitimate."[18]

EQUAL PARTICIPATION

The second consideration turns on the question of equal access to the discussion within the PoP event. It is equally as important that all students be able to participate fully in the debate as it is that the topic not include discriminatory perspectives (indeed, the two are closely linked). Given the Northern High School teachers' conversation in the case, I assume that they have no desire to intentionally discriminate against transgender students. That is to say, if the given topic is discussed in the PoP format, the teachers want to ensure that transgender students will not be *intentionally* degraded. However, what cannot be ruled out is whether the discussion can *un*intentionally trigger contempt for particular groups or become offensive speech.

Simply including some controversial topics in educational curriculum can limit how much and how able students whose identities are called into question will participate in the classroom, since the affected persons may likely feel threatened and withdraw from the discussion space. To put it more generally: enabling discriminatory statements in educational institutions creates a climate of mistrust and fear that contradicts both the pedagogical and ethical goals of educational institutions.

However, to bring a difficult topic to discussion does not automatically imply that some groups would be offended or feel themselves callously exhibited as examples. They may feel more upset if their teachers preemptively exclude such a discussion on the grounds of protecting these students' feelings. This is because addressing certain controversies carefully and thoughtfully can serve to make invisible positions visible, and can give voice to those personally affected by the stakes of the controversy. Deciding which topics may or may not be discussed can also demonstrate a lack of faith in students' abilities to handle difficult conversations. Students who experience controversies under the right circumstances (such as through caring relationships in the classrooms) may actually demonstrate increased participation. Dealing with controversial issues can thus have a positive impact on the emotional development of young people. They may develop a better understanding of their feelings and attitudes, gain self-confidence, and learn to consider controversies and conflicts as a normal and necessary part of democracy.[19]

Such an effect, however, is contingent on the general social climate of the society. In a society in which racist, sexist, and/or homophobic attitudes are prevalent, and discrimination is ubiquitous, the individuals belonging to the discriminated-against groups are likely to have the least power and therefore the least degree of participation and opportunity to voice their opinions. We must also consider the strong need for peer approval within student groups, and that fears of setting oneself apart from peers by expressing contrary viewpoints could inhibit students from expressing themselves freely. The process of dealing with divergent perspectives could easily transform differences of opinion into inequality and discrimination when certain perspectives are—even unintentionally—devalued or marginalized.

CONCLUSION

The PoP curriculum case at Northern High School allows some general conclusions. Civic education should not shy away from working out differences among individuals who disagree. However, it is legitimate only if it serves democratic purposes and is not exploited for political partisanship. Learning both *what* to treat as controversial and *how* to engage in respectful dialogue with people whose values differ from one's own is important for the protection and strengthening of democracy and for the promotion of a culture of human dignity.

Tetyana Kloubert is acting professor and deputy chair for adult education at the Catholic University of Eichstätt-Ingolstadt, Germany, as well as a faculty member at the University of Augsburg, from which she received her PhD. Having trained in both Ukraine and Germany, she researches problems of civic education and indoctrination in Eastern Europe, Western Europe, and the United States.

Creating Principled Debates by Choosing Debate Principles

Rich Frost

The simple answer to the question of whether students should not just be allowed, but encouraged and even required to participate in public debates about the basic rights of transgender people is a resounding "No." Melissa and Jack's instincts are the moral compass of this story; it is inappropriate, and potentially damaging, to put students' basic humanity up for debate in a forum like PoP just because it is "empirically controversial." The more difficult answer to tease out is just when topics should be considered worthy of public debate and, as hinted at by Melissa, taught as "open questions" to students. What principled criteria can allow us to distinguish between topics beyond mere polling data? Given the constraints and goals of the PoP program, as described, I argue that these teachers have a responsibility to independently evaluate whether something is controversial *and* should be taught as an open question in the form of a public debate based on two lines of inquiry: 1) whether both sides of the alleged debate are based in verifiable, empirical facts, and, relatedly, 2) whether both sides' arguments are based in values endorsed by, or at least not excluded by, the school itself. When applied to the case at hand, it is clear that another forum would be better for teaching issues around the rights of transgender students.

FACT-BASED PERSPECTIVES

I first ask whether the arguments made against transgender rights are based in verifiable, empirical facts. This criterion is pulled directly from the goals of the program itself, in which the teachers note that the program is meant to compare "evidence-based" arguments that are based in "sound reasoning" and "critical thinking." However, the debate over transgender student rights has been rife with misrepresentations, myth, and unsupported conjecture. Frankly, it is telling that Patricia and Tim resort primarily to their responsibility to not make decisions for students when making their arguments; the case could hardly be written with a substantive defense of the position that transgender students should *not* be allowed to use facilities consistent with their gender identity, because those arguments are generally based in demonstrably faulty assumptions and beliefs.

For example, through scouring news articles, court documents, and public debates, the most commonly cited reasons for the anti-trans position include privacy and safety.[20] Tim mentions this, saying that "I think a lot of folks—some of our families included—sincerely believe that allowing people to choose which bathroom to use presents a real safety issue." This calls into question whether there is a legitimate privacy or safety issue. But when given the opportunity to demonstrate the necessity of these bills to protect safety and privacy, lawyers, anti-trans advocates, and legislators have consistently been unable to come up with concrete examples or empirical data. For example, after North Carolina passed a prohibition (known as HB2) that directed state agencies, including public schools, to designate multiple occupancy bathrooms and changing rooms for use only by students based on their biological sex, a Republican-appointed federal judge noted that "no party has indicated that the pre-HB2 legal regime posed a significant privacy or safety threat to anyone in North Carolina."[21] In fact, research suggests that transgender people are disproportionately likely to be the *victims* of assault in public restrooms. No credible data supports the assertions that a single transgender person has ever assaulted someone in a bathroom; that allowing transgender people to use bathrooms and facilities consistent with their gender identity will lead to an increase in cisgender people "posing" as trans for nefarious purposes; or that existing laws against assault, "peeping," indecent exposure, trespass, and so forth are insufficient to protect people in these spaces.[22]

When it comes to Northern High, it is important to consider how the inclusion of perspectives that have no empirical grounds relate to the goals of "critical thinking" skills, "sound reasoning," and "evidence-based" arguments, which the PoP teachers emphasize throughout their discussion. I agree with the teachers that these are important skills for students to develop, and that the PoP curriculum helps do just that. However, debates are only effective insofar as we can agree on what constitutes a reasonable argument, what should be persuasive, and how to evaluate the merits of any particular position. Allowing one side of a debate to rely on classic fallacies or to present arguments unsupported—or even refuted—by the relevant empirical data undermines the entire purpose of holding debate forums. Additionally, an underlying goal of the PoP forums, referred to several times by both sides of the argument, is to promote "democratic citizenship." Ensuring that debates are based in factual perspectives and logical, sound arguments is crucial to cultivating these important civic values that strengthen our democracy in the long term.

SCHOOL VALUES

The second question to consider is whether each argument is steeped in values endorsed by the school. For example, an argument in favor of slavery on the basis of the supremacy of White people would not be accepted as a legitimate values-based argument in American schools today. While the use of "values" may scare some people as a cover for political preferences, schools actually already outline values that they hope to inculcate in their students. I ask not that this school select novel or controversial values in order to cherry-pick PoP topics, but merely that they utilize values that they already emphasize when they are making their selections. Some values that emerge over the course of the teachers' discussion include familiar educational values: critical inquiry, political engagement, empathy, and understanding across difference. Other values often taught in schools might include kindness, respect, good judgment, and courage—values that were explicitly encouraged in the public schools I myself attended.[23] While I leave it to the reader to determine whether the values asserted by anti-trans activists are merely a pretext for transphobic instincts, a strong case can be made that teaching both sides of the debate over transgender rights as equally meritorious would not promote these values because one side of the debate is not steeped in said values. Regardless, as the arguments espoused by anti-trans activists also fail the first principle, the topic—if it is to be engaged with at all—should be explored in a non-PoP forum.

FINAL THOUGHTS

Some who disagree with me may suggest that I have created a straw man of the array of arguments opponents might present by focusing on strong opposition to bathroom access. After all, the teachers mention some compromise-based positions, such as increasing access to single-user bathrooms. But while there may be some debate between different kinds of accommodations, this misdirect attempts to dance around the fundamental political question, which is essentially whether to recognize transgender identities at all—as noted by Patricia saying that "[w]hen I was in school I was taught that sex was biological" and "transgenderism is a controversial issue." Further, these kinds of compromise positions do not fit the format of PoP debates, in which students are asked take a definitive, oppositional stance. If the desire of the teachers is to explore the nuances of how to *best* work with transgender students, I would submit that a different forum would be more appropriate than the diametrical opposition inherent in the PoP-style debate hall.

This brings me to a final point. Patricia repeatedly refers to not including transgender rights as a PoP debate topic as "censorship." This fundamentally misconceives the concept of censorship. The PoP forum is a single part of a larger educational system with very particular goals. It serves as a component of the larger curriculum, not as the only means of education in the school. Removing something from consideration because it is a poor fit for PoP does not mean that teachers have to eliminate something from the curriculum altogether; it just means that it might be best taught in a different manner. Further, if the mere choice to not select a topic was "censorship," then an infinite number of potential topics are, de facto, "censored" by not being considered by the teachers to begin with. As long as nondiscriminatory, defensible, and explicit criteria guide the decision-making process, it is both acceptable and desirable to remove some topics from consideration. Was it censorship to recognize that trade with China was inappropriate *for that particular forum* and should instead be taught elsewhere? Certainly not; it was a question of trade-offs, priorities, and finding the very best topics for a program with limited bandwidth, particular goals, and unique hazards. Rather than viewing taking issues off the table as "censorship," the criteria I have laid out serve to demonstrate which issues are best suited for PoP consideration and which issues are best suited for some other form of pedagogy. By making these decisions in a principled manner, students can learn about crucial contemporary issues, schools can teach and transmit their values, and our democracy can still be served by the important mission of programs like the PoP debates.

Rich Frost is an attorney at the Education Law Center in Newark, New Jersey, where he works to find novel solutions to prevent and ameliorate the impacts of bullying in schools.

CHAPTER 8

Bending Toward—or Away From—Racial Justice?

Culturally Responsive Curriculum Rollout at Arc Charter

TATIANA GERON AND MEIRA LEVINSON

Sophie Biel watched second-year teacher Ethan Frankel dismiss his eighth graders out of the social studies classroom. Ms. Biel was the instructional support specialist for Arc Charter Schools, a small Northeastern charter network. She was visiting Ethan's classroom in Arc Coastal Middle School to coach him on implementing Arc's new social studies curriculum. The culturally responsive curriculum, whose goal was to "portray diverse experience and perspectives in global and American history while challenging racial and cultural intolerance, injustice, and oppression,"[1] had already been successful with the teachers at Arc Downtown. But, Sophie thought to herself as Ethan approached her desk, grinning, she might have her work cut out for her at Arc Coastal.

"So, how do you think that went?" Sophie asked as Ethan sat down.

"I thought it was excellent!" Ethan beamed. "They were so engaged! They had so much to say about the connections between Jim Crow laws and our twenty-first-century legal system. This new curriculum is awesome, Ms. Biel."

"Ok, so engagement was positive. I noticed you fed off the energy in the room, too," Sophie responded, cringing inwardly as she recalled how Ethan had enthusiastically affirmed a student's statement that White people shouldn't become police officers. "Any deltas, or things you wish had gone differently?"

"Well," Ethan ran a hand through his red curls. "Honestly, a couple of times I didn't really know how to push the conversations in the right direction. I mean, this is why I wanted to teach social studies! Honest conversations about the problems in our country today! But I noticed that Kaeden and Emmalee, and some of the other, um, White kids?" He looked furtively at Sophie as he mentioned race, and then continued. "They weren't participating as much. And, like, I'm not sure how much I can really say either, as a White male, right?

"That unpacking privilege exercise you had us do at the last PD was really good, by the way," Ethan added hastily. "But to tell the truth, it was the first time I'd thought about racism like that. I really want my students of color not to feel marginalized in *my* classroom, like you said. But am I oppressing them just by being in a position of authority?"

He looked at Sophie like she had all the answers. She took a deep breath, unsure where to start. Just then, the bell rang, and Ethan jumped up. "I have to go supervise lunch today. Can we talk more about this in our next session? I'm really looking forward to it."

Sophie nodded, and Ethan bounded out. She admired Ethan's willingness to tackle the difficult topic of structural racism in his classroom and was grateful for his burgeoning self-awareness. But the fact of the matter was that the lesson had been extremely difficult to watch. Ethan had gone off script very early, encouraging his students to share their experiences with the criminal justice system without setting up discussion norms or boundaries. Despite their previous coaching, his facilitation still lacked nuanced understanding. Sophie was worried that Ethan's teaching was simplifying students' views on race and the justice system, not rendering them more complex as the curriculum intended.

Sophie had taken the position of instructional support specialist after nine years teaching English language arts at Arc Downtown, the flagship of the network's five schools. Originally drawn to teach in an urban charter to fight for social justice, the past nine years had taught her just how complicated that fight was. A queer, White woman who grew up working class, Sophie was constantly thinking about the intersectionality of race, class, gender, and sexuality marginalization, and how it manifested itself in the school system. At Arc Downtown she'd found a team of similar-minded educators who pushed each other's thinking and engaged in activism together. Sophie hadn't wanted to leave the classroom, but when she and her wife adopted their daughter, she'd decided to take a more flexibly scheduled position that allowed her to work with schools across the network.

She'd been thrilled to learn that her first project was to revamp the Arc social studies curriculum, an endeavor she and her Downtown colleagues had been pushing for years. Though she would never claim to be an expert on racial justice, she felt her greatest strength was to listen to and learn from others' experiences—and she'd seen her share of what worked and what didn't when having difficult conversations with students. After four months of developing the curriculum at her former school, Sophie was continuing the process with Coastal, starting with a full-day training and following up with twice-monthly observations and check-ins. Her goal was then to roll the curriculum out in Arc's other three schools the following semester, although that would be up to the central administration, contingent on the successful pilot at Coastal.

Sophie's two days a month at Coastal were jam-packed with department meetings and observations; today, her fifth visit, was no different. But as her heels clicked down the hallway on her way to her next meeting, Sophie pondered for the umpteenth time how different Coastal was from Downtown. While Downtown served a mixed-income group of students of color, Coastal's student body mirrored the predominantly White and working-class demographics of its small, former port city. At Downtown, the curriculum change had been catalyzed by veteran teachers who created their own units that addressed issues of race and power in history. Sophie was concerned that her team had underestimated what it meant to put a social justice curriculum in the hands of the mostly White and younger teachers at Coastal, many of whom had never considered the need for such a curriculum.

She knocked on Tiana Shepard's classroom door, and the seventh-grade social studies teacher opened it with a smile. Tiana had taught at Downtown for six years before shifting to Coastal last year. Having worked together to develop the new curriculum, both women were proud of the work that Tiana's students were doing with the unit on early colonial history. "I was hoping you'd help me look through some student work," Tiana said. "I've been having the kids write journal pieces for homework. Some of them already know more than I do about the massacres and enslavement of the Taino following Columbus' arrival on Hispaniola. Other kids have grown up being force-fed the old story, though. I'm having trouble meeting all the kids where they're at."

Tiana held up one piece of notebook paper for Sophie to see. "Tyler, for example. This kid is a sweetheart, and he's really taking this new curriculum to heart. He wrote, *Today I learned that Columbus forced the Taino to work themselves to death in the gold mines. I used to think that he was a hero, and now I'm not sure what to think. Does this mean that other people who I think are heroes will end up being the villain, too? What about me—am I a villain for thinking he was so great? Is everything I've learned in school a lie?!*

Sophie smiled at the seventh grader's dramatic phrasing, but Tiana continued. "And, to make things more complicated, I got an email from his mom this morning. She was concerned after Tyler spent all dinner talking about the atrocities European explorers committed in the New World. I think her exact words were, 'Are you teaching him to hate himself because he's Italian? Are you teaching hatred of White people?'"

Tiana sighed. "I'm not here for this White fragility thing, Sophie. Obviously, I care about my students, but I care about them learning the *truth*. And when I was growing up, did any of my White teachers care that they were teaching history that made us Black kids feel uncomfortable and upset? No way. Our world is changing, and besides, this"—she gestured to the "Columbus—Hero or Villain?" sign she'd tacked on her bulletin board—"this is the truth. It's our duty as teachers to disrupt the cycle of power. I've dealt with this kind of thing before, here, so I'm ok talking to Tyler's mom about celebrating different perspectives and empowering each other to do good in the world, so on and so forth. But she cc'd Principal Barry on that email."

Sophie groaned.

"You might want to report this to the higher-ups at Arc," Tiana said. "They need to know that some real parental pushback is possible."

"You're right," Sophie agreed. "But I don't know how much backup you're going to get. I don't think they really understand what the curriculum is about—and I'm worried this could make the rollout harder to the rest of the network." As Tiana's face fell, Sophie hastened to change the mood. "But that's not on you! You're doing such great work. I just have to figure out how to sell it to the central office."

Tiana smiled. "This is the revolution, right? We'll keep fighting the good fight. Even if it takes up our whole lunch break."

* * *

Sophie's last consultation of the day was with Lucy Cross, the sixth-grade social studies teacher. Lucy was in her fourth year teaching and had grown up in the same town as Coastal, but beyond those basic facts, Sophie didn't know her very well. When she knocked on Lucy's door, Lucy was grading papers at her desk and looked surprised to see Sophie.

"Oh, hi!" Lucy smiled and gave Sophie an apologetic look. "I'm sorry, I completely forgot we were meeting today."

"Is now still a good time?" asked Sophie.

"Sure, I have a few minutes." Lucy pulled a chair for Sophie up to her desk. "To be honest, though, I'm not sure how much we have to meet about, and I don't want to waste your time."

"Don't worry, you're on my schedule," Sophie tried to reassure her. "How did the south-up map lesson[2] go today?"

"Oh, well, I didn't do that lesson. It's an interesting idea, but I need to teach my students the *right* way to read a global map. That's hard enough, and the south-up map will just be confusing to them. I decided to focus on teaching the core concept really well this week. In past years this has built a great foundation for the rest of our year."

Sophie was taken aback. Lucy was still smiling, with no indication that she meant to be combative, but Sophie felt her own hackles raise. "But that's exactly the rationale behind this lesson—that students deserve a different perspective on geography than what has traditionally been considered 'the correct way' to view a globe. Particularly with many of our students' families coming from countries that were dominated by Northern groups—many teachers have found that this kind of lesson engages them in the geography curriculum in a new way."

"Yeah, but shouldn't that wait until after the state test? I'm sure *you* get it," Lucy leaned in toward Sophie. "If I have to choose between teaching a lesson that's rigorous, and teaching one that's culturally responsive, I'm going to choose rigorous, right? Don't get me wrong, I think it's good for some teachers to roll out this new curriculum, but not for me."

"Um," Sophie began, but Lucy barreled on.

"Also, talking about race when I'm trying to teach geography is confusing. It distracts the students from the core curriculum; they get so riled up! I'm just sorry you have to be put in the middle of it," Lucy said sympathetically. "It's got to be tough having to be the advocate for this."

"It's not tough for me. I really believe in this curriculum—for all kids." *She thinks I agree with her because I look like her,* Sophie realized. But Lucy was already backtracking.

"No, of course—I believe in all the kids, too. That's why I want to stay focused on the important stuff. Besides, we have our international potluck coming up, and that's always a great way to celebrate Coastal's diversity," Lucy grinned as she ushered Sophie out of her classroom.

* * *

Sophie walked toward the teachers' lounge, feeling disoriented. She knew introducing the curriculum would be bumpy, but she hadn't anticipated that three months in, she would still be encountering so many different challenges. How on earth, she wondered, was she going to manage the rollout to three more schools?

Raised voices down the hallway caught her attention, and she watched Ethan Frankel's classroom door spring open. Two girls rushed out, one White, one Black. Ethan followed, looking bewildered.

"Make her take it back!"

"You know it's true!"

"My dad's a cop! Take it back!"

Ethan had to block the two from getting physical. Sophie quickened her pace. Principal Barry appeared at the other end of the hall first. "Ladies? Mr. Frankel? Why are we yelling in the hallway?"

"She's saying my dad is racist! My dad isn't racist! You're racist for saying that!"

"You can't call me racist! What's wrong with you?"

"Ladies! Mr. Frankel, go back in the classroom and write me a report, I'll take care of this. Ladies, come with me. Nia," he turned to the Black student. "This is the second time you'll be in my office this week! That's grounds for suspension. Let's go."

* * *

Sophie's heart was still pounding as she entered the teacher's lounge. With relief, she saw her close friend and former Downtown colleague, David Garcia, standing at the microwave. "Soph! How's the day going?" he greeted her with a fist bump.

"I just spent fifteen minutes helping Ethan Frankel reset his class." Voice shaking, Sophie explained what happened in the hallway.

David shook his head. "Unfortunately, I'm not surprised. Brandon's dad told me last week he was *not* happy that his son was being taught about racism by 'some White kid who can go home with his privilege when school gets out,' while Brandon's got to think about this every day of his life."[3]

"Do you think the curriculum could be hurting kids, students of color especially, more than it helps?" Sophie thought of Principal Barry threatening Nia with suspension and shuddered. "The power dynamics here are so difficult. I've also got teachers who think teaching race is a distraction, and parents who worry that the curriculum is teaching their White children to hate themselves for being White. Central office could hear this and pull their support—not only here, but for the whole network. You know how they value curricular coherence across their schools. Downtown would be devastated."

David looked pensive. "You're doing a good job, Soph, but I wonder—I can't believe I'm saying this, but I wonder if Arc's ready for a curriculum that actually takes a hard look at race. I'm one of what, four adults of color who work at Coastal full-time? And I spend my days telling students to walk silently in the halls and nod no matter what the teacher is saying. Not exactly liberation pedagogy. If Arc isn't even challenging the status quo in how we hire teachers or set school culture, why should we think that teachers can do it in their classrooms with students?

"I don't know, though," David abruptly reversed himself, "as King said, we can't keep waiting. 'Freedom is never voluntarily given by the oppressor'—and this curriculum isn't going to start teaching itself."

As David hurried out to meet his next class, Sophie felt her stomach clench. Implementing this curriculum was a moral imperative, she was sure. In fact, the challenges of carrying it out at Arc Coastal seemed to make it even more necessary. But thinking of Ethan's capacity and Lucy's perspective, the parental pushback, and the hallway fight, it was impossible to ignore the real harm that students could experience if the curriculum were taught badly. Could she continue to defend the curriculum implementation at Coastal—let alone the rollout across the network—given what she had seen?

Creating Culturally Responsive Curricula for All

Janine de Novais

Sophie believes that implementing the new culturally responsive curriculum at Coastal is "a moral imperative." Nonetheless, she cannot ignore the very concrete challenges she sees each time she visits the school: young teachers with the best intentions but lacking the pedagogical acumen and depth of understanding to handle the new curriculum (Ethan); experienced teachers who believe the curriculum is not rigorous and thus, not a priority (Lucy); and importantly, students and families whose identities and worldviews are challenged by the new curriculum. As we accompany Sophie on her visit to Coastal, we resonate with her question: Could she—should she—continue to defend the curriculum implementation at Coastal, and its rollout across the Arc network, "given what she had seen?"

The answer to the question is a resounding "Yes." The reason, I argue, is that an unstated assumption shapes the way most of us—educators, scholars, policymakers, students, and parents—think about culturally responsive curricula like that which Sophie is trying to build across the Arc network. We think that such curricula are specifically and only for students of color. The truth, however, is that any curriculum that is rigorous, accurate, deep, and relevant to the lives of students must be culturally responsive. If we are worthy to call ourselves educators in our particular time and place in the world, implementing culturally responsive curricula is an educational imperative.

THE ROLE OF EDUCATION IN MULTICULTURAL DEMOCRACY

As frustrating Sophie may find Lucy's comments, they are representative of the thinking of many people. Given that the initial push for a culturally responsive curriculum was (rightly) motivated by the notion that a majority of students in public education were not taught content that related to their experiences, and that these students were, generally, students of color and students from lower socioeconomic strata, many have come to understand these curricula as "what kids of color and/or low-income students need." Culturally responsive curricula, including but not limited to Ethnic Studies, are seen as innovations without which "certain" students cannot succeed academically. Consistent with this, the most common response to Lucy's point of view is usually twofold: (a) To argue, as Sophie does, that culturally relevant curricula are good for *all* kids without specifying why; (b) To argue that culturally responsive curricula are rigorous. While points (a) and (b) are not wrong, they are not our best arguments.

The fact is that, most standard curricula, in being monocultural at best, or ethnocentric and racist at worse, are, by definition, *not rigorous*. To draw on an example from the case, if an educated person presents the view that Columbus was a hero who "discovered America" and brought civilization to its indigenous peoples, that person will be criticized for historical inaccuracy and misinformation.[4] And yet, we behave as if teaching the full historical record is something we should only do to be "inclusive" of some students.

Thus, teaching culturally relevant curricula is something we *must* do to be accurate, to be rigorous, and to be effective as educators. To say that not teaching culturally relevant curricula to White students will not harm them as much as it will harm students of color, is to pretend to not watch the news every day. Every day we witness what it means to live in a multicultural, unequal democracy where people are not educated to share a common understanding of that society. And of that multiculturalism. And of that inequality.

Our society—indeed our world—brims with cultural heterogeneity and difference. Students have to grapple with this as a fact, not as an innovation or an accommodation that a dominant cultural group offers another. If critical multicultural curricula (a.k.a. culturally relevant curricula) are by definition the only truly rigorous ones, then it becomes an educational imperative to deliver said curricula to *every* student as soon as possible.

This is, of course, easier said than done. It is no secret that most schools operate under less than ideal circumstances all the time. Class sizes are too large, too many teachers are inexperienced, too few teachers are teachers of color, STEM departments are understaffed, guidance counselors are overworked, and on and on. Nonetheless, it is not customary to not teach the standard curriculum because we do not find the most ideal conditions in which to do it. No school says, "You know what, let's not teach fractions to these third graders because the classes are too large, and the teacher is a novice who is struggling to teach fractions." Schools bend over backward, as they should, to prepare to meet mandatory requirements for core content. It is only by missing the point that *culturally relevant curricula are core content* that we make excuses for their absence from most classrooms.

We should ask ourselves, when we stall on reforming long-outdated curricula across schools, whose dignity and sense of belonging are we willing to compromise further, put on hold longer, fail to honor yet again? And we should ask ourselves why we are comfortable with this wait. After all, Dr. Martin Luther King Jr. famously warned us in his "Letter from a Birmingham Jail" that "Wait has almost always meant Never," and that "justice too long delayed is justice denied."

PRACTICAL PROBLEMS

This is not to deny the challenges Sophie faces in implementing a culturally responsive curriculum at Coastal. But we can think of these challenges as comprising the cultural "soil" of Coastal. This soil needs to be prepared and transformed, so that the "seeds" of this new culturally responsive curriculum can grow.[5]

Consider the challenge Ethan embodies. Less experienced teachers like Ethan have to be engaged in academically rigorous professional development in order to develop not just their content knowledge but also their pedagogical skills around teaching the new curriculum. This is not something that can be accomplished by a single training from Sophie and periodic class observations, but rather something that requires a community of practice for teachers and a long-term commitment to said professional community of practice.

Arc needs to provide teachers like Lucy both the directive and the tools for integrating culturally responsive curricula into their rigorous, standards- and test-driven teaching. Telling Lucy that culturally relevant curricula are rigorous will amount to nothing if she is not given tools for aligning said curriculum with what the state requires her to teach. Again, this is a larger effort, over a longer period of time, than what Sophie alone can accomplish.

Teachers have to spend the necessary time building a sense of community and instilling norms of academic discourse and debate within their classrooms. Once such a climate is in place, students can engage each other and this new complex and challenging content. Once students and teachers feel empowered in their engagement with the new curriculum, they will become better able to interface with reluctant families; they will become the new curriculum's best ambassadors.

Finally, Arc should offer families opportunities, through family engagement events grounded in the new curriculum, to experience the possibilities of learning about issues of racism and inequality in academically rigorous ways. Families should also be encouraged to visit classes, participate in discussions, and become part of the change happening at Coastal.

The practical challenges Sophie encounters at Coastal echo the broader problems our society faces right now. These problems are: the widespread lack of knowledge that most of us have about the true history of this country; the misunderstanding that "telling the truth" about said history is about appeasing people of color, when really it is about being accurate; and how we do not work on creating strong communities where we can teach and learn about said history in challenging but productive ways. We are used to not telling the truth about the difficult aspects of our history, we are used to raising an argument about "rigor" to distract from what's missing from curricula, and we are used to not talking or learning about any of this in culturally mixed company.

As both deeply rooted and widespread challenges in the cultural soil of Coastal, these issues must be tackled. But they cannot be tackled *before* the curriculum is introduced *because it is only when the curriculum is introduced that these issues surface.* In other words, the challenges Sophie sees are there to remind her and her colleagues at Coastal that they are not simply introducing a new curriculum; they are transforming who they are. In this way, they represent all of us in this country at this time; they represent our problems, sure, but they also represent our possibilities.

Janine de Novais is an assistant professor in the College of Education and Human Development at the University of Delaware. She works at the intersection of race, culture, education, and democracy.

Weighing Harm

White Fragility and Antiracist Resistance in Australian Education

Margot Ford, Daniella J. Forster,
and Kevin Lowe

While we all agree with the moral imperative to teach social justice issues, especially those tackling issues of race and racism, Sophie raises a very real dilemma. Issues of race and racism are often greeted with visceral responses that can indeed cause harm unless the issues are understood in all their complexities and contradictions. In this respect, Sophie's challenges feel very familiar to us in Australia. Although Australia and the US have different histories, each nation grapples with an overlay of multifaceted issues surrounding discourses of race and racism in education and more broadly in public spaces.

Australia generally lauds itself as a successful multicultural society, as over 90 percent of the population has a migrant past. In contrast to our national narrative of multicultural success, however, Australian history features repeated examples of systemic racism perpetrated particularly against Aboriginal and Torres Strait Island Indigenous communities. Indigenous Peoples currently make up 3 percent of the overall Australian population, reaching as high as 35 percent in some remote areas.

As in the United States, Australian educators' attempts to teach the truth about the past can be met with resistance from parents, and even active backlash from the public in the press and on social media. In light of these examples of *White fragility*—that is, a state in which even a minimum amount of racial stress becomes intolerable, triggering a range of defensive moves—we believe that changes are necessary not only in schools like Arc Coastal, but also in the broader public.[6] We begin by examining Ethan's practices and how Sophie can help mitigate the harm he causes while strengthening his and others' reflectiveness about race and racism. We then offer an example from Sydney of the harm that can result when social justice work in schools spills over into the public sphere. We conclude with recommendations for how educators and policymakers can promote antiracist education even as White fragility threatens to derail such initiatives and perpetrate harm on others.

CHALLENGING THE STATUS QUO: SOME STRATEGIES

Of all the teachers Sophie encounters at Arc Coastal Middle School, Ethan may be the most challenging (although we note we could write a whole commentary about Lucy, as well!). Ethan seems well-intentioned, even enthusiastic about teaching about race and racism. Yet his naivete and lack of self-awareness could cause real damage. When White people first encounter the truth about past injustices and recognize the present consequences of that injustice, they may (over)compensate with a form of White guilt. This may then trigger White fragility, as they think they are (now) doing the right thing and as a result become highly sensitive to criticisms. We see these risk factors in Ethan: poor pedagogical choices due to White guilt combined with overconfidence that he is now doing the right thing.

Sophie needs to walk a fine line with Ethan as she keeps him committed to the program, whilst also critiquing his approach. He needs intense intervention so he realizes that in order to effectively teach about racism he needs to continually question his own practices. Since Sophie's time is limited, she could pair him up with Tiana. Tiana knows the curriculum well, and they could act as critical friends in the absence of Sophie. In Australia, there are also online resources available, endorsed by education authorities, that she could introduce him to.[7]

At the same time, neither Tiana nor Sophie may yet want to introduce Ethan to the concept of White privilege—or at least, not encourage him to use the concept in his class. Teaching about race requires sensitivity, empathy, and understanding for all students who may feel threatened. White students and families who are struggling economically may be alienated by the idea that they enjoy White *privilege*. Perhaps examining social justice from the point of view of socioeconomic status first, where shared experience of economic struggle becomes something all the students can relate to, will help engender empathy for antiracist work later in the school year.

Students at Arc Coastal may also benefit from the creation of safe spaces for White and Black students to talk out their feelings. This might have prevented harm to Nia, who was apprehended by the principal during an argument that spilled into the hallway. Such spaces might also help Principal Barry understand that it is reasonable for students to have strong reactions to challenging material about race and racism.

"LITTLE CHILDREN SHOULD NOT BE EXPOSED TO THAT"

At the moment, Sophie is concerned about negative reactions from teachers, administrators, and parents. There is risk, though, that these tensions could become a public concern, as occurred here in 2017.

In Australia, teachers are now required to embed Indigenous issues throughout the curriculum in at least a limited way.[8] One of the topics students may study is the "Stolen Generations," or the history of government-mandated forced separation of Indigenous children from their parents.[9] (This occurred in the United States, as well.) In particular, the Stage Three (upper primary) history curriculum descriptor requires students to "investigate the significance of ONE of the following in the *struggle for the rights* and *freedoms* of Aboriginal and Torres Strait Islander peoples," with the Stolen Generations as one option.[10]

As a result, in August 2017, upper primary students (ten- and eleven-year-olds) in an affluent, White-dominant North Sydney school culminated their historical inquiry by performing a play about the Stolen Generations. Some children represented nuns directing (or as some commentators stated, abusing) Indigenous children taken by forcible removal from their families between 1910 and the 1970s. In another scene, children held placards saying "Sorry" to represent the famous Sydney Bridge walk protest of May 28, 2000, which called for a formal apology to the Stolen Generations. As the students had learned, Prime Minister Kevin Rudd finally delivered the apology in 2007.

A few parents in the audience were startled by the content; one parent in particular took offense and went on local radio to voice his displeasure. Local and national newspapers took up the story, releasing a cacophony of outrage on social media and showing the full force of White fragility. People claimed that the play was "bloody disgraceful" and "an appalling betrayal."[11] They charged that children were "being used as political pawns" and that the "cultural left" were "indoctrinating students with Marxist-inspired, politically correct ideologies."[12] Little was heard of other parents who were quite supportive of the play.[13]

The government's response was the most concerning. New South Wales education minister Rob Stokes said there was "a powerful lesson here in how to present sensitive historical issues in schools in ways that are not seen as biased or overtly political."[14] Rather than strongly support the teacher and the school for teaching the required curriculum, the department launched an investigation. The school principal and teachers were thus prevented from speaking publicly. While others tried to present a counternarrative arguing that "discomfort should not be a reason not to teach our children about the facts of important events in Australia's history," this was largely drowned out, despite strong evidence that claims of multiple parent complaints was hyperbolic media confection.[15]

We share this narrative to demonstrate that White fragility can result in harm for a range of stakeholders, including teachers. All those involved in teaching antiracist curricula need to have protective strategies, including support from colleagues, parents, and those in leadership positions. The saturation of anger, disgust, ambivalence, and fear exhibited in mainstream media exposes the reach of taken-for-granted White vulnerability to perceived threats to White privilege in Australian society.

STRATEGIES TO ACHIEVE LONG-TERM EDUCATIONAL TRANSFORMATION

Despite the risks, we reiterate that it is so important to continue this work. Recognizing the potential points of harm, and implementing strategies to minimize these for all students, is critical in the planning stage. Supporting teachers like Ethan and Tiana and preparing them for their own personal journeys is also crucial. Sophie cannot do this alone. School and district (or charter network) leaders must also take responsibility for supporting the important work being done, recognizing that there are risks involved, and acknowledging that social change takes time. They should also take proportionality of harm into account, as the discomfit that some White students and parents may experience is significantly less than the harms of systemic racism experienced by students of color every day. We urge Sophie and her team to continue to rock the boat, but be mindful of bringing all students and their families with them on the journey.

Dr. Margot Ford, a senior lecturer in the School of Education at the University of Newcastle, Australia, has worked in a range of social justice aspects in education for several decades. She specializes in Indigenous education and race and racism, and examines ways to support students from low socioeconomic backgrounds both in school and higher education.

Dr. Daniella J. Forster is a senior lecturer who teaches educational philosophy and ethics at the School of Education, University of Newcastle, Australia. She writes about moral complexity in teacher education, codes of conduct, educational ethics, and other topics including collective academic publishing and community coproduction.

Dr. Kevin Lowe, a Gubbi Gubbi man from South East Queensland, is a senior research fellow at Macquarie University, Australia. He has been a teacher in schools, senior curriculum manager for Technical and Further Education (post-secondary education), and educational researcher working in Aboriginal education, Indigenous policy analysis, curriculum, and community and school engagement.

Slow Down to Make Real Change

Teresa Rodriguez

I identify as a cisgendered, biracial (Peruvian/Irish) woman who was born into a mixed first/second generation immigrant, Catholic, middle-class family with access to educational opportunity. I am also a former middle and high school history teacher who has had the privilege to work in both suburban and urban public districts, urban public charter schools, and a K–12 private school. As a result, the work of teaching "diverse experiences and perspectives in global and American history while challenging racial and cultural intolerance, injustice, and oppression" that Arc Charter Schools is taking on is close to my heart. In fact, I am frequently in the seat that Sophie Biel finds herself in. She is right to think that "she might have her work cut out for her" when pursuing a culturally responsive curriculum. Having tried myself for many years to teach an inclusive history of the United States, I can attest that there are fewer models than there should be.

With the benefit of Monday-morning quarterbacking, I would humbly suggest that Sophie and her team—like all idealists—seem to have underestimated the work that is required for this effort to be adopted successfully. In order to bring this important work to fruition, Sophie needs to take two crucial steps. First, she needs to get buy-in from the entire Arc Coastal community, including families. Second, she needs to slow down. It's always tempting to try to enact systemic reform by issuing guidelines, curricular scripts, and so forth. But this curriculum will succeed only if the individuals who will actually be teaching this curriculum long-term are given time and support for personal transformation, not just systemic transformation. If Sophie can accept that the necessary timeframe for her curricular reforms is long (just like the arc of the moral universe), she will be able to build on her admirable preliminary work and successfully address the new challenges she is facing at Arc Charter Network.

TO GO FAR, GO TOGETHER

Sometimes as educators we try to innovate under the radar. We try not to call attention to ourselves and our work because we are unsure of our plans and want to see what parts of an idea will work and what parts should be abandoned outside of a spotlight or public eye. We are trying to experiment responsibly. In making a major curricular change such as this, however, I suggest that Sophie and her team should involve families from the get-go. Consider the famous proverb, "If you want to go fast, go alone. If you want to go far, go together." Arc Coastal needs to work together with parents to bring about far-reaching curricular reform by sharing sample lessons with families and asking for their feedback. This will invite scrutiny, but it will also allow parents to engage more with their children about the questions raised in the curriculum. It will also defuse parents' potential suspicion or even anger if they lack detailed information about the course.

ENABLING SOCIAL TRANSFORMATION THROUGH PERSONAL TRANSFORMATION

In a column entitled "Good Leaders Make Good Schools," *New York Times* columnist David Brooks argues, "We went through a period where we believed you could change institutions without first changing the character of the people in them. But we were wrong. *Social transformation follows personal transformation*"[16] (italics emphasis mine.) The teacher profiled at the beginning of this case, Ethan Frankel, demonstrates the importance of Brooks' insight. Despite his enthusiasm for teaching to transform a racist and White supremacist society, Ethan is not ready to do so because he has not transformed himself. He is still at what Darnisa Amante labels "Stage 0" of this work.[17] Until he develops a sufficient understanding of his own identities as a White man and an authority figure in a diverse classroom, he will be unable to help his students develop their own identities through the curriculum and ask questions in a healthy and responsible way. When Ethan fails to set up discussion norms and boundaries, for example, he demonstrates that he has not had many opportunities to engage in discussions about equity and oppression in his intellectual life. If he had, he would understand the power that norms can have to ground a group discussion in respect and honesty. Relatedly, the ultimate goal of this history curriculum is to understand the complexity of the world we live in, but Ethan is not comfortable with that himself. He thus needs more time to practice and watch others before he works with students independently.

One way that he could grow in this area while also contributing to the curriculum development and testing at Arc Coastal is if he observed Sophie teaching his class every week or two. She could model for him how to set positive classroom discussion norms, handle difficult questions as a White, queer woman, and negotiate authority with students in a mutually supportive way. At the same time, since he would know his students better than she, he could offer suggestions for how to work with specific students. Sophie would also likely benefit from piloting the curriculum at Arc Coastal, since adjustments will undoubtedly need to be made. Downtown and Coastal have such different student demographics that the latter may need different background information or instructional approaches than the former.

Piloting the curriculum may also increase Sophie's confidence in ultimately handing it off to others. As a teacher who knows the power of writing her own curriculum and the taxing effort it requires, I get nervous when I hear teachers are being "given a script." Yes, curricular guides, scope and sequence documents, generative questions, and other resources are always helpful, but *scripts* sound like an effort from central administrators to lessen the teacher's own intellectual role and contribution. As the case itself demonstrates, curricular scripts will not help teachers like Ethan (or Lucy) unless and until they undergo personal transformation—and once they do so, they will both want to engage as intellectuals in coconstructing the curriculum.

MOVING FORWARD

Piloting the curriculum in Ethan's classroom will take time—an obviously scarce resource in Sophie's world. But slowing down the rollout, and introducing it gradually with deepened professional development opportunities, rather than all at once with only spot visits to classrooms, will actually strengthen its implementation in the long run. As we all know, when it comes to encouraging deep thinking and learning, less is more. Of course, there will never be a perfect time, nor enough days of professional development for teachers like Ethan to feel prepared. But the one full day of training plus twice-monthly observations that Sophie offered seem inadequate to support the whole of this new curriculum. Hence, she might want to introduce pieces of this curriculum in a slow and deliberate way, even if it feels inadequate at the beginning.

I realize my reflection has mainly been critical of Sophie's efforts, but I appreciate her initiative. Arc's central office must understand that just as science courses are updated as scientific knowledge changes, history classes must also be revised regularly in light of the most recent scholarship. Keeping an outdated curriculum which does not include sources of information from all parts of our American history is immoral, undemocratic, and no longer an option. It has led people to embrace misinformation that damages our democracy. As Paolo Freire puts it, "washing one's hands of the conflict between the powerful and the powerless means to side with the powerful, not to be neutral."[18]

When Sophie presents a curriculum challenging racial and cultural intolerance, injustice, and oppression, she knows that some people will feel uncomfortable. As the saying goes, "Racism is so American that when we protest racism the average American thinks we are protesting America." By summoning up new energy to continue to offer opportunities for teachers and parents alike to learn, question, and share, Sophie can help ensure the long-term success of this curriculum. This will allow what is currently *her* curriculum to become the *school's* and *community's* curriculum—one that will ultimately help our democracy itself bend toward justice.

Teresa Rodriguez is a former high school history teacher, former middle school counselor assisting students and families with high school selection, and current school administrator who seeks to enable family, school, and community connections. Throughout her twenty-two years as an educator, Teresa has tried to support students, teachers, and families by offering resources, encouraging dynamic two-way communication among families and schools, and continuing in the work despite her many missteps.

Considerations for the Ethical Implementation of Culturally Responsive Curricula

Winston C. Thompson

As is true of many of the vignettes in this collection, an entire book could be written about the ethical issues present within this fascinating, frustrating, and (for many) rather familiar case. Limiting myself to brief comments, I would like to focus on three areas of the case that might serve as openings for further exploration of similar/related circumstances.

In what follows, I would like to respect Sophie's sense of certainty regarding the "moral imperative" that the culturally responsive curriculum should be pursued. Certainly, other persons in her position might conclude that their previous and current experiences give them sufficient support for another conclusion, but Sophie's commitment seems firm. Sophie does not seem to be asking *if* she should be implementing this curriculum but, instead, wondering *how* to do so well, given the context of Arc Coastal and all that has transpired. That in mind, I would like to suggest a few matters that may influence her next steps: the types of discomfort in the case, the tough work of teaching teachers, and the unequal effects on students.

TYPES OF DISCOMFORT

In Sophie's final reflections on what she's witnessed at Arc Coastal, she expresses concern regarding the impact of the curricular implementation on those involved. This suggests a worthy moral precept and might serve as some guidance in how she ought to proceed.

Looking for evidence of potentially harmful impact, it would seem that Sophie can, at least, readily point to various experiences of discomfort at Arc Coastal. Though this might be a promising start to Sophie's attempts at ethical implementation of the curriculum, I don't think that we have good reasons to believe that the presence of discomfort is necessarily evidence that any of the involved parties have been morally wronged. Nonetheless, categorizing the types of discomfort present in relation to the new curriculum may grant Sophie clarity in determining what to prioritize in her responses. Without detailing the specifics of Arc Coastal, here are a few overlapping ways that Sophie might begin to consider discomfort as she proceeds.

Firstly, some morally defensible and beneficial projects might entail reasonably intense and/or necessary discomfort (or even pain!) in their pursuit.[19] A curricular shift toward greater engagement with race and culture may well be such a project. Additionally, attempts to empower members of groups long disadvantaged can often strike some members of advantaged groups as an uncomfortable (or even painful!) erosion of the "natural" order; it upsets for them reliable "facts" of the world.[20] Sophie might consider these feelings to be instances of justifiable discomfort in the service of beneficial outcomes, which likely constitute the very core of her commitment to the curriculum.

Of course, some discomfort might not fit this description. Some discomfort (or pain!) carries little to no redeeming consequence, or is far too intense to be justifiably visited upon another person. For example, were the curriculum actually teaching students to literally hate themselves on the basis of their racial or ethnic identities, it would run afoul of this moral boundary. Sophie ought to avoid contributing to instances of unjustifiable discomfort and, as such, may wish to prioritize identifying and resolving those discomforts that truly belong to this category.

Secondly, Sophie might consider whether a discomfort is narrowly pedagogical or more broadly social. By this I wish to suggest that, on one hand, some of the discomfort at Arc Coastal might be caused by poor pedagogical practices. Perhaps some teachers' novice attempts to realize the goals of the curriculum have resulted in the discomfort that some students, parents, and teachers have thus far experienced. Sophie might attend to a pedagogical shortcoming by more directly attempting to shift pedagogical practices.

On the other hand, the relative racial/cultural homogeneity/hegemony of the school (and the wider community, the country, and its history, etc.) might have created a context in which even the best (or otherwise sufficiently good) pedagogy about race and/or culture results in feelings of discomfort among those involved. In this situation, we might view the social circumstances as the ultimate source for discomfort, such that even the best teacher, outfitted with an ideal curriculum, will not be able to avoid this outcome of teaching the material—think again, for example, about Tiana's conversation with Sophie regarding teaching the Columbus lesson. Sophie might regard this broad context as beyond her immediate power, and while it may be intimately related to her sense of the urgency of the new curriculum, its full resolution might not be a prerequisite for the present implementation efforts.

Finally, adding further complexity to the potential categories of discomfort, Sophie might wish to compare the different categories of discomfort experienced by students, parents, teachers, and others related to the school. Generally speaking, in prioritizing her responses, how might she rank the various combinations of types of discomfort and the persons experiencing them? Even if the answers to these questions do not come easily, they may be invaluable in providing a structure within which to consider how best to address the particular needs of implementation at Arc Coastal.

TEACHING TEACHERS

Of the many elements of this case ripe for ethical consideration, Sophie would do well to start by engaging the teachers' relationship to the new curriculum.

Teacher response to the new curriculum seems to span a rather wide spectrum. Some teachers (e.g., Ethan Frankel) are excited about the aims of cultural and racial responsiveness, yet seem ill-equipped to achieve through the curriculum what Sophie envisions. Other teachers (e.g., Lucy Cross) view the new curriculum as incorrect, nonrigorous, and/or unimportant, such that they are unwilling to teach it. In both cases, it might be helpful for Sophie to think about how these teachers are taught about the curriculum they are expected to teach. Casting the teachers as students themselves may be helpful to Sophie's goals.

Taking teachers seriously as competent learners who are attempting to make sense of race, culture, social power, and this new curriculum, requires more than simply placing the new lessons in their mailboxes. It likely requires some real opportunities to discuss, debate, disagree, and more. This in mind, carefully structuring this opportunity to study the curriculum's aims, and the decision to implement it at Arc Coastal, might allow teachers to challenge their own ideas/values and those of their colleagues. Sophie has had some success teaching this curriculum to students and working to challenge colleagues at Arc Downtown. As such, it is possible that renewed attention to reflectively teaching the teachers at Arc Coastal, perhaps drawing upon the resources of experienced coteachers (e.g., David Garcia and, potentially, Tiana Shepard) and effectively framing some of the aforementioned discomfort with the curriculum as a pedagogical opportunity, might bear good fruit.

Certainly, as is true for many lessons well-taught to mature students, the real possibility exists that some teachers will arrive at conclusions that differ from Sophie's own. This shouldn't be feared; otherwise, advocates of the new culturally responsive curriculum run the risk of holding the reductive view that all who disagree with them are merely insufficiently educated on the relevant topics. Rather, in respect for teachers' professional expertise and autonomy, and the degree to which the proper treatment of these subjects likely requires ongoing work, Sophie might count it a victory that teacher disagreement stemming from these educational exchanges focuses on the *actual* curriculum rather than uninformed, imagined caricatures of it. Incremental though it may seem, this is real progress on a serious set of concerns.

UNEQUAL EFFECTS

Acknowledging the insights of the previous sections, Sophie would do well to observe that persons within the school are not equally vulnerable or advantaged relative to the new curriculum, its subject(s), and its echoing effects. Indeed, this might be the most important consideration of all.

While it would be a simple matter to assert that the new curriculum should establish shared norms of communication in order to avoid hallway skirmishes of the sort Sophie observed on her way to the teachers' lounge, this does not mean that an ethical implementation will necessarily avoid heated exchanges. It is entirely possible that the ideal implementation of the curriculum may lead students to recognize racism and/or identify racists. Students may even come to view themselves as having a legitimate moral obligation to speak out against racism and racists. That could easily lead to a heated exchange (even if expressed within the established communication guidelines) if another student's family member or their action is directly or indirectly highlighted. Perhaps, even under ideal circumstances, these types of difficult moments are entailed within a responsible embrace of the new curriculum.

Currently, as a literal bystander, Sophie doesn't have sufficient information to determine whether Nia made a responsible and informed claim. It is entirely possible that she is wholly in the wrong and fully culpable for the verbal dustup. That said, Sophie may have sufficient evidence to begin considering the ways in which Nia might be more vulnerable than some of her classmates. As a Black girl at Arc Coastal, it is entirely possible that her authentic engagement with the curriculum might be read as aggressive and/or confrontational when articulated through her raced/gendered body in ways dissimilar to her peers. Sophie would do well to consider how that fact, and its consequences, might steer her efforts in the difficult work ahead.

Winston C. Thompson is assistant professor of philosophy of education at The Ohio State University. Thompson's scholarship explores ethical/political dimensions of educational policy and practice in pluralistic, democratic societies.

(How) Can Curriculum Leverage the Disruption of Oppression?

Deborah Loewenberg Ball and Darrius Robinson

In this case we are introduced to Sophie Biel, a teacher who is now an "instructional support specialist" helping other teachers implement a new culturally responsive social studies curriculum in her charter network. Following the successful implementation of the curriculum at Arc Downtown, Sophie begins to have serious questions about implementing the curriculum at another school in the network, Arc Coastal. One morning, two months into her work at Coastal, she visits three teachers. Ethan, enthusiastic about the new curriculum, is a novice who is newly encountering ideas about racism and how his own identity carries privilege and power of which he has been unconscious. Inexperienced, he lacks the skills needed to effectively implement the curriculum. Tiana is experiencing parental pushback about whether she is teaching anti-Whiteness. Lucy is unengaged with the curriculum, choosing to focus instead on "rigor" and preparing her students for testing. After the meetings, Sophie witnesses a racially charged altercation between two of Ethan's students that is poorly managed by the principal. Disturbed, Sophie talks with David Garcia, a colleague with whom she used to work at Downtown. David notes the structural barriers at Coastal, from control-oriented behavioral rules, to lack of diversity among the teachers, to patterns of bias in disciplinary actions. For Sophie, these events constitute evidence that the new curriculum might be causing more harm than good for students. Sophie begins to wonder whether it is wise to continue to support the rollout of the curriculum at Coastal. We wonder, too.

MORE THAN CURRICULAR CHANGE

The challenges at Coastal mirror the endemic problems that threaten the implementation of any new curriculum. Inadequate professional development, resistance from teachers and parents, and misaligned administrative support have derailed many new curricula. Consider, for example, the adoption of a new mathematics curriculum. Districts routinely adopt new math curricula with considerable effort in selection and rollout, yet face disappointing results when modest professional development leaves teachers without adequate support to make the changes entailed and to deal with parents' concerns. Inside the classroom, too, students sometimes end up confused when teachers are underprepared for the change in instructional approach or focus. Several years later, the process begins anew with a new curriculum selection process.

Still, this revolving door of curriculum change rarely requires a fundamental shift in the content delivered or calls for the school to adapt at a structural level. The fact that schooling has remained relatively unchanged as curricular shifts have come and gone is evidence of this point. Curricular shifts are often aimed at increasing opportunities to learn within the existing structures. Whether it is a reordering of the topics covered or a shift in instructional foci, the underlying goal is to use the available resources within a classroom more effectively to support student learning.

The social studies curriculum effort at Coastal involves more. It asks teachers to engage students in critical perspectives on the historical racial narratives that dominate the usual social studies curriculum, and that reflect normalized White, Christian, binary gender, and middle-class experience. Teaching this new curriculum requires teachers to consider their own intersectional identities and those of their students; to attentively establish norms for talking about race, gender, and class; and to communicate sensitively with parents about the goals and importance of the curriculum. Understanding the many ways that their students will bring their experiences into the class's work, and anticipating how that work will affect relationships and power dynamics in their classroom, places additional demands on the teachers. It requires in particular that they consider explicitly the broader historical, political, and societal environments in which such an antiracist curriculum sits. They will need to confront the fact that implementing the curriculum in this context—in which school norms, policies, and rules reproduce patterns that marginalize students of color and members of other oppressed groups—creates untenable tension between life in the school and the content and discourse of the curriculum.

DO IT RIGHT OR DO IT RIGHT NOW?

There is urgency at the core of Sophie's dilemma. She is confronting two choices—to proceed with implementation or to halt it. On one hand, it is urgent that Coastal students have the opportunity to engage with a culturally responsive social studies curriculum that constructively contends with the racism, injustice, and intolerance that permeate history. Driven by the moral imperative of the change needed, and the proven track record of the curriculum at Downtown, Sophie could decide to accept that it will take for time for the curriculum to take productive root at Coastal and stay the course, meeting with and supporting the teachers as they adapt and learn. This option might seem to reflect determination and commitment to the much-needed but difficult work of disrupting the racism and oppression too often reproduced in schools. Persistence is crucial to that work.

On the other hand, the interactions with Ethan and Lucy are worrisome, and they raise questions about the prospects for improvement without a different plan to guide and support implementation. The racial incident involving the two girls from Ethan's classroom and the pattern of bias revealed in the principal's reaction make visible the dangers inherent in unskilled use of the curriculum. Opening up classrooms in these ways, without care, could reinforce rather than disrupt racism. The alternative, then, might be to concede that Coastal is not ready for this curriculum. The teachers might not be prepared to implement it with care, even with Sophie's help. Sophie, just adjusting to her new role, might not be prepared to support the implementation effectively. The school might not be ready to address the systemic patterns of racism that permeate the school's policies and practices, which are at odds with the goals of the curriculum. Driven by the imperative to protect students, halting the implementation of the curriculum would reduce the potential of harmful effects on students.

Yet halting it does not completely remove the risks. Students will continue to be exposed to the usual harms of an uninspiring, culturally assaultive curriculum and, moreover, will continue soaking in the racism of the broader society in which they are growing up. Although both are grounded in important considerations, neither of these options is ideal. Coordinating these imperatives, rather than pitting them against each other, would require a more nuanced course of action, one that would entail understanding both the power and limits of curriculum as a resource for changing teaching and learning more fundamentally.

Curricular materials can have a considerable impact on shaping the ways in which teachers engage students with academic material and how they understand and respond to their students. For example, they have helped engender fundamental changes in the collective wisdom regarding the enactment of teaching and learning in classrooms. Culturally responsive curricula, in particular, seek to radically alter students' engagement with academic material by tempering its often abstract and esoteric nature with connections to students' cultural knowledge and experiences.

Although advocating for the new social studies curriculum is necessary, advocacy alone is insufficient to produce radical outcomes for students. The promotion of such a curriculum must be accompanied by the support necessary to ensure that it is implemented sensitively and with skill. The question with which Sophie contends should not be whether or not to proceed with the rollout, but rather what more must she and others do to support its successful implementation. What support does Ethan need to continue to develop an understanding of his racial identity and develop his capacity to foster productive conversations? What support does Lucy need to understand that culturally responsive lessons and rigorous ones are not mutually exclusive? How can parents be informed of the school's commitments in ways that preempt common misunderstandings and that help Tiana contend with families' resistance? What does Sophie herself need to learn to develop the sensitive and complex skills involved in her new role as an instructional coach? What structural adjustments need to be made at the school level to contend with the discrepancies between the overall school climate and goals of the curriculum that David mentions? And what adjustments at the network level? These questions highlight the need to address the critical factors that will impact the implementation of the curriculum.

So—is it wise for Sophie continue to support the implementation of the curriculum at Coastal given what she is seeing? This is the wrong question to ask. Given the conversations that Sophie has with David and Tiana, it is clear that the conditions at Downtown had primed it for such a curriculum to be implemented successfully. At Coastal, Sophie has to build the commitments and capacity needed to advance the use of the curriculum there. Therefore, the critical, and more productive, question is whether the network leadership can—and whether they will—commit to providing the resources and support it will take to make effective and sensitive implementation at Coastal possible.

Deborah Loewenberg Ball is the William H. Payne Collegiate Professor of education at the University of Michigan and the director of TeachingWorks. *Ball is a scholar and practitioner of teaching and teacher education, focusing on elementary mathematics as a critical context for developing the power of teaching to disrupt racism, marginalization, and inequity.*

Darrius Robinson is a doctoral student and a Rackham Merit Fellow in the University of Michigan School of Education. An experienced elementary teacher and coach, his research explores how students make sense of instructional reform efforts.

Holding Complicated Truths Together Enhances Rigor

Clint Smith

I was born and raised in a city that was filled with statues of White men on pedestals and Black children playing beneath them—where Black people played trumpets and trombones to drown out the Dixie song that still whistled in the wind. In New Orleans there are over one hundred schools, roads, and buildings named for Confederate soldiers and slave-owners. For decades, Black children have walked into buildings named after people who didn't want them to exist.

What name is there for this violence? What do you call it when the road you walk on is named for those who imagined you under the noose? What do you call it when the roof over your head is named after people who would have wanted the bricks to crush you?

When I was a child I did not have a language for this, and it was not until much later in my life, through the work of teachers and texts, both formal and informal, that I have developed an ability to speak to the way that our country creates myths about who we are and who we have been. As a high school teacher, part of what I attempted to do in my classroom was to ensure that my students were equipped with the tools and the language to accurately name the world around them. I did not want them to experience the sense of paralysis I felt in knowing something was wrong, but not knowing how to name it as such. Tiana articulates a similar idea in the case study when she says, "It's our duty as teachers to disrupt the cycle of power." And Sophie's efforts to create a more culturally responsive social studies curriculum across her school network is born out of the same commitment.

Beyond providing the language for a young person to name the world around them, engaging with the histories we too often fail to name helps us better understand the contemporary landscape of inequality. One cannot begin to understand what happened to Michael Brown in Ferguson, Missouri, without understanding the decades-long history of state-sanctioned housing segregation that created the conditions of the community in which he lived. One cannot begin to understand what happened at the White supremacist rally in Charlottesville, Virginia, without taking into account the ways in which the Sons and Daughters of the Confederacy warped the narrative of the Civil War into an ahistorical caricature of itself. One cannot begin to understand what happened to the nine victims of the Charleston church massacre without making sense of how, two hundred years ago, South Carolina was one of the single most important slave ports in the United States.

And yet, we find ourselves in a moment where our collective understanding of American history is wholly inadequate and purposefully inaccurate. According to the Southern Poverty Law Center, only 8 percent of US high school seniors in 2018 were able to identify slavery as the central cause of the Civil War.[21] Eight percent. The other 92 percent named "states' rights" or "the economy" as its central cause. They're not wholly incorrect to name the economy, but if they don't understand that in 1860 the four million Black slaves were worth more than every American bank, factory, and railroad combined, then they misunderstand how enslaved human beings *were* the economy.

The percentage of students who misunderstand the role of slavery in shaping the trajectory of this country is actually a microcosm for a much larger, more pernicious phenomenon in American life. Which is to say, we are so committed, often unconsciously, to the idea of American exceptionalism, that we often suppress anything that would render our history, and thus our country, unexceptional. In our classrooms across the country, our textbooks soften the contours of America's most violent deeds and most malevolent people to present something more palatable, even if it is, as a result, dishonest. What is also true is that in the process of excavating unexplored truths, we simultaneously must wrestle with what it means to hold virtue and violence at once.

In my primary and secondary education I was taught that Abraham Lincoln was the great emancipator. I was taught that by sheer force of will and by the moral might of his pen he freed the slaves and set America on a trajectory of freedom and equality. I was not taught that in 1858, during the famous Lincoln-Douglas debate, Lincoln stated the following:

> I am not, nor ever have been, in favor of bringing about in any way the social and political equality of the white and black races . . . I am not nor ever have been in favor of making voters or jurors of Negroes, nor of qualifying them to hold office, nor to intermarry with white people; and I will say in addition to this that there is a physical difference between the white and black races which I believe will forever forbid the two races from living together on terms of social and political equality. And inasmuch as

> they cannot so live, while they do remain together there must be a position of superior and inferior, and I as much as any other man am in favor of having the superior position assigned to the white race.[22]

While Lincoln believed slavery was immoral, this passage illuminates how he also believed—at the same time—that Black people were neither equal to nor capable of living alongside their White counterparts. The fact that students are rarely invited to grapple with this dimension of Lincoln's thought reflects the larger phenomenon in the pedagogy of American history in which those who are presented as opposing slavery, abolitionist or otherwise, are then assumed to have also believed in racial equality. But we know clearly that this was not the case. Lincoln seriously considered multiple plans for Blacks to recolonize in Central and South America both before and after emancipation.[23] The truth, as Lincoln makes evident, is that it is fully possible for one to believe that Black people should not be held in forced bondage, and also fully possible that one still believes Black people to be inferior. It's important to be clear about both beliefs, so that we are precise in our account of what the various actors in American history stood for and what they did not.

To be clear, there is much to admire about Lincoln. He possessed a laudable capacity to evolve in his political thinking, he led the nation through its most uncertain time and won a war that preserved the Union, and he did indeed act courageously in signing the Emancipation Proclamation. But that does not mean we should ignore the more unsavory aspects of his legacy. It is essential that we help students learn how to hold these complex truths as one in order to more fully understand the origins of our country, how those ideals wove their way into foundational policies we have always leaned on—and how these origins shape what our country is today.

Any culturally responsive history curriculum must hold these complicated dualities at once. The United States is a country of great opportunity, but we must wrestle with how certain opportunities are contingent on different facets of one's identity. The United States has provided economic mobility for millions of people, but we must wrestle with the history of violence and exploitation that helped to generate its economic foundation. The United States has freed millions around the world from despots and genocide, and we must wrestle with this same country's pervasive history of barbarous imperialism. These are all parts of what make this country what it is. Teachers attempting to bring American history into the classroom should not singularly focus on a false narrative of American exceptionalism, just as they should not singularly focus on its violence without accounting for its virtues.

Toward the end of the case, Lucy states, "If I have to choose between teaching a lesson that's rigorous, and teaching one that's culturally responsive, I'm going to choose rigorous . . ." Lucy's perspective is one shared by many educators—those who believe a pedagogy meant to interrogate dominant modes of thinking about and seeing the world is one that is mutually exclusive from intellectual rigor. This could not be further from the truth. If anything, asking students to complicate their beliefs, and hold together a complex set of facts that don't fit neatly into a specific ideological position, demands a level of cognitive dexterity that is often missing in our social studies curricula. We do not have to choose between a rigorous lesson and a culturally responsive one. Our current political moment, and indeed our nation's history, demands both.

Clint Smith is a PhD candidate at the Harvard Graduate School of Education and author of the poetry collection Counting Descent *(Write Bloody Publishing, 2016). His essays, poems, and scholarly writing have appeared in the* New Yorker, *the* Paris Review, *the* Atlantic, *the* Harvard Educational Review, *and elsewhere.*

CHAPTER 9

Talking Out of Turn

Teacher Speech for Hire

ELLIS REID, MEIRA LEVINSON, AND JACOB FAY

After wearing a Black Lives Matter pin at school on Election Day 2016, long-time substitute teacher David Roberts was permanently banned from subbing for Clovis West High School in California. Clovis has a clear policy that prohibits employees from engaging in "political activities" during the workday, which Roberts was judged to be directly violating. Roberts responded with surprise and perplexity, maintaining, "A pin that reads 'Black Lives Matter' is not a political button. It is a peaceful request to end this violence. It is not a protest. It is not intended to be anti-police and does not imply that black lives matter more than other lives. It simply says they matter, too."[1]

Roberts' interpretation of Black Lives Matter (BLM) as apolitical may seem quirky or even disingenuous, given that BLM's own guiding principles describe BLM as "an ideological and political intervention in a world where Black lives are systematically and intentionally targeted for demise."[2] At the same time, Roberts perhaps understandably viewed his button as a way to support students of color on what everybody recognized would be an emotionally trying day. "That's why I was doing it: to show solidarity to the kids," Roberts explained to the *Fresno Bee*. "They really appreciated it." Roberts also questioned the district's commitment to political neutrality. "Clovis Unified claims you have to be neutral, but they're not neutral. There's a set of beliefs you're expected to have there."[3]

That same week, halfway across the country, fifth-grade teacher Mika Yamamoto of Renaissance Public Academy in Mt. Pleasant, Michigan was fired for informing a group of students "that, on that particular day she felt less safe than ever, because our country had just elected a president who had openly spoken out against women, people of color, the LGBTQ+ community, and other people he felt were different than him."[4] The school principal, Yamamoto alleged in a lawsuit filed after her termination, told her that "the community [was] not ready for [her] voice"—which happened to emanate from the only teacher of color at Renaissance. He also told her that her views would be better suited for a big city like New York or Chicago.[5]

The 2016 election season is of course not the first time that teachers have been fired (or threatened with termination) for expressing political perspectives that were out of sync with the surrounding community. In 2009, Lawrence (Kansas) High School history and government teacher Tim Latham claimed his contract was not renewed because he criticized Barack Obama in class and maintained a school-affiliated website that was "too patriotic," including links to a number of military academies, branches of the armed services, and military history sites.[6] Latham further charged that after a student complained about how he was teaching the 2008 presidential election, his assistant principal told Latham to stop "picking on Obama in class."

In his defense, Latham agreed that he had compared Obama's level of experience unfavorably with John McCain's extensive public service, but claimed, "I didn't cover anything else that wasn't already covered by anybody else in the news."[7] As for his website, he insisted his links to things like the US Military Academy at West Point were totally relevant to his job as a high school history teacher—a job he had held for nineteen years in numerous districts, although this was his first year in comparatively liberal Lawrence, Kansas. In the end, his contract was renewed for a second year after an outpouring of student and public support, but he continued to feel under scrutiny for expressing conservative perspectives that contradicted his superiors' more liberal politics.

Deborah Mayer also found herself on the wrong side of community consensus while teaching current events in her fifth-grade social studies class in Bloomington, Indiana.[8] Mayer regularly taught current events using *TIME for Kids*, a district-approved, educational newsweekly. In January 2003, Mayer led a class discussion about a *TIME for Kids* article that discussed recent peace marches protesting the then-impending war in Iraq. In response to a student's question about whether or not she would ever participate in one of these marches, Mayer told her class that when she drove past protesters waving "Honk for Peace" signs, she honked her horn. Before going to war, she explained to the class, it's important to look for peaceful solutions, just like students are taught to do when problems arise on the playground.

Although the discussion lasted all of five minutes—and Mayer claims she wasn't in the habit of sharing her political opinions with the class—parents complained, prompting a sit-down conversation between Mayer, the school principal, and the parents. During the meeting, the principal made clear to Mayer that there were to be no more discussions of her stances on controversial political issues. Her contract was not renewed at the end of the year.[9]

Mayer subsequently sued the district in federal court, alleging that her termination infringed on her First Amendment right to free speech. She ultimately lost her case, however, on the grounds that "the school system does not 'regulate' teachers' speech as much as it *hires* that speech. Expression is a teacher's stock in trade, the commodity she sells her employer in exchange for a salary."[10] In other words, once Mayer signed her contract with the district, the content of her expression in the classroom was wholly subject to the authority of the school administration.

This does not mean that teachers have *no* First Amendment rights—but those rights are entirely outside of the classroom walls, and they are in practice increasingly limited. In *Pickering v. Board of Education* (1968), the US Supreme Court found in favor of Illinois high school teacher Marvin Pickering, who had been fired for writing a letter criticizing the local school board to the town newspaper. In overturning his firing, the court ruled that "a teacher's exercise of his right to speak on issues of public importance may not furnish the basis for his dismissal from public employment."[11] In a subsequent case, however, the Supreme Court clarified that the speech of any public employee is only protected when its subject is a matter of public concern.[12] Most recently, the Supreme Court held in *Garcetti v. Ceballos* (2006) that any speech made by a public employee in the course of their duty does not receive First Amendment protection. Although the case law is thus far unclear, it is quite possible that teachers may be fired if they speak out even in public forums on educational issues in their district.[13]

In a number of additional cases involving the First Amendment rights of teachers, courts have reliably sided with school districts.[14] In *Boring v. Buncombe County Board of Education*, a 1998 case illustrative of the reasoning behind much of this case law, the Fourth Circuit Court of Appeals held that "it is far better public policy . . . that the makeup of the curriculum be entrusted to the local school authorities who are in some sense responsible, rather than to the teachers."[15] The court thus found against a teacher who had been transferred from her high school over a curricular disagreement. Although the teacher had violated no official district policy, the court affirmed the district's right to set the curriculum and to deal with dissenting teachers as it saw fit.

Arguably, the relationship between teachers and school boards suggested by the Fourth Circuit is appropriate. Local school boards are democratically elected. In important respects, their decisions represent the democratic consensus of their community. Why should an individual teacher—whether because they support Black Lives Matter or because they oppose Barack Obama—reasonably expect to exercise individual control over the content of the curriculum set by an elected school board? In at least some cases, vesting ultimate authority over curricular decisions in the school board clearly seems like the right decision. In *Webster v. New Lenox*, the Seventh Circuit Court of Appeals ruled against social studies teacher Ray Webster, who had sued after being banned from teaching creationism to his junior high school students.[16] Given the youth and impressionability of young people like those in Webster's classroom, the court ruled, a teacher doesn't have the right to "ignore the directives of duly appointed education authorities."[17] The idea that Webster ought to have the constitutional right to unilaterally revise a district-mandated curriculum to include creationism seems, at best, far-fetched.

At the same time, teachers' lack of classroom speech protections could lead them to avoid discussing controversial political issues with their students altogether. Even teachers who consistently take pains to hide their own political beliefs from their students may very well worry about crossing a line during a particularly difficult discussion. The political questions being debated today—from immigration to gun rights, health care to police brutality—directly touch the lives of young people across the country. Teachers who choose to facilitate discussion around these issues must recognize that students may feel offended or even personally attacked by statements that teachers make in the classroom—even when they are simply responding to a student's question, as Deborah Mayer did in answering her fifth grader's question about "honking for peace." Research has shown conclusively that students gain civic knowledge, skills, and virtues when they learn in an "open classroom climate" that encourages them to explore divergent perspectives.[18] It would be unfortunate for our shared civic life, indeed, if teachers shied away from fostering such a culture because they feared for their jobs.

Furthermore, what school boards see as political activism, a teacher may see instead as protecting his students' psychological safety. Roberts believed his Black Lives Matter pin showed solidarity with students whose lived experiences caused them to feel under threat; his convictions were strengthened by the fact that Black students made up only five percent of the student body at Clovis West. Similarly, Yamamoto understood her speech as necessary to protecting her school's most vulnerable students. Both Roberts and Yamamoto contend that multiple students came up to thank them for their support.[19] One irony is that it is precisely when one group is in the minority that its members may need protection or support that members of the majority discount as "politicized" and "special treatment." Particularly when teachers find themselves out of step with the majority culture and allied with a minority student group, then, they may take actions that they view as nonpolitical—such as helping students feel safe and supported—but others see as deeply political and even partisan.

Even when the psychological well-being of students isn't in question, teachers, administrators, and parents may still have a hard time coming to consensus about the distinction between encouraging political discussion and politicking. Where Latham believed he was encouraging his students to critically evaluate both major party candidates for president, the school board saw partisanship. Mayer's encouragement to students to explore peaceful solutions before turning to war could also be read as a nonpartisan approach to teaching fundamental civic values—but that is not how her principal or some parents saw it. Similarly, even though Yamamoto's statement to her students was factually accurate—she *was* feeling scared, and President-elect Trump *had* openly spoken out against the groups she named—it was nonetheless interpreted as partisan critique.

The possibility for disagreement over what constitutes partisanship puts teachers in a vulnerable position. Knowing the state of First Amendment protection for teacher speech, it may be the rational decision for a teacher today to steer clear of controversy in the classroom. However, that would mean that students are deprived of the opportunity to explore important political issues in a supportive and relatively safe setting. Moreover, if teachers who represent views different from those prevailing in the local community are encouraged to avoid leading students in investigations of controversial political issues, that may mean that students never confront divergent and opposing viewpoints. In light of the hyperpartisanship that marks American politics today, this kind of self-censorship may be particularly troubling.

Together, these considerations suggest important questions for school administrators, teachers, and society at large. Does the view that teachers are essentially "hired" speech provide teachers the capacity to maintain an open classroom climate in which students are encouraged to explore new ideas? Ought teachers in K–12 public schools enjoy some degree of academic freedom in order to maintain a classroom where inquiry and the robust exchange of ideas are the norm? And who should ultimately decide what problematic partisanship looks like in the classroom?

It's Not What Teachers Say; It's Why

JONATHAN ZIMMERMAN

What's the proper role of a teacher in the United States? In 1856, children's author and educator Jacob Abbott gave a simple, straightforward answer: to support the status quo. Teachers "could lead students only to accept, not to question, the existing order," Abbott wrote. They were hired to reflect "the will of [their] employer," he added, so they had "no right to wander away from that purpose."[20]

Exactly 150 years later, a federal court used eerily identical language in sustaining the dismissal of Deborah Mayer. In reply to a student's question—"Have you ever attended an antiwar protest?"—Mayer had the temerity to say that she had driven by a protest and had honked her horn approvingly. And that was enough to get her fired! Upholding her district's decision not to renew her contract, the court declared that "the school system does not 'regulate' teachers' speech as much as it *hires* that speech. Expression is a teacher's stock in trade, the commodity she sells her employer in exchange for a salary." Jacob Abbott couldn't have put it any better himself.

A CASE FOR TEACHERS' RIGHT TO FREE SPEECH

The free speech rights of teachers are at a low tide, as all of these cases vividly illustrate. But teacher rights have ebbed and flowed between Abbott's time and our own, which should also give us at least a small buoy of hope. Progressive Era teachers invented the "current events" lesson and used it to debate controversial public issues until World War I abruptly cut off any such discussion. Teachers in the 1930s and 1940s explored questions of poverty and inequality, before the Cold War made these subjects verboten. The 1960s and 1970s witnessed another burst of classroom debate, especially surrounding the Vietnam War and civil rights, which lasted roughly until the "back to basics" movement of the 1980s.[21] After that, the rise of test-driven accountability systems—starting in the states, and culminating in the federal No Child Left Behind Act of 2001—reduced the time that teachers could realistically devote to controversial questions; meanwhile, court rulings like the one against Deborah Mayer limited teachers' right to address such issues at all. If it's not going to be on the test that the kids have to take, why teach it? And if it's too risky to teach, why take the risk?

That's not for me to say. As a tenured full professor at an American university, I have immensely strong academic freedom protections; our public school teachers don't. It would be precious—and, frankly, preposterous—for me to encourage teachers to address issues which I can discuss without fear, but which might get them fired. But perhaps I can help frame a case for why they should have more freedom, and what the rest of us should do in support of that.

The most obvious reason is that teachers are—or should be—"priests of our democracy," as Supreme Court justice Felix Frankfurter wrote in 1952.[22] School is our chief public institution for producing democratic citizens. More than any other public employees, then, schoolteachers are charged with inculcating the skills and habits of democratic life: reason, civility, tolerance, and—yes—discussion. But they can't do that—or, at least, they can't do it well—if they are prohibited from engaging in the very practices that they're supposed to teach. Here I borrow from Alexander Meiklejohn, perhaps the most important American philosopher that Americans know the least about. "It is obvious that the teacher must be free to do what he is trying to get his students to do," Meiklejohn wrote in 1938. "To require our teachers to say to their pupils, 'I want you to learn from me how to do what I am forbidden to do,' is to make of education the most utter nonsense."[23] Teachers are political beings, just like the rest of us. And it makes no sense to pretend otherwise when the kids are in the room.

At the same time, however, Meiklejohn cautioned teachers against using their authority to impose their politics on young minds. That was indoctrination, not education. "Our teachers must be advocates, but they may never be salesmen or propagandists," he warned.[24] But which was which? And how can you tell the difference? Teachers are the adults in the room, and they're also usually required to grade students. Won't the students gravitate to the teacher's point of view, either because they respect the teacher or because they want to curry favor?

That's always a danger. To make the case for teachers' free speech rights, then, we also have to ask the right question: freedom for what? Was the speech aimed at challenging minds, or at changing them? The most important question is not what a teacher said; it's why she or he said it. By wearing a Black Lives Matter button, was David Roberts simply expressing "solidarity" with students of color? Or was he also trying to sway his students in favor of BLM's political platforms, on policing and other contested issues?

Was Mika Yamamoto's comment, like Roberts' button, an effort to support her school's minority populations? Or, by expressing disgust about the election of Donald J. Trump, was she seeking to turn students against Trump as well? Did Tim Latham want to widen students' political perspectives about Barack Obama, or did he want them to adopt his perspective about Obama? And in sharing her views on the war in Iraq, was Deborah Mayer trying to get the class to share them, too?

ASSESSING MOTIVE

These aren't easy matters to resolve, because they speak to one of the most ineffable aspects of human behavior: motive. And it's precisely because motive is so ambiguous that we should give teachers the benefit of the doubt about it. In the same way that defendants are held innocent until proven guilty, our assumption should be that teachers are working to expand minds rather than to indoctrinate them. And the burden should always be on the employer to prove otherwise. So if a school district wants to discipline or dismiss a teacher for something she said, it should have to show that the remark was part of an effort to propagate the teacher's point of view.

How would you do that? The first step would be to ask the teacher what she or he was trying to accomplish, which is something that didn't seem to happen in any of these cases: school leaders simply told the teachers to stop a certain behavior, without inquiring about why they had started it. The next step would be to talk to multiple students about their own perceptions of the teacher, which doesn't appear to have occurred here either. Yes, at least one student complained about Tim Latham's anti-Obama comments. But a much larger number spoke up on his behalf after the district declined to renew his contract, which makes one wonder why school officials didn't think to interview them beforehand.

Maybe the real problem here is that not enough of our school leaders—and, most of all, not enough of our school patrons—actually *want* teachers to engage students in discussions of controversial issues, especially if the discussion engages opinions other than their own. That speaks to an inherent tension in what I'm calling "democratic" education: how can it be democratic if big swaths of the demos—you know, the people—don't want it? I don't know the answer to that, of course, but here's what I do know: nothing will change until those of us who do want this kind of instruction join hands to demand it. And we're more likely to get it if our school districts hire teachers from a broad range of backgrounds, especially from those that aren't heavily represented in those districts. So the good liberal burghers of

Lawrence, Kansas, should try to recruit more conservative teachers like Tim Latham, just as the conservative precinct of Mt. Pleasant, Michigan, should hire more liberals like Mika Yamamoto. And in all of our communities, we should rally behind teachers whose opinions we don't share; otherwise, our pleas for "dialogue" and "discussion" will look like yet another effort to inscribe our particular perspectives and prejudices. Of course our teachers should be free to say what's on their minds. But that probably won't happen until more of us are willing to open our own.

Jonathan Zimmerman teaches education and history at the University of Pennsylvania. He is the author of six books and coauthor (with Emily Robertson) of The Case for Contention: Teaching Controversial Issues in American Schools *(Chicago, 2017).*

Why States Must Protect Teachers' Academic Freedom

Randall Curren

Three days after Deborah Mayer admitted to her students that she "honked for peace" when asked whether she would ever participate in a peace march, she faced an angry parent in a meeting convened by Victoria Rogers, the principal of her elementary school. "He stood up and started pointing his finger in my face. I felt very threatened," she told a reporter.[25] She recalled him then demanding, "I want her to promise never to mention the word *peace* in her class again!"[26] Rogers reportedly insisted that Mayer comply with his demand and announced later the same day that teachers were not to discuss peace. Rogers then cancelled Peace Month, an annual fixture of the curriculum that was to begin in two weeks. The anger concerning Mayer's "unpatriotic" stance on peace apparently inspired further complaints about her, which parents were allowed to file on Title IX Sexual Discrimination and Harassment grievance forms. These complaints had nothing to do with sexual discrimination or harassment, and they were evidently placed in her personnel file without administrative review, at great cost to her subsequent employability.[27]

If Mayer's account of these events is accurate, she was one of countless victims of the misdirected patriotic rage that swept the US in the aftermath of the attacks of September 11, 2001. The invasion of Iraq in March 2003 cut short the UN weapons inspections that had all but conclusively demonstrated that it posed no threat, and there was in any case no evidence that Iraq had played any role in the 9/11 attacks. There was no basis in national interest or the norms of international justice for invading Iraq, and doing so proved to be not only a catastrophic injustice but one of the costliest foreign affairs disasters in US history. Mayer was meanwhile denied due process by a principal who seems to have overreacted to a parent's unreasonable demand that teachers not even refer to something that was evidently part of the curriculum. It is ironic that in caving in to that demand, Rogers failed to exercise the very pedagogical and curricular authority that the courts aim to protect in limiting teachers' First Amendment claims. The courts' aim has been to protect the authority of public officials to establish standards of acceptable educational practice. Mayer may have violated one such standard, but Rogers' violation of the public trust was more flagrant and more damaging.

CAN TEACHERS PROMOTE FREE SPEECH IF THEY LACK IT?

This case raises challenging questions about teachers' academic freedom and the extent to which First Amendment protection of free speech applies to teachers' speech in the classroom. Does regarding teachers' speech as "hired" and "wholly subject to" the authority of the school administration allow teachers to model and cultivate the intellectual and civic virtues essential to a healthy democracy? How can teachers model inquiry in which they are not allowed to engage? How can they model the responsible exercise of free speech rights if courts deny they have such rights in the classroom? My answer to these questions is that a policy of regarding teacher speech as hired does not *preclude* such aspects of good teaching. The courts' retreat from regarding teachers' free speech rights as applicable to their teaching *strengthens* the ability of public authorities to ensure that such good teaching occurs, even as it removes an obstacle to administrative interference with good teaching. This implies that teachers' First Amendment rights are at best a deeply flawed ground on which to stake the academic freedom essential to good teaching.

Consider by way of analogy that this commentary is an example of "writing for hire." The assignment was to write a case commentary that was twelve hundred to fifteen hundred words in length, jargon-free, for a general audience, in sections with headings, illuminating "aspect(s) of the case" that I find interesting. As a writing for hire, this commentary is "wholly subject to the authority" of the editors and publisher, who could refuse to publish it if it did not meet their specifications. They would be rightly indifferent to any free speech claim I might stake in defense of deviations from those specifications. Yet, this authority is entirely compatible with us sharing the common purpose of modeling reasoned inquiry about a matter of vital public interest, and the terms of the contract leave adequate scope for academic freedom of the kind needed to fulfill this common purpose.

There is no reason in principle why teachers' contracts could not be analogous in all of these respects, even as courts deny the applicability of teachers' First Amendment rights to their teaching. What matters is not the fact of their speech being wholly subject to administrative authority, but whether that authority is shaped by responsibilities and terms of employment that accord teachers the degree of academic freedom they need to teach well. These specifics of administrative authority and terms of employment should be codified in state-level specifications of educational aims, standards of acceptable educational practice, and norms of teacher impartiality in orchestrating classroom discussion of controversial matters.

ACADEMIC FREEDOM AND IMPARTIALITY

A basic premise of education is that it is to our advantage to know the truth and make rational decisions, both in our private lives and as citizens of a democracy. In order to cultivate the intellectual and civic virtues this premise implies, teachers must have the academic freedom to lead students in forms of inquiry. Teachers must model and nurture responsiveness to relevant forms of evidence and reasons, allowing students to go where the evidence and reasons lead them. In doing this, teachers must convey the perspective and logic of the subjects they teach with integrity, modeling such intellectual virtues as open-mindedness, curiosity, and respect for evidence.

It is also important to recognize that meaningful inquiry is limited not only by students' maturity, but also by the complexity of the forms of evidence and reasoning involved and whether the answer to a question is truly open. For example, some matters that remain controversial in the court of public opinion, such as biological evolution and climate change, are not open questions within the relevant sciences. It is misguided to think that anyone without expertise in the research methodologies of these fields can meaningfully judge the evidence for themselves. In such cases, curricula and teachers should be true to the perspectives and findings of the relevant sciences, recognizing that with respect to matters within the competence of established sciences, scientific consensus is the ultimate arbiter.

It is unclear whether the modeling of virtues of inquiry in matters that students *can* meaningfully address requires teachers to sometimes reveal their personal views on controversial *open* questions—as Deborah Mayer did. Students are naturally curious about the beliefs of their teachers, but if teachers reveal their beliefs, they may undermine students' diligence in taking responsibility to ensure that their own beliefs are warranted by evidence and sound reasoning. Their curiosity may be satisfied by knowing what their teachers think, when it would be much more beneficial for them to practice thinking through questions for themselves. In order to provide such practice, teachers must be able to examine open questions with their students, considering the grounds for different views that students can meaningfully engage, and modeling open-minded and impartial assessment of the merits of those grounds.

Impartiality and neutrality are not the same. Impartiality in judging the merits of ideas is an intellectual virtue, whereas neutrality in the face of compelling evidence is not. The evidence concerning climate change is now overwhelming, for instance, so teacher neutrality with respect to it is indefensible. There is no educational or civic merit in maintaining neutrality in the face of such evidence. Students should learn what constitutes evidence in diverse fields of study from teachers who model respect for evidence. Impartial respect for evidence will sometimes require teachers to contest the faulty grounds on which widely held views are predicated, but it does not compel them to volunteer their own all-things-considered judgments about controversial open questions. Even in college classrooms in which six or seven different ethical analyses of a topic such as capital punishment are examined, sound pedagogy might compel a teacher to acknowledge that grounds for reasonable disagreement remain.

CONCLUSION

The court held that "Mayer was told that she could teach the controversy about policy toward Iraq, drawing out arguments from all perspectives, as long as she kept her opinions to herself. The Constitution does not entitle teachers to present personal views to captive audiences against the instructions of elected officials."[28] I find the constitutional stance reasonable, and the analysis I have suggested implies that if this is indeed what Mayer was told, then she may have had enough academic freedom to teach the controversy well. However, the analysis also implies that states must do more to establish and defend standards of educational practice that protect the academic freedom essential to cultivating intellectual and civic virtues. Mayer's own account of the events suggests that although she may have erred in revealing her personal view of antiwar demonstrations, her principal and district failed to defend her academic freedom to teach the curriculum she was hired to teach. She seems to have been much more a victim of partisan defiance of public educational authority than a perpetrator of it.

Randall Curren is professor and chair of philosophy and professor of education (secondary) at the University of Rochester, and was the Ginny and Robert Loughlin Founders' Circle Member at the Institute for Advanced Study in Princeton, New Jersey, for 2012–13. His most recent works include Why Character Education? *(Wiley-Blackwell, 2017),* Living Well Now and in the Future: Why Sustainability Matters *(MIT Press, 2017), and* Patriotic Education in a Global Age *(University of Chicago Press, 2018).*

Free Speech, Accountability, and Public Trust

The Necessity of Neutrality

Joshua Dunn

In public schools, students have more free speech rights than their teachers. While this fact seems strange, its strangeness largely dissolves upon reflection. Students are compelled to attend school but no one is forced to be a teacher. As well, no one has a right to be a teacher, and, therefore, no one has a right to teach a certain way. Teachers might want to openly declare their political preferences in class because they think it is either their moral or educational duty, but they do not have a right to do so.

While teachers' rights can properly be limited, this does not tell us whether it is good to do so. Perhaps there are pedagogical and social benefits to giving teachers greater latitude in the classroom. This could be true in individual cases; however, for the broad run of cases the prudent decision for teachers and school boards is to follow a principle of neutrality, not endorsing one political side or the other in the school or classroom.

OPEN CLASSROOMS, NEUTRAL TEACHERS

Since research indicates that students learn valuable civic lessons from an open classroom environment where exploring different viewpoints is encouraged, we must ask what practice most likely encourages that environment. Individual teachers may be able to reveal their personal preferences and not silence dissenters, but it is implausible that in general that is the best strategy for encouraging discussion. Teachers are in a position of authority and can dramatically affect the life prospects of students. Students understandably will self-censor to avoid offending the person who controls their grade.

The conduct of the teachers discussed in this case exposes how students could be silenced by their teachers and raises questions about their judgment and fitness for the profession. David Roberts' claim that a Black Lives Matter button was not a political statement and that he just wanted to show "solidarity [with] the kids" is beyond fatuous. Would he have called a button with "Blue Lives Matter" merely "a peaceful call to end this violence" against the police? And did he give any consideration to how children of police officers in his class would feel about that button? Just months before he wore that button to school, eight police officers were murdered by activists claiming sympathy with the Black Lives Matter movement. He would certainly claim that it would be wrong to indict all of BLM because of their actions, but the same reasoning would apply to the police. He claimed he wanted to show solidarity with "the kids" but apparently only some kids. Similarly, would students supporting Barack Obama have felt more or less free to speak up in Tim Latham's class after he negatively compared Obama's professional experience to McCain's? It was clear that he was endorsing McCain and questioning the judgment of those supporting Obama. As well, Deborah Mayer broadcasting that she thinks it is important to look for peaceful solutions before going to war expressed a position so banal that it dripped with condescension and trivialized a matter of immense political and moral importance. Who would disagree with her except the congenitally bellicose? Does it not imply that anyone who disagreed with her must not want to find a peaceful solution and would that not discourage students who agreed with President Bush from speaking up?

These examples point to the risk of "moral grandstanding" in education. The philosophers Brandon Warmke and Justin Tosi have defined moral grandstanding as participation in moral discourse for self-promotion.[29] It does not matter if the speaker truly believes what she is saying. In fact, she most likely does. Instead, the perniciousness of moral grandstanding comes from the desire to appear morally superior. This corrodes public discourse by increasing cynicism and promoting even greater polarization. Cynicism increases because people suspect that moral discourse is about "showing that you are on the side of the angels" rather than honest deliberation. It increases polarization, since speakers engage in a "moral arms race" and make "increasingly strong claims" which "signal that one is more attuned to matters of justice and that others simply do not understand or appreciate the nuance or gravity of the situation."[30]

These problems are heightened in education precisely because students are supposed to be learning how to honestly deliberate across lines of difference. Instead of teaching students to critically evaluate and discuss complex and contentious areas of political disagreement, the grandstanding teacher instead models dogmatism and self-righteousness. Good people like me, they imply, simply want to stop the violence, or want qualified leaders, or want peace rather than war, while those who do not support them must want the opposite.

NEUTRALITY EQUALS PROTECTION

Practicing neutrality can protect teachers and, rather than discouraging controversial subjects, liberate them to take on those topics in the classroom by inoculating them from accusations of indoctrination. A teacher can tell his students that the conditions of his contract forbid him from revealing his political preferences and, thus, students should not assume that any arguments he advances represents his position. The only way that students would know their teacher's politics is if he always took the conservative or liberal side.

As well, there are many ways of making sure that divisive topics are discussed in homogenous communities. Force the students to debate the issue, and require students to defend the position they oppose. This would satisfy the rule of neutrality and provide a powerful lesson in civic deliberation. It also would help students, and teachers, overcome the problem of confirmation bias, the tendency of all of us to accept findings which fit our assumptions. Surely it would be useful for Trump supporters to have to advance arguments for why he should not be president, and for his opponents to explain why someone would support him. These kinds of exercises are not difficult to implement, and the only thing preventing teachers from doing so is not wanting their students to think through opposing viewpoints.

NEUTRALITY AND PUBLIC SUPPORT

An additional reason for teachers to practice neutrality is that support for public education depends on it. If the public believes that only certain viewpoints are allowed, or that classrooms are ideologically one-sided, support for public schools will erode. While there will be some right-wing teachers, like Tim Latham, who push conservative positions on their students, more than likely they will come from the left. Not without reason do conservatives suspect that public schools are hostile territory. Teachers' unions are notoriously left-wing, with their financial support almost entirely going to liberal candidates and causes. Colleges of education are overwhelmingly left-wing, with some even going so far as trying to impose Orwellian ideological litmus tests on students.[31] One study based on campaign contributions found that teaching, and in particular high school teaching, is one of the most Democratic-leaning occupations in the country.[32] And when schools assign Howard Zinn's *A People's History of the United States*, a book so bereft of scholarly merit that the socialist historian Michael Kazin dismissed it as "obtuse and dogmatic," a "Manichean fable," and a "polemic,"[33] conservatives, or for that matter anyone who does not share Zinn's crude caricature of American history as one entirely of oppression and exploitation, reasonably wonder whether their children are being educated or indoctrinated.

When officials allow their teachers to be openly partisan in school, they risk doing even more to alienate one-third to one-half of the electorate. Even ideologically homogenous districts could undermine financial support for public education, since some school funding comes from the state rather than just from local taxes. Why, legislators may reasonably ask, should public dollars go to support those who will use those resources to push their partisan agenda on students? Some state legislatures have already targeted universities for these reasons, and K–12 education only makes itself a similar target when teachers can depart from the norm of neutrality during the school day.

THE NECESSITY OF POLITICAL ACCOUNTABILITY

At some point, public employees must be accountable to the people who pay their salary. In public education, the obvious place to locate that accountability is with elected school boards who must respond to taxpayer and, particularly, parental concerns. A school board's decision can be debated and discussed and ultimately overturned through the political process. If teachers take offense at the idea that they are nothing more than "hired" speech, they are free to choose another career that they find less insulting. Teachers may view it as part of their job to evangelize for their political preferences, but if the people who hired them disagree, they should proselytize on their own time.

Joshua Dunn researches the courts and education as professor of political science and director of the Center for the Study of Government and the Individual at the University of Colorado Colorado Springs. He is the author of Complex Justice: The Case of *Missouri v. Jenkins (University of North Carolina Press), coeditor of* From Schoolhouse to Courthouse: The Judiciary's Role in American Education *(Brookings Institution Press), and Legal Beat columnist for* Education Next.

Boundaries, Ambiguity, and Teacher Ingenuity

Creating a Safe Environment in Singapore

Jasmine B.-Y. Sim and Lee-Tat Chow

Healthy political development among youths remains contingent upon their exposure to diverse and multiple perspectives, nurtured through safe classroom environments that enable them to develop views for themselves.[34] It is a common expectation for teachers to maintain silent neutrality, especially in handling political or religious issues, to ensure that students' views are not—intentionally or otherwise—influenced one way or another. Arguably, if students are to be respected as citizens, then the school curriculum and teachers should allow for students "to reflect on issues, on their own beliefs and values and on the society in which they wish to live."[35] The cases outlined in "Talking Out of Turn" bring to the surface the issue of teacher neutrality: whether teachers, in adhering to their roles as professionals employed by the school, diminish their ability to meaningfully engage students with a substantial diversity of ideas crucial for the latter's growth.

As researchers immersed in a context outside the US—our experience is with the educational system in Singapore—we would be remiss to forgo the opportunity to offer a different perspective to this debate. The following commentary offers a glance at how teacher neutrality might function in a soft-authoritarian state, providing a point of contrast and contemplation in the discussions on teacher neutrality.

CITIZENSHIP EDUCATION IN SINGAPORE

In Singapore, the government relies on a survivalist discourse that emphasizes the vulnerability of the small nation-state. This discourse provides a strong justification for the authorities' interventionist approach of governance that is "essentially paternalistic."[36] Unlike the United States, Singapore's education system is centralized under the government's authority and openly serves as an instrument for state formation. As stated plainly by the Ministry of Education, education in Singapore endeavors "to mould the future of the nation by moulding the people who will determine the future of the nation."[37] Education in this sense is "primarily for the benefit of the community and not the individual."[38] Teachers are public servants, who must pledge "to guide our students to be good and useful citizens of Singapore" by imparting to them "a sense of commitment and belonging to Singapore."[39] This is markedly different from the educational vision in the US, which emphasizes the importance of preserving autonomy and developing students' independent voices.

Under Singapore's centralized education system, formal citizenship education is implemented through a state-crafted curriculum, particularly via social studies. Social studies teachers find themselves faced with the stacked burdens of adhering to the mandated curriculum, while also preparing their students for a compulsory national examination required by the subject.[40] Like the nation itself, the social studies curriculum prescribes consensus over contention. The core values of consensual politics and social harmony are hailed as essential for national survival and are consequently hardwired into the citizenship curriculum.[41] It is thus difficult, amidst a climate of consensus and perceived national fragility, for one to raise contentious issues without appearing antagonistic. The circumstances that teachers in Singapore are embedded in are, to say the least, opposite to those in the US.

COMPARATIVE CHALLENGES OF CIVIC EDUCATION

Yet, what strikes us as intriguing is that despite the polarities between the US and Singapore education systems, teachers in both contexts face similar difficulties in addressing controversial issues. Both US and Singaporean teachers face censorship and fear of reprisal. One of the central issues in "Talking Out of Turn" stems from the treacherously fuzzy line between the exploration of contentious issues and the advocacy of partisanship, making it difficult for teachers in the US to discuss controversies with their students; consequently, it might be simpler—albeit problematic—to avoid controversial issues in the classroom altogether. The teachers involved in the cases appeared to be caught off-guard in the absence of oversight.

In Singapore, this issue takes the form of "Out of Bounds markers" (OB markers), a uniquely Singaporean political lexicon, constructed by authorities, that demarcates certain topics such as race, religion, and politics as sensitive. In turn, sensitive topics demand restraint from teachers when discussing these topics. The implementation of these markers, however, seems to shift according to who pushes the limit; it remains ambiguous as to when these limits will be enforced. In this vein, many citizenship teachers in Singapore err on the side of caution when it comes to the teaching of controversial issues for fear of crossing the line, preferring to adhere closely to curricular boundaries set by the authorities in the classroom.[42]

As civil servants, teachers in Singapore are expected to maintain neutrality when presenting different perspectives to students, but further than that, they are also expected to orient students toward safeguarding the well-being of the community as a priority over the students' personal, religious, or political views, in order to produce citizens that are "committed to the well-being of the society and nation."[43] Here, we note that the avoidance of controversial issues by Singapore teachers is not driven—as it is for US teachers—by concerns of exerting undue influence upon students, but rather that discussing controversial issues may result in victimizing certain ethnic groups, thereby jeopardizing social cohesion and endangering national survival.[44]

In the presence of centralized educational structures, the boundaries that teachers are expected to operate within are made clear at the outset, protecting them from public scrutiny insofar as they keep within the limits. We recognize, however, that the price is a heavy one, as the autonomy of Singapore teachers under these circumstances appears nonexistent. Yet, as noted before, the enforcement of OB markers is ambiguous, and empirical research conducted on local schools have found clever ways through which Singapore teachers have manipulated their circumstances to introduce controversial issues into classrooms.

Most notably, despite its heavy emphasis on building consensus and avoiding conflict, part of the social studies syllabus encourages teachers to "activate students' prior knowledge and challenge their assumptions" through questioning, and to present "multiple perspectives . . . for their consideration."[45] Technically adhering to the official syllabus, research has found that many Singapore teachers place heavy emphasis on presenting multiple perspectives in their classroom discussions of issues.[46] This loophole, so to speak, has been utilized by teachers as a means to inject controversial issues into the classroom, channeling dissenting views and even their personal views (as they admit in interviews) to students, but presenting them as *a* perspective among others for students' "consideration." While teachers may freely discuss issues from all perspectives, they do so on the provision that—in according with national guidelines—they refrain from advocacy and that discussions do not breed division among students.

Thus, where teacher neutrality arises in the US as a matter of preserving autonomy (of students or teachers), neutrality in Singapore education is propelled by the efforts of the centralized authority to maintain consensus and avoid social discord. Although the autonomy of Singapore teachers remains limited by a monitored educational climate, there is still room afforded—relying on the creativity of teachers—for the exploration of diverse ideals and sensitive issues, as long as they are engaged under the agenda of social cohesion. In a rather counterintuitive way, it is the imposition of boundaries, and the fixed role of professionally hired civil servants, mixed with a degree of ingenuity by the teachers in Singapore, that provide them with a safe environment to hash out difficult issues and different perspectives with their students.

Jasmine B.-Y. Sim is an associate professor in the Curriculum Teaching and Learning Academic Group, National Institute of Education, Nanyang Technological University, Singapore. Her research interests include civic and citizenship education, social studies and democratic education, and school-based curriculum development.

Lee-Tat Chow is a research assistant in the Humanities and Social Studies Education Academic Group. He holds a master of Buddhist studies degree from the University of Hong Kong.

The Perils of Warning Teachers About "Political" and "Partisan" Speech

Mica Pollock

I see two tensions at the core of this case. Each tension is related to an open question: *should* we clarify "allowable" teacher speech in our current historical moment? I am conflicted about clueing teachers in to the limits of their own speech, because efforts to clarify what teacher speech is allowed—that is, *legally* permissible—can both encourage and discourage teachers from engaging students with the issues of our time. Similarly, efforts to clarify what teacher speech is "partisan" and what is not can both encourage and discourage teachers from engaging students with challenging social and political issues.

CLARIFYING ALLOWABLE SPEECH

Teachers worried about their jobs understandably seek clear lines on what speech is allowed when it comes to speaking out about social and political issues. Before we speak, we all want to know: which speech could get us in legal or professional trouble?

As a scholar who often writes to teachers, I myself quietly seek this same clarity. I tend to ask teachers to speak up on key social issues, with young people's well-being in mind. And so, I want to be sensitive to the constraints of teachers' jobs and the "rules."

At the same time, we may risk chilling teachers' willingness to engage students with those key social issues if those clarifications come in the form of warnings, especially if these warnings are necessarily vague. I worry about sentences in the case like these: "This does not mean that teachers have *no First Amendment rights*—but those rights are *entirely outside* of the classroom walls, and they are in practice *increasingly limited*," and "*[I]t is quite possible that* teachers may be fired if they speak out *even in public forums on educational issues* in their district" (emphasis added). To my ear, the case's warnings imply that it is likely best to avoid anything vaguely controversial.

Indeed, the harshness of such warnings masks the broader space that does exist for allowable teacher speech. That's because, in many ways, allowable speech is ultimately a decision for school leaders in each context and situation—meaning that teachers' speech is often allowed until someone complains and the school/district/board administration decides otherwise.

In an era when students really need to hear teachers' voices modeling what it looks like to consider tough, controversial issues as participants in a democratic society, I believe that teachers should adopt a "speak and ye might be punished, but still, try to engage the issues of our time" stance. Doing so would enable them to focus on what really matters: first, engaging students in difficult conversations about the world they live in; and, second, building relationships with their students, the colleagues they struggle to talk with, the families who might complain, and the administrators who will in the end decide what they will be punished for saying.

CLARIFYING PARTISAN SPEECH

This case uses several terms that the authors imply are fundamentally different without defining the distinction. Two examples: the authors caution readers about teacher speech that is "deeply political and even partisan," and ask us to consider "the distinction between encouraging political discussion and politicking."

In the Trump era, teachers really need terms like *partisan* or *political* clarified. Vague uses of these terms can obstruct teachers' efforts to support their students in the world we live in. Today, some educators are labeled partisan if they simply challenge hate or bullying on their own campuses; engage students in dialogue about real, controversial issues; or just affirm that all students have the right to learn safely in school.[47] A teacher in New York was told not to engage a longstanding, historically grounded lesson about Columbus Day because it was "too controversial." An Oregon teacher received a letter from parents angry that she *might* say something negative about Trump when teaching about the Magna Carta. Educators in Arlington, Virginia, faced criticism for hanging up signs with phrases like "diversity strengthens us" and "science is real." The parents who complained called those messages too partisan and political for school.

My understanding of the word *partisan* is that teachers shouldn't indoctrinate students to take specific positions on candidates and ballot measures. For example, they should not tell students to encourage their parents to vote to approve this bond measure or go vote for candidate X. This seems like a clear line to hold. But this does not include teaching students how to weigh these issues for themselves and make thoughtful, evidence-based decisions.

Furthermore, worries about partisanship all too often extend beyond this line. For one thing—as Deborah Mayer's case suggests—teachers are often criticized for being partisan if they tell students what they personally think about any political issue, even if their explanation is not accompanied by encouragement to vote or take a particular position. To avoid being partisan, some argue, teachers should enable students to explore various sides of the issue without *ever* letting on what they themselves think. I worry that this level of restriction asks teachers to pretend they are not human beings struggling to make evidence-based claims in a debatable world.

Indeed, nearly every social and political issue in the Trump era seems to be deeply political or partisan. In an era when the government denies climate science, to teach climate science at all seems partisan to some; I've talked to science teachers in rural-suburban Pennsylvania who feel this very pressure in their schools. Similarly, in an era when the government promotes untruths about immigrants and crime, to teach the facts of immigrant contributions (or the justice system) seems partisan to some.

I think we need to clarify that in the Trump era, teaching about the facts—or even taking the side of facts—is not partisan. An administrator or parent with anti-immigrant views may call it partisan or political if a teacher repeats aloud the legal fact that public K–12 schools may not exclude students based on immigration status. But this is just a legal fact—go read *Plyler v Doe.*[48]

Today, labeling teacher speech as partisan is a critique so overused that it has become a weapon to shut down not just teachers themselves, but the actual teaching of facts. I could easily imagine a parent complaining that a teacher's lesson challenging basic ideas of White supremacy was too political and partisan for public school. But what if, upon closer examination, the teacher was simply marshalling evidence to explore how White supremacy (that is, "the belief that white people are superior to those of all other races, especially the black race, and should therefore dominate society") is a real, though false, idea in the world, with centuries of consequences.[49] A refusal to discuss the concept leaves students unable to discuss one of the major dynamics of US history and, of course, one of the major recent events of the Trump era: the White supremacist rally in Charlottesville, Virginia. Further, *challenging* this belief with fact-based understanding (for example, demonstrating that "races" were historically produced and are genetically invalid, and that no social subgroups of humans are inherently superior to others) is not partisan but just teaching facts.

Further, because the premise of White supremacy is actually *false*, shouldn't a teacher's job be to offer evidence solely on the true side? It is ridiculous to think that in order to teach about Charlottesville from a nonpartisan perspective, teachers should honor debunked eighteenth- or twenty-first-century claims that "White" people are more worthy or more smart. Sure, teachers could explain that these ideas define White supremacist thought, but they should also make sure that students understand that *those ideas are falsehoods.*[50] Is that partisan? I think it's teaching facts.

It should not be partisan to study facts. It should also not be considered partisan to stand up against hate and to protect students' well-being, two actions core to teachers' everyday jobs.[51] Because here's the real core tension of this moment: because some government actors have promoted intolerance and distorted facts, *teachers who speak up against hate or for students, facts, and learning are accused of being politically partisan.*

THE REAL GOAL: ENGAGING STUDENTS

Rather than warning teachers vaguely about discussing "the political" or being partisan, it's perhaps best to keep our eye on the prize: supporting and developing teachers' efforts to skillfully engage students in conversations about the world they live in. To do this, teachers need considerable latitude to talk about social and political issues using evidence—perhaps even in ways that push against the warnings discussed in this case. In the end, perhaps, unions, school boards, educator collectives, and the wider parent/family community must keep rallying to protect teachers' efforts to talk with students about the world.

Mica Pollock, an anthropologist, is professor of education studies and director of the Center for Research on Educational Equity, Assessment, and Teaching Excellence (CREATE) at the University of California, San Diego. Her newest book is Schooltalk: Rethinking What We Say About—and To—Students Every Day *(The New Press, 2017).*

Protecting Students' Rights to Think Critically

CURTIS ACOSTA

One year into the Trump presidential administration, the anxiety that various communities in the US felt after election day has only increased. Many youth and their families live with the constant threat of deportation, find themselves banned from entering the country, and endure a deluge of hateful, racist messages from national, state, and local officials. The anxiety and fear is real for African Americans, Chicanxs/Latinxs, women, Muslims, and LGBTQ individuals—as well as advocates for these communities. With divisive rhetoric and policies polarizing our national discourse in mainstream and social media, it seems prudent that classroom teachers would choose to engage in respectful and critical dialogue about the state of the nation. After all, public schools have an important responsibility to foster the courage to fulfill our civic responsibilities and reject the amplification of fear and hate reflected in the creation of dehumanizing public policy. Unfortunately, the examples in this case illustrate a much darker reality for educators who want to embrace controversial and critical issues in the classroom. This is an experience that I am familiar with as a former teacher of Mexican American studies (MAS) in Tucson—a program that was attacked by powerful Arizona politicians and eventually banned through state legislation in 2012.

Reflecting on this experience, I want to underscore the important relationship between the boundaries of teacher speech and the free speech rights of students in the classroom. Teachers have the opportunity and responsibility to create dynamic learning environments for students to formulate, test, and reassess ideas. To limit the potential of those learning environments by censoring such ideas could adversely affect the First Amendment rights of students. I saw this firsthand in Tucson.

MEXICAN AMERICAN STUDIES IN TUCSON

MAS was targeted and dismantled due to the anti-Mexican and anti-immigrant sentiments in Arizona during the early 2000s. Both the sitting attorney general and the state superintendent of public instruction in Arizona at the time claimed that our highly successful academic program was teaching partisan and anti-American content to students. They firmly believed that my colleagues and I were radicalizing and indoctrinating our students, while refusing to visit our classes or investigate in good faith. Arizona officials arbitrarily used controversial statements in our curriculum as evidence against our program, taking them at face value and without pedagogical context. Citations that included revolutionary expressions by Chicanx/Latinx historical figures were used as violations of the state law, while comparable rhetoric used by the founding fathers in the Revolutionary War era—in our district adopted textbook no less—were deemed innocuous. Under the authority of the attorney general and the state superintendent, our curriculum was banned, and our books were boxed up and stored in a warehouse if they reflected themes such as oppression, race, ethnicity, and class.

In the summer of 2017, after a seven-year legal battle and five years after the termination of our program, we were finally able to have our day in court and prove that racial animus was the motivating factor in eliminating MAS. Judge A. Wallace Tashima ruled that the attacks on our program by the former attorney general and state superintendent infringed on students' First and Fourteenth Amendment rights. Judge Tashima's decision is a critical moment for academic freedom. It exposes, on the one hand, how political motives are often at the center of cases that are disparaged as too controversial for the classroom. On the other hand, Tashima's decision affirms how important it is that teachers are empowered to create educational spaces that meet the needs of their students. In other words, by empowering teachers we can empower students.

This is what such a relationship can look like in practice. Every year, MAS students produced a play based on counternarratives of the Tucson experience. Through their original play, our students became aware of their own historical space and place. They identified stories in their community of the Chicanx experience that the mainstream Tucson media typically silenced. They then used ethnographic research methodologies to interview *Tucsonenses* about the history, present social realities, and future of Tucson. Their research became dramatic monologues, performed on stage with guidance from myself and experts in theater from the University of Arizona. Their growth from consumers to producers of knowledge was real. But the power of the project rested on the interdependence and connection among students, teachers, and community members, who together cultivated a critical, humanizing, and healing experience through an academically rigorous and artistic journey of discovery and expression. Performing these counternarratives for our community was an emotional and moving experience for all involved. As the saying goes in our Chicanx community, *la cultura cura*, the culture cures.

THE MYTH OF NEUTRALITY

My experience suggests that it is a struggle to keep such educational possibilities alive. When teachers risk creating spaces outside traditional classes, they are often accused of imposing their own views on students or of violating the ideal of neutrality. But neutrality, as an educational ideal, is a myth. No one—teachers, administrators, schools boards—can teach or support teaching from a position of neutrality. If the Clovis example does not make it clear that school districts, their governing boards, and their personnel all have political beliefs and biases, consider the generations of deplorable evidence in respect to the miseducation of youth of color in US schools, of which MAS is one small chapter.

However, neutrality is too often used as a political weapon. In the case of MAS in Tucson, the local school district where the program was once created and housed refused an invitation from our legal team to join the remedy meetings and hearings with the court and the state, claiming that they needed to stay neutral. In hindsight, the idea that these meetings and hearings could be neutral when the court ultimately found one of the parties to have violated the First and Fourteenth Amendment rights of the Mexican American students in Tucson seems absurd. Why would a school district create false equivalencies between those who affirm our common humanity and challenge racist policies and agendas and those who instigate and foster racial animus? Is neutrality used in these cases just as a substitute for fear?

Yet that is the power of faux neutrality in education. Taking any stand, even one that supports legality over illegality in our case, seems too controversial to touch. And what is the likely outcome of framing racial and social justice as "too political?" Silence, fear, and the false sense of neutrality is tantamount to submission to racist agendas. How can fear ever inspire us to find peace, justice, and equality? As Dr. Martin Luther King Jr. said, "Silence is betrayal." It is a language of the status quo—the language of being complicit and fearful of confronting injustice and hate.

Although school districts should continue to resist political campaigning on their campuses, we must also require them to follow the law and to protect the rights of students. Abdicating responsibility to do so, by hiding behind the myth of neutrality, can cause harm to the students, educators, and district staffs. Fear of being deemed too controversial by local media or community groups is not a justification for refusing to demand justice. However, it is equally important to emphasize that schools are not places for political ideologies to be expressed or conveyed in a dogmatic fashion by educators or the institution as a whole. As educators, we need to fight attitudes of fear that drive us away from our responsibilities to provoke critical thinking and reflection in our classrooms, so our students can grow in their own courage and participation in our democracy. We need to be as courageous as our students, the Dreamers, LGBTQ students, and other youth who have not let the anxious and troubling times discourage them from living inspired and impassioned lives.

WHERE DO WE GO FROM HERE?

As can be seen in the cases from the chapter and my own experiences as a teacher in MAS, ideologues using public education to further their own political agendas and beliefs, or to silence the scope and diversity of thought and ideas that have been produced in our country and around the world, is a very real phenomenon. If educators continue to be intimidated or sanctioned for cultivating civic discourse, then our democracy is made that much more impotent. Perhaps this new legal precedent will be a shield for educators to responsibly present material to students that may be divergent to community consensus. However, it is clear that school districts and their governing boards must protect educators who want to expose students to multiple perspectives on issues that may conflict with political agendas from public officials or a tyranny of the majority. Educators must continue to cultivate critical dialogue and encourage students to explore their beliefs in a manner that is civically responsible, respectful to their peers, and reflective of the tenets of our country. We must challenge reactionary and fearful policies that not only stagnate education, but divide, silence, and diminish our common humanity.

Curtis Acosta is a former Mexican American studies teacher in Tucson. He is the founder of the Acosta Educational Partnership and an assistant professor of language and culture in education at the University of Arizona South.

CHAPTER 10

Educating for Civic Renewal

MEIRA LEVINSON AND JACOB FAY

This book is designed to be *used*, in addition to being read. This is not to disparage the act of reading, which can itself be a transformative activity. As philosophers, in particular, we are both committed to the proposition that ideas and arguments matter. By shifting how readers formulate a problem, understand its dimensions and possibilities, or conceive of potential solutions, a piece of writing has the power to enact change—at least inside readers' heads, and often in the world at large, as well. We thus discuss below a variety of concepts and themes that are illuminated across multiple cases and commentaries, anticipating that readers may benefit from seeing the intellectual threads that stitch chapters together. We imagine this discussion will be useful also to professors who are trying to decide whether and how to incorporate the book into their syllabi. We hope that the cases and commentaries will prove useful in a wide variety of courses, including teacher education, educational leadership and administration, social studies methods, civic education, educational policy, political theory, philosophy of education, public policy, school law, race and multiculturalism, and related areas. By drawing out some of the key themes, we intend to help instructors see how the materials in this book may fit into their courses.

At the same time, however, we would be disappointed if this book were viewed solely as a text to be read *about* the politics of democratic education, rather than a tool to be used to *enable* democratic education and engagement with diverse others. For, as we explained in the first chapter of this book, we intend the cases and commentaries in this book to foster (or provoke) conversation in departmental and faculty meetings, parent-teacher organization evenings, school board development sessions, student government meetings, middle and high school classes, city halls, and state houses. These are the places in which we should be engaging with one another about schools' roles and responsibilities in a struggling democracy. People frequently avoid having such explicit conversations because of how risky they feel. It is difficult and even scary to talk about contentious political issues with people who we don't know well, who we don't have reason to trust, who have power over us (or over whom we have power), with whom we disagree, or in front of whom we feel we have to maintain a facade of objectivity, neutrality, or even omniscience.

The cases in this book are designed to make these conversations less scary and more possible. This is not because they smooth out the disagreements or hide the controversies. To the contrary, it is because they normalize such disagreement. They make it clear that good, caring, honest, smart, thoughtful people can have very different views about what educational policies or practices are essential for realizing core democratic values in divided societies. In the final section of this chapter, therefore, we offer a variety of ways in which educators, policy makers, parents, and others who care about realizing civic ideals in and through schools can lift the cases and commentaries off the page and use them to enable hard but necessary conversations with others.

DISCORDANT ROLES FOR SCHOOLS EDUCATING IN AND FOR DEMOCRACY

We deliberately selected cases for this book that delve into quite disparate dilemmas surrounding schools' roles in and for democracy—from regulation of teacher speech, policies around charter school design, school culture initiatives, and digital monitoring of students, to choices about curriculum, district partnerships with law enforcement, teacher preparation and support, and districtwide responses to student activism. We did so in part to help educators, policy makers, and families navigate the wide array of challenges they face in the current political climate. Taken together, the cases and commentaries are designed to affirm the existence of, and to provide some guidance through, the multiple struggles exacerbated by democratic discord in schools.

The diversity of cases and commentaries also illuminates three distinct civic roles that schools play educating *in* a democracy as well as educating *for* democracy. First, public schools have responsibilities in democracies as legal agents of the state, responsible for implementing democratically enacted public policies and laws. "Eyes in the Back of Their Heads 2.0" demonstrates schools' responsibilities in this role, as they are tasked with protecting students from cyberbullying and from inappropriate digital content. Second, schools exist in democracies as *objects* of adults' and students' ongoing democratic expression and engagement. "Particular Schools for Particular Students," for example, shows how adults engage civically through cultural havens like the Bari charter school, while "School Walkouts and Civil Disobedience" shows how students use walkouts and other forms of protest to transform their schools in a very different way into objects of democratic expression. Third, as we noted in chapter 1, schools are sites of civic preparation for future democratic citizens. Fulfilling this role drives the teachers in "Politics, Partisanship, and Pedagogy," for example, as they wrestle over how to teach their tenth graders about controversial issues; many of the commentaries about "School Walkouts" similarly emphasize schools' responsibilities to provide students with high-quality civic education and curricular content.

Schools face complex challenges in fulfilling any one of these roles in times of partisan contestation and civic upheaval. It is hard to implement public policies when they are in flux, to function as objects of civic engagement when mutual mistrust is high and sympathy is low, and to teach the next generation of citizens when the very aims of civic education are in doubt. Schools also struggle when the roles themselves come into conflict: when their obligations to prepare future citizens are stymied by curricular requirements or restrictions imposed by current citizens, for example, or when young people's civic vision and activism clash with school and district policies.[1]

We see these struggles at play in many of the cases. "Eyes," for instance, details not only how schools as agents of the state are legally obligated to protect students from inappropriate digital content, but also how fulfilling such obligations may stymie schools' attempts to teach students about their own civil liberties and democratic rights against a surveillance state. In "Walkouts," likewise, we see how students' civic engagement via marches and walkouts risks coming into conflict both with district attendance and discipline policies, and with adults' views about young people's ideal civic roles. Sometimes teachers find themselves at the center of democratic discord over their responsibilities; as "Talking Out of Turn" reveals, for instance, they may lose their professional security and even their jobs if administrators or parents conclude that they have overstepped their appropriate civic roles. "The Price of Safety," meanwhile, highlights how people's disagreements over the state of society itself—Is it safe or under threat? Should new arrivals be welcomed or feared? Whose interests should be taken into account?—can buffet school board members and district leaders as they attempt to fulfill all three roles of schools in a democracy.

As many of our commentators argue, however, these conflicts need not be inevitable. In his commentary on "Eyes," for instance, Erhardt Graeff proposes that schools adopt "participatory design and popular technology principles" to involve students and families in coconstructing the digital surveillance technologies that will be used to monitor them. Such ideas flip the script of surveillance being used by agents of the state on citizens, and instead offers citizens agency in democratically guiding state action, and it helps schools foster rather than impede students' digital civic learning. Jonathan Boisvert, Keegan Bonds-Harmon, Innocense Gumbs, and Jalissa Mixon similarly reframe schools' roles in their commentary on student walkouts. As high schoolers themselves, they argue that by not impeding student activism, schools can help students strengthen their civic skills and demonstrate their civic commitments to improving their community when they walk out. Conversely, some commentators on "Talking Out of Turn" argue that teachers may be wrong to perceive their choices as subject to role conflicts. Precisely by adhering to public regulations over their speech, Joshua Dunn argues, teachers can protect themselves from reaching fatuous or misguided personal judgments about the neutrality of their partisan beliefs. Jasmine Sim and Lee-Tat Chow likewise argue that by adhering to strict government-imposed restrictions over "out of bounds" speech, teachers in Singapore are counterintuitively able to foster open classroom climates in which to discuss many controversial issues. While schools face both acute and perennial challenges of educating in and for democracy, therefore, many potential conflicts may be resolvable with creativity and seeing the problem from a different angle.

ADDITIONAL THEMATIC CONNECTIONS

Reading across the cases and commentaries, as opposed to focusing solely within any one chapter, reveals a number of additional cross-cutting themes that repay further investigation. We discuss the first few in detail, and then for reasons of space provide briefer accounts of additional themes:

Just as schools are pulled between educating as agents *in* democracy and as sites *for* democracy, they also are forced to contend with the *permeable boundaries* between the society in which they are embedded, on the one hand, and the more idealized school community designed to protect students from the divisions and hardships characteristic of the outside world, on the other. Many of the cases in this book arise in this breach along the boundary between school and society. In "Walling Off or Welcoming In," for instance, Jersey City K–8's School Culture Committee wrestles with the impossibility of walling the school off from a generally toxic political culture. District officials in "The Price of Safety" are similarly riven over how county-wide gang violence should be addressed within the schools, and whether the boundary that had been drawn around schools to keep law enforcement out should be reconfigured. Teachers in "Politics, Partisanship, and Pedagogy" confront another aspect of drawing boundaries, as they debate which authentic political disputes in the broader society should be given space within the school in their "Power of Persuasion" curriculum. This question of mirroring society also arises in "Eyes" and "Walling Off," as people raise questions about how closely students' rights within the school should track adults' civil liberties in the broader polity. Finally, "Walkouts" raises the challenges of boundary-crossing in the other direction, as students leave the boundaries of their schools to try to make change through public protests and marches.

Insofar as the primary responsibility of any state is to protect its citizens (and ideally others living within its borders) from threats, it should perhaps not be surprising that a book about civic ethical dilemmas will be in large part about dilemmas of *safety and protection*. But it is still sobering to consider the range of threats arising in these cases and commentaries with which schools must contend, and/or that they risk perpetrating: harassment, bullying, racism, suicide, deportation, silencing, ignorance, marginalization, gang violence, segregation, civil liberties violations, arrest, suspension and expulsion, physical violence, emotional violence, job loss, and so on. In part as a consequence, one could read this book as an inquiry into *vulnerability*: who should be considered vulnerable and deserving of state protection in the educational context, why, and how?

Given the cases' consistent dive into questions of safety, it should also probably not surprise us that *surveillance, law enforcement, and discipline* are also pervasive considerations. "Eyes" is entirely focused on digital surveillance of students, of course, and "The Price of Safety" both explicitly asks whether a school district should partner with law enforcement and implicitly raises questions about sheriffs' ethnoracially biased surveillance and disciplining of Latinx students. But the civic implications of school-sponsored surveillance arise in other cases, as well. "Walling Off" hinges on how schools interpret and fulfill legal antibullying mandates, and on educators' interfering in such normally private decisions as whom to be friends with or how to play with blocks. "Bending Toward—or Away From—Racial

Justice" features multiple examples in which people are in effect surveilling and disciplining one another, from the parent who contacts the principal to complain about Tiana's teaching her son to hate his heritage, to the principal's threatened suspension of Nia, and to Sophie's observations of school practices as an instructional coach for the charter network. The teachers in "Talking Out of Turn" find their jobs on the line thanks to surveillance and discipline at the hands of parents and administrators; district officials in "Walkouts" have to contend with all of these considerations, from coordinating with law enforcement to monitoring students.

Themes of *inclusion and exclusion* also run through many cases and commentaries. "Particular Schools" asks whether de facto segregated "haven" charter schools create inclusive communities for some students and families at the cost of excluding others, or even of excluding those same families from broader civic membership. "Walling Off" asks how schools can create a robustly inclusive school culture when both students and teachers express sentiments that others experience as exclusionary. "The Price of Safety" prompts reflection about undocumented students' tenuous status within schools, as their solid legal standing (thanks to *Plyler v. Doe*) is unsettled by the presence of law enforcement. Both "Politics" and "Bending Toward . . . Justice" investigate how curricular choices and pedagogies may exacerbate some students' experiences of exclusion while helping other students feel recognized or included.

Student and teacher speech are obviously the focus of "Walling Off," "Talking Out of Turn," "Politics," and "Walkouts." But they also arise in interesting ways in "Eyes," as schools subject digital communication to automated content analysis, and in "Bending Toward . . . Justice," as teachers like Ethan contend with the challenges of setting norms for student speech while also enabling open dialogue about complex topics. Questions about the meaning and significance of *identity*—including how people's personal identities intersect with their civic identities and opportunities—also permeate these cases and commentaries. Many revolve, for instance, around students' and families' real or perceived Muslim, undocumented, Latinx, Trump-supporting, transgender, Black, Somali, activist, gang-involved, Aboriginal, immigrant, radicalized, White, and other identities. *Teachers'* identities are also at stake in "Politics" and "Particular Schools." Finally, we encourage readers to consider how considerations of *partisanship*, *parental voice*, *civil rights*, *curricular design*, and *district-level policy* (among numerous other themes) also provide insight across multiple cases and commentaries. As we consider the ethical dimensions of democratic discord around schools, in other words, we can benefit from multiple entry points.

USING THIS BOOK TO ENGAGE IN DEMOCRATIC EDUCATION AND CONVERSATION WITH DIVERSE OTHERS

Thus far, we have discussed cross-cutting connections among the cases and commentaries, assuming (as editors tend to do in a concluding chapter) that readers will have read through the book in order to gain systematic insight into civic ethical dilemmas in education. As we mentioned earlier in this chapter and in chapter 1, however, there is a different way to use this book, which we are also committed to supporting: namely, using cases and commentaries as prompts for collective democratic engagement around hard problems.

Each case is written so that it can be read on its own, with no background preparation. At under six pages, each case or commentary can also be read by most native English speakers in about ten minutes.[2] Hence, parent-teacher organization members, participants in a districtwide professional development session, pre-service teachers in training, public policy students, or department of education staffers could read a case and immediately launch into a discussion of the issues at stake. As we explain in chapter 7 of *Dilemmas of Educational Ethics*, and on the justiceinschools.org website, facilitators can use a generic discussion protocol to lead a collective discussion (or a set of small group discussions) about the case. See "Normative Case Study Discussion Group Protocol" on the page following for a slightly modified version of that protocol.

We recommend spending at least an hour in order to have a full case discussion, including time for reflection about the process itself in addition to the substance of the case. But we are well aware that teaching-team meetings, professional development workshops, and undergraduate class sessions are often far shorter than that; we ourselves have conducted case discussions in just twenty-five to thirty minutes by sacrificing the process reflection portion of the protocol (questions 5–7).

Having led discussions with up to 150 people at a time, we can also attest to small groups' abilities to self-facilitate discussions using the protocol or other guiding materials. We recommend discussion groups of five to ten people; since one of their purposes is to enable challenging conversations among people with a diverse range of views and experiences, however, we also suggest erring on the side of making groups slightly too big rather than too small. No matter whether the conversation is among one large group or scattered among a number of smaller groups, we recommend that facilitators pause the conversation at various points to consolidate and summarize groups' responses before moving on. Because the cases raise so many

NORMATIVE CASE STUDY DISCUSSION GROUP PROTOCOL

1. What is the dilemma in this case? For whom is it a dilemma?
2. Why is this a dilemma?
   A. What values or principles are at stake? Do people disagree about which values matter, which should take precedence, or how they apply in this case?
   B. What practical and/or policy considerations are at stake? Do people disagree about which considerations are relevant, which should take precedence, or how they should be addressed in this case?
3. What choices are available, and to whom?
   A. How does each of these choices frame and address the issues at stake?
   B. For each choice, what is gained? What is lost?
4. What do you think should be done in this case, and by whom? Why?
5. What have you learned from talking about this case that might apply to other ethical dilemmas in education?
   A. What principles or values are you thinking about for the first time, or thinking about in a new way?
   B. What policies or practices are you thinking about for the first time or in a new way?
6. What value is there, if any, in talking through a case like this with others?
   A. What did you learn about yourself?
   B. What did you learn about others?
   C. What did you learn about your institution, organization, or broader context?
   D. What did you learn about the process itself?
7. Is there anything else you want to bring up or discuss?

interconnected challenges, conversations can quickly move from one topic to the next, and it can be hard for people to remember ideas that had seemed incredibly salient even ten minutes earlier. When a number of small groups are having separate conversations, too, they may find it useful to hear what dilemmas other groups have uncovered as a means of expanding their thinking. Facilitators may find it challenging to summarize a fast-moving case discussion the first time they do so; over time, however, they will come to recognize some of the themes that frequently arise and can organize their account of the discussions accordingly. They can also help connect groups' spontaneous insights with ideas from the commentaries.

As any good teacher knows, no one pedagogy can meet all needs or learning objectives. In our own teaching and professional development work, we have taken a number of additional approaches to using the cases and commentaries. These include:

- "four corners" discussions, where people take a stand on a particular claim and then talk with others who have different views
- "fishbowl" conversations among a small group, sometimes in defined roles, while others listen in on the conversation and then discuss what they heard with respect to both substance and process
- "town hall" meetings in which people take on different commentators' or others' perspectives to discuss the case with one another
- seminar discussions, often drawing on additional philosophical or other scholarly materials
- opportunities for participants to create visual representations (using pipe cleaners, construction paper, tape, and other simple craft materials) or other artistic interpretations (through podcasts, videos, and even interpretive dance!) of the key tensions and choices at stake in a case
- "found poem" creations in which participants choose first a sentence, then a phrase, then a word from the case and/or commentaries that they read aloud without pause or comment (we stand in a circle, with everyone reading first their sentence, then going around the circle again to share the phrases, then finally the words—it sounds simple but can be surprisingly profound)
- introducing the case through "readers' theater," using scripts we have created for some of the dialogue-rich cases (see justiceinschools.org for "Walling Off" and "Politics" scripts, as well as scripts for other cases on the website)

We have been grateful, furthermore, to learn from many K–12 and university educators about other ways in which they have used cases to promote democratic deliberation and reflection in their work.[3] One common assignment is to have students write an original commentary, sometimes from their own perspective, and sometimes from the perspective of an assigned theorist (e.g. Rawls, Bourdieu, Noddings) or other scholar. We have seen terrific work from education students who interviewed teachers, principals, and guidance counselors about their views of a case and then wrote reflective essays. There are a number of creative ways to extend the case through role-playing. Participants may be asked to continue the dialogue past where the written case ends; or, somebody in a particular role may take an action (such as disciplining a teacher or supporting a student's choice to speak up about a controversial topic), with others then required to respond from their roles. We have seen powerful pre-service and in-service professional development in which participants were asked to apply their learning from a case discussion to their own dilemmas or cases, and even to write up cases with one another for future discussion and deliberation. Educators have also created lesson plans and taught these and other cases to their own middle and high school students. Depending on the teacher and their learning goals, they have used the cases in their full and unedited form, created abridged versions, introduced them through readers' theater, created fictional scenarios focused on middle or high school student protagonists, and "chunked" the cases so that students have the opportunity to pause and talk, track changes in their thinking, and check for understanding at determined points throughout the case.

Even the best lesson plan in the world, of course, does not guarantee success. As a wise veteran teacher reassured one of us when a class went badly early on in our teaching career, children (and adults) throw tantrums even at Disneyland. Furthermore, insofar as these cases tackle the quite profound tensions that can arise under conditions of democratic discord, it would be foolish for us to pretend that conversations about the cases will themselves never succumb to toxic hostility. We found it challenging to keep case discussions consistently productive in the first few months following President Trump's inauguration, for instance, as we grappled with the implications of his norm-shattering rhetoric and actions. Some of our students felt sufficiently threatened by his election, too, that they were disinclined to give others the benefit of the doubt when they expressed ideas that seemed ill thought out or even dangerous.

At the same time, our students recognized the importance—perhaps now more than ever—of crossing partisan boundaries, trying to understand others' experiences and perspectives, and creating spaces for mutually respectful dialogue. It is at times of greatest democratic discord that we are most in need of collective engagement. We recommend, therefore, that groups talk with one another up front about these challenges, and set norms for conversation at the start. Coming to know one another as people—with families, hopes and dreams, silly hobbies, pets—can also help to create a culture of mutual trust and respect. Finally, these cases and commentaries are themselves designed to provide tools for educators, policy makers, parents, and students to address contentious issues *before* they tear apart a community. That way, when a politically fraught decision does go wrong—or is interpreted by some as having done so—communities can draw upon their understanding of analogous events and recognize that this is an anticipated, even inevitable, feature of democratic life. They can also draw upon the dispositions toward collective engagement that they have developed in order both to address the immediate rupture and to continue the hard but necessary work of constructing a mutually rewarding democratic future.

Notes

FOREWORD

1. Philip Jackson, *Life in Classrooms* (New York: Holt, Rinehart, and Winston, 1968), 149.
2. Herbert R. Kohl, *The Discipline of Hope: Learning from a Lifetime of Teaching* (New York: Simon & Schuster, 1998).
3. John Rogers et al., *Teaching and Learning in the Age of Trump: Increasing Stress and Hostility in America's High Schools* (Los Angeles: UCLA Institute for Democracy, Education, and Access, 2017), https://idea.gseis.ucla.edu/publications/teaching-and-learning-in-age-of-trump.
4. Marcelo Suárez-Orozco, Carola Suárez-Orozco, and Adam Strom, "A Lesson in Civility: The Negativity Immigrant Students Hear," *Kappan Online*, http://www.kappanonline.org/suarez-orozco-stroma-lesson-in-civility-immigrant-students-negativity.
5. Facing History and Ourselves, *Eyes on the Prize: America's Civil Rights Movement 1954–1985* (Boston: Blackside, 2006), https://www.facinghistory.org/books-borrowing/eyes-prize-study-guide.

CHAPTER 1 (Schools Of, By, and For the People)

1. For a fuller account of the effects of fast norm-shifting on educators, see Meira Levinson and Ellis Reid, "The Paradox of Partisanship," *On Education. Journal for Research and Debate*, 1, no. 1, 2018, https://www.oneducation.net/no-01-march-2018/the-paradox-of-partisanship or doi: 10.17899/on_ed.2018.1.3.
2. Bill Bishop, *The Big Sort: Why the Clustering of Like-Minded America is Tearing Us Apart* (New York: Mariner Books, 2009); Diana Hess and Paula McAvoy, *The Political Classroom* (New York: Routledge, 2014); Cass Sunstein, *#Republic: Divided Democracy in the Age of Social Media* (Princeton, NJ: Princeton University Press, 2017).
3. Hess and McAvoy, *The Political Classroom*, 4.
4. Meira Levinson, *No Citizen Left Behind* (Cambridge, MA: Harvard University Press, 2012).

5. Danielle Allen, *Education and Equality* (Chicago: University of Chicago Press, 2016); Peter Levine, *We Are the Ones We Have Been Waiting For* (New York: Oxford University Press, 2013); David E. Campbell, Meira Levinson, and Frederick M. Hess, eds., *Making Civics Count* (Cambridge, MA: Harvard Education Press, 2012); Levinson, *No Citizen.*
6. John Dewey, "Education and Social Change," in *The Collected Works of John Dewey, 1882–1953: Electronic edition* (1937/1987).
7. Meira Levinson discusses the first of these dilemmas in chapter 5 of *No Citizen Left Behind.*
8. Meira Levinson and Jacob Fay, eds., *Dilemmas of Educational Ethics: Cases and Commentaries* (Cambridge, MA: Harvard Education Press, 2016), 3–4.
9. Jal Mehta, "Toward Pragmatic Educational Ethics," in Levinson and Fay, eds., *Dilemmas*, 18.

CHAPTER 2 (Walling Off or Welcoming In?)

This case is a work of fiction, inspired by our own experiences in classrooms, discussions with current classroom teachers, survey data collected by *Teaching Tolerance*, and media coverage of political tensions in schools. See Maureen B. Costello, "The Trump Effect: The Impact of the Presidential Campaign on Our Nation's Schools," *Teaching the 2016 Election* (Montgomery, AL: Southern Poverty Law Center, 2016), https://www.splcenter.org/20160413/trump-effect-impact-presidential-campaign-our-nations-schools.

1. See "Anti-Bullying," New Jersey Education Association (NJEA), http://www.njea.org/issues-and-political-action/anti-bullying. New Jersey's Harassment, Intimidation, and Bullying law defines these terms as "any gesture, any written, verbal or physical act, or any electronic communication, whether it be a single incident or series of incidents, that is reasonably perceived as being motivated either by any actual or perceived characteristic . . . that takes place on school property, at any school-sponsored function, on a school bus, or off school grounds . . . that substantially disrupts or interferes with the orderly operation of the school or the rights of other students, and that a reasonable person should know, under the circumstances, will have the effect of physically or emotionally harming a student or damaging a student's property, or placing a student in reasonable fear of physical or emotional harm to his person or damage [to] his property." The law creates an extensive accountability framework that requires, for example, all school employees or those under contract to report qualifying incidents to the principal on the day of the incident, and requires the New Jersey Department of Education to assign a grade to each school based on reported incidents of harassment, intimidation, and bullying.
2. See "We The People," Amplifier, https://amplifier.org/wethepeople/ for images of the posters, which Shepard Fairey created for the 2017 Women's March following President Trump's Inauguration.

3. See Dana Liebelson, "School Asks Teachers To Take Down Pro-Diversity Posters, Saying They're 'Anti-Trump,'" *HuffPost*, February 21, 2017, http://www.huffingtonpost.com/entry/school-pro-diversity-posters-trump_us_58ac87b9e4b0e784faa21446.
4. Maureen B. Costello, *The Trump Effect: The Impact of the Presidential Campaign on Our Nation's Schools*, and *After Election Day: The Trump Effect* (Montgomery, AL: Southern Poverty Law Center, 2016), https://www.tolerance.org/magazine/publications/the-trump-effect-spring-2016 and https://www.tolerance.org/magazine/publications/after-election-day-the-trump-effect; John Rogers et al., *Teaching and Learning in the Age of Trump: Increasing Stress and Hostility in America's Schools* (Los Angeles, CA: UCLA Institute for Democracy, Education, and Access, 2017).
5. "Charles Murray," Southern Poverty Law Center, https://www.splcenter.org/fighting-hate/extremist-files/individual/charles-murray.
6. James A. Banks, "Improving Race Relations in Schools: From Theory and Research to Practice," *Journal of Social Issues* 62, no. 3 (2006), 607–14; Walter G. Stephan and Cookie White Stephan, "Intergroup Relations in Multicultural Education Programs," in *Handbook of Research on Multicultural Education, Second Edition*, ed. James A. Banks and Cherry A. McGee Banks (San Francisco, CA: Jossey-Bass, 2004), 782–98.
7. Samuel L. Gaertner et al., "Across Cultural Divides: The Value of Superordinate Identity," in *Cultural Divides: Understanding and Overcoming Group Conflict*, ed. Deborah A. Prentice and Dale T. Miller (New York: Russell Sage Foundation, 1999), 173–212.
8. Elizabeth G. Cohen and Rachel A. Lotan, *Designing Groupwork: Strategies for the Heterogeneous Classroom, Third Edition* (New York, NY: Teachers College Press, 2014).
9. Gordon Allport, *The Nature of Prejudice, 25th Anniversary Edition* (Reading, MA: Addison-Wesley, 1979/1954).
10. Elizabeth G. Cohen and Rachel A. Lotan, "Producing Equal-Status Interaction in the Heterogeneous Classroom," *American Educational Research Journal* 32 (1995): 99–120.
11. Robert E. Slavin, "Cooperative Learning and Intergroup Relations," in *Handbook of Research on Multicultural Education*, ed. James A. Banks and Cherry A. McGee Banks (New York: Macmillan, 1995), 628–46.
12. Frances E. Aboud, "Modifying Children's Racial Attitudes," in *The Routledge International Companion to Multicultural Education*, ed. James A. Banks (New York: Routledge, 2009), 199–209.
13. See Banks, "Improving Race Relations," and Aboud, "Modifying Children's Racial Attitudes."
14. James A. Banks, *An Introduction to Multicultural Education, Sixth Edition* (New York: Pearson, 2019).

15. Banks, *Introduction to Multicultural Education.*

CHAPTER 3 (School Walkouts and Civil Disobedience)

This case is constructed from real events. Names, dates, figures, and quotations have been collected from online media sources. We are deeply thankful for the work of the *Oregonian/OregonLive*, Oregon Public Broadcasting, *Willamette Week*, KGW.com Portland, *Portland Mercury*, the *Portland Tribune*, *FightBack!News*, KOIN 6, the *Seattle Times*, KING 5 Seattle, and Seattle Wishesh.

1. Nina Mehlhaf, "PPS Students Stage Mass Walkout to Protest Trump Election," KGW 8, November 14, 2016, https://www.kgw.com/article/news/pps-students-stage-mass-walkout-to-protest-trump-election/283-351794630.
2. Rob Manning and Bryan M. Vance, "PPS Students Walk Out in Protest of Donald Trump's Election," Oregon Public Broadcasting, November 14, 2016, http://www.opb.org/news/article/portland-public-schools-walkout-protest-donald-trump/.
3. "Students Walk Out of School, March Through Portland," *The Oregonian/OregonLive*, November 14, 2016, http://www.oregonlive.com/portland/index.ssf/2016/11/students_walk_out_of_school_pr.html.
4. Casey Parks, "Fed Up with Anti-Latino Sentiment, Hundreds of Portland High Schoolers Leave Class," *The Oregonian/OregonLive*, May 23, 2016, http://www.oregonlive.com/education/index.ssf/2016/05/portland_latino_students_prote.html.
5. Nicole Dungca, "'Save Our Core': Da Vinci Middle School Students Walk Out to Protest Changes," *The Oregonian/OregonLive*, May 20, 2014, http://www.oregonlive.com/portland/index.ssf/2014/05/save_our_core_da_vinci_middle.html; Nicole Dungca, "Wilson High School Students Walk Out in Support of Teachers: PPS News," *The Oregonian/OregonLive*, December 13, 2013, http://www.oregonlive.com/portland/index.ssf/2013/12/wilson_high_school_students_wa.html; Nicole Dungca, "Cleveland High School Students Protest Standardized Testing," *The Oregonian/OregonLive*, April 18, 2013, http://www.oregonlive.com/portland/index.ssf/2013/04/cleveland_high_school_students.html; Chapin Gray, "Student Anti-war Protests Sweep U.S.," *FightBack!News*, March 23, 2008, http://www.fightbacknews.org/2008/03/studentantiwarprotests.htm; https://archive.org/details/WalkOutHighSchoolPortland2008AntiWar.
6. Trevor Ault and Emily Sinovic, "#NotMyPresident Student Protesters March, Block Traffic," KOIN 6, November 14, 2016, http://koin.com/2016/11/14/students-protest-trump-at-pioneer-square/.
7. "Students Walk Out of School, March Through Portland."
8. Dungca, "Wilson High School Students Walk Out."
9. Bethany Barnes, "Emails Show Tension, Rifts in Wake of Lincoln High's Walkout Over Bond Delay," *The Oregonian/OregonLive*, October 10, 2016,

http://www.oregonlive.com/education/index.ssf/2016/10/emails_show_tension_rifts_in_w.html.
10. Barnes, "Emails Show Tension."
11. Wm. Steven Humphrey, "Portland High School Kids Are Skipping School to Protest Trump," Blogtown (blog), *Portland Mercury*, November 14, 2016, http://www.portlandmercury.com/blogtown/2016/11/14/18693932/portland-high-school-kids-are-skipping-school-to-protest-trump.
12. Max Norman, "Walkout Increased Student Divide," *Portland Tribune*, June 1, 2016, http://portlandtribune.com/fgnt/37-opinion/309729-187473-walkout-increased-student-divide.
13. Samantha Swindler, "Student Protests About More Than Just a Banner," *The Oregonian/OregonLive*, May 25, 2016, http://www.oregonlive.com/washingtoncounty/index.ssf/2016/05/student_protests_about_more_th.html.
14. Swindler, "Student Protests."
15. Swindler, "Student Protests."
16. Shasta Kearns Moore, "Records: PPS Board Member, Principal Were in Feud over Lincoln Walk-out," *Portland Tribune*, October 10, 2016, http://portlandtribune.com/pt/9-news/326707-206009-records-pps-board-member-principal-were-in-feud-over-lincoln-walk-out.
17. Shuly Wasserstrom, "PPS: 'Outside Organizations' Encouraging Protests," KOIN 6, November 21, 2016, http://koin.com/2016/11/21/pps-outside-organizations-encouraging-protests/.
18. Nicole Dungca, "Cleveland High School Senior: Students Will Stand on the Picket Line with Teachers if Strikes Come," *The Oregonian/OregonLive*, January 15, 2014, https://www.oregonlive.com/portland/index.ssf/2014/01/cleveland_high_school_senior_s.html.
19. Mehlhaf, "PPS Students Stage Mass Walkout."
20. Tim Becker, "Middle Schoolers Walk Out to Protest Teacher Leaving," KOIN 6, October 5, 2016, http://koin.com/2016/10/05/middle-schoolers-walk-out-to-protest-teacher-leaving/.
21. Tombdragon, November 23, 2016 (11:48 a.m.), comment on Tony Hernandez, "Student Protesters Dispute Police, School District Statements," *The Oregonian/OregonLive*, November 22, 2016, http://www.oregonlive.com/portland/index.ssf/2016/11/student_protesters_dispute_pol.html.
22. Jared Cowley and Sara Roth, "Portland Public Schools Defend Lockout at Benson High School," KGW 8, September 13, 2016, http://www.kgw.com/news/education/asb-leaders-criticize-pps-for-benson-high-lockout-during-walkout/317245966.
23. Moore, "PPS Board Member, Principal Were in Feud."
24. Rachel Monahan, "Benson, Lincoln Student Leaders: District Official 'Must be Held Accountable' for Lockout," *Willamette Week*, September 12, 2016, http://www.wweek.com/news/2016/09/12/benson-lincoln-student-leaders-district-officials-must-be-held-accountable-for-lockout/.

25. Bethany Barnes, "Portland Public Schools Ordered Lockout as Lincoln High Protesters Headed to Benson," *The Oregonian/OregonLive*, September 9, 2016, http://www.oregonlive.com/education/index.ssf/2016/09/portland_public_schools_called.html.
26. Mehlhaf, "PPS Students Stage Mass Walkout."
27. "School Board Voices Support for Rights of Students," Des Moines Public Schools, http://www.dmschools.org/2016/11/school-board-voices-support-for-rights-of-students/.
28. Associated Press, "Thousands of Seattle Students Walk Out of School to Protest Trump," *Los Angeles Times*, November 14, 2016, http://www.latimes.com/nation/nationnow/la-na-seattle-trump-protest-20161114-story.html; Elisa Hahn, "Seattle Students May Walk Out Monday in Protest," KING 5, November 12, 2016, http://www.king5.com/news/local/seattle/seattle-students-may-walk-out-monday-in-protest/351120016.
29. Hahn, "Seattle Students May Walk Out Monday in Protest."
30. "Responding to School Walkout Demonstrations," *Lessons Learned from School Crises and Emergencies* 3, no. 1 (2008), Readiness and Emergency Management for Schools Technical Assistance Center, https://rems.ed.gov/docs/LL_Vol3Issue1.pdf.
31. Moore, "PPS Board Member, Principal Were in Feud."
32. Portland Student Action Network's Facebook page, accessed January 17, 2016, https://www.facebook.com/pg/portlandstudentactionnetwork/about/?ref=page_internal.
33. PSAN Facebook page, accessed July 26, 2017, https://www.facebook.com/events/409041256106119.
34. PSAN Facebook page, accessed July 26, 2017, https://www.facebook.com/pg/portlandstudentactionnetwork/about/?ref=page_internal.
35. Casey Michel, "How Liberal Portland Became America's Most Politically Violent City," *Politico*, June 30, 2017, http://www.politico.com/magazine/story/2017/06/30/how-liberal-portland-became-americas-most-politically-violent-city-215322.
36. This case was distributed to commentators in July 2017 and for fidelity's sake has not been updated since. It is important to note, however, that following the horrific February 2018 school shooting in Parkland, Florida, students across the nation (and globe) organized school walkouts to protest gun violence and support gun control reform. In March and April 2018, hundreds of thousands of students—perhaps as many as a million K–12 students—organized and participated in school walkouts in thousands of schools across the country.
37. Shawn Ginwright and Julio Cammarota, introduction to *Beyond Resistance! Youth Activism and Community Change: New Democratic Possibilites for Practice and Policy*, ed. Shawn Ginwright, Pedro Noguera, and Julio Cammarota (New York: Routledge, 2006), xiii–xxii; Anne Ríos-Rojas, "Beyond Delinquent

Citizenships: Immigrant Youth's (Re)Visions of Citizenship and Belonging in a Globalized World," *Harvard Educational Review* 80, no. 1 (April 2011): 64–94; Beth C. Rubin, "'There's Still Not Justice': Youth Civic Identity Development Amid Distinct School and Community Contexts," *Teachers College Record* 109, no. 2 (February 2007): 449–81.

38. Michelle J. Bellino, *Youth in Postwar Guatemala: Education and Civic Identity in Transition* (New Brunswick, NJ: Rutgers University Press, 2017).
39. Thea R. Abu El-Haj, *Unsettled Belonging: Educating Palestinian American Youth After 9/11* (Chicago: University of Chicago Press, 2015).
40. Constance A. Flanagan et al., "Schools and Social Trust," in *Handbook of Research on Civic Engagement in Youth*, ed. Lonnie R. Sherrod, Judith Torney-Purta, and Constance A. Flanagan (Hoboken, NJ: Wiley, 2010), 307–29.
41. Bradley A. U. Levinson, "Citizenship, Identity, Democracy: Engaging the Political in the Anthropology of Education," *Anthropology & Education Quarterly* 36, no. 4 (December 2005): 329–40.
42. Joel Westheimer and Joseph Kahne, "What Kind of Citizen?: The Politics of Educating for Democracy," *American Educational Research Journal* 41, no. 2 (January 2004): 237–69.
43. Meira Levinson, *No Citizen Left Behind* (Cambridge, MA: Harvard University Press, 2012).
44. Michelle J. Bellino, "The Risks We Are Willing to Take: Youth Civic Development in 'Postwar' Guatemala," *Harvard Educational Review* 85, no. 4 (Winter 2015): 537–61.
45. Levinson, *No Citizen Left Behind*; Roderick J. Watts, Matthew A. Diemer, and Adam M. Voight, "Critical Consciousness: Current Status and Future Directions," in *Youth Civic Development: Work at the Cutting Edge: New Directions for Child and Adolescent Development, Number 134*, ed. Constance A. Flanagan and Brian D. Christens (San Francisco, CA: Wiley, 2011), 43–57.
46. Thea R. Abu El-Haj, "Becoming Citizens in an Era of Globalization and Transnational Migration: Re-imagining Citizenship as Critical Practice," *Theory Into Practice* 48, no. 4 (Fall 2009): 274–82; James A. Banks, "Diversity, Group Identity, and Citizenship Education in a Global Age," *Educational Researcher* 37, no. 3 (April 2008): 129–39; Peter Levine and Karol E. Soltan, eds., *Civic Studies: Approaches to the Emerging Field* (Washington, DC: Bringing Theory to Practice, 2014).
47. Nathan Heller, "The Big Uneasy," *New Yorker*, May 30, 2016: 48–55.
48. Harry C. Boyte et al., *Awakening Democracy Through Public Work: Pedagogies of Empowerment* (Nashville, TN: Vanderbilt University Press, 2018).
49. Marie Ström, introduction to *Taking the Lead: Ordinary People, Extraordinary Stories*, by Jenni Samdaan, Marie-Louise Ström, and Jo Tyler (Cape Town, South Africa: IDASA.

50. Nomthi Skhosana, quoted in "Making a Real Difference: Nomthi Skhosana and the Vukani Community Development Organization," in *Taking the Lead: Ordinary People, Extraordinary Stories*, 44–45.
51. Ronald Koziol and Peter Negronida, "Drop School Boycott, Dr. Redmond Urges," *Chicago Tribune*, October 18, 1968; James Redmond, in *Proceedings: Board of Education of the City of Chicago* 1 (July 10, 1968–December 26, 1968): 700–704; Dionne Danns, *Something Better for Our Children: Black Organizing in Chicago Public Schools, 1963–1971* (New York: Routledge, 2003), 80–86.
52. Admittedly, middle school children may be too immature to assess risks and adequately react to them. Helping them cultivate such skills might not be the best use of their time at their developmental stage.

CHAPTER 4 (The Price of Safety)

This case is a work of fiction, inspired by the research of Jennifer Chacón and by news coverage of similar challenges facing communities around the US. We are grateful to Carlos Aguilar, Jay Lee, and Sarah Mehrota for outstanding research assistance, and to Carlos Aguilar, Stephany Cuevas, Deborah Jewell-Sherman, Paul Reville, Irvin Scott, Elizabeth City, Ellis Reid, Jacob Fay, and students in Harvard's 2017 PhD in Education Proseminar for their feedback on prior drafts of the case.

1. This program is based on the Gang Resistance Education and Training Program, a national program that is an active partner with the Office of Juvenile Justice and Delinquency Prevention. Dana Peterson et al., "National Evaluation of the Gang Resistance Education and Training (G.R.E.A.T.) Program: School Personnel Survey Report" (St. Louis, MO: University of Missouri-St. Louis, 2009), https://www.great-online.org/About/Evaluation#_ftn2.
2. Peterson, 35.
3. Gang Resistance Education And Training Program, Middle School Component, https://www.great-online.org/Home/About/MiddleSchool.
4. See Office of the Attorney General of Florida, "Florida Gang Reduction Strategy 2008–2012," http://www.floridagangreduction.com/webfiles.nsf/WF/KGRG-7FVPNR/$file/GangReductionReportWEB.pdf.
5. This is a paraphrase of Detective Sergeant Michael Morino, Nassau County Police Department's gang investigation squad commanding officer, as quoted in Dan Lieberman, "MS-13 members: Trump makes the gang stronger," CNN, July 28, 2017, https://www.cnn.com/2017/07/28/us/ms-13-gang-long-island-trump/index.html.
6. Chongmin Na and Denise C. Gottfredson, "Police Officers in Schools: Effects on School Crime and the Processing of Offending Behaviors," *Justice Quarterly* 30, no. 4 (2011): 619–50, doi:10.1080/07418825.2011.615754.
7. "Delegation of Immigration Authority Section 287(g) Immigration and

Nationality Act," Immigration and Customs Enforcement (US Department of Homeland Security, 2018), https://www.ice.gov/287g.

8. Stephen Kang, "The Trump Administration Is Detaining Immigrant Kids for Gang Membership Without Evidence. So We Sued," *ACLU blog*, August 14, 2017, https://www.aclu.org/blog/immigrants-rights/immigrants-rights-and-detention/trump-administration-detaining-immigrant-kids.
9. Jennifer M. Chacon, "Students and the Deportation Machine" (unpublished manuscript, accessed July 2017), Microsoft Word file.
10. *FERPA General Guidance for Parents* (US Department of Education, 2015), https://www2.ed.gov/policy/gen/guid/fpco/ferpa/parents.html.
11. *Plyler v. Doe*, 457 US 220 (1982).
12. *Plyler v. Doe*, 221.
13. Aaron Kupchik and Geoff Ward, "Race, Poverty, and Exclusionary School Security: An Empirical Analysis of US Elementary, Middle and High Schools," *Youth Violence and Juvenile Justice* 12, no. 4 (September 2013): 332–354.
14. Kupchik and Ward.
15. *Vernonia School District 47J v. Acton*, 515 US 646 (1995), finding no Fourth Amendment violation in the school's random drug testing of high school student athletes; *Board of Ed. of Independent School Dist. No. 92 of Pottawatomie Cty. v. Earls*, 536 US 822 (2002), finding no Fourth Amendment violation in the school's random drug testing of high school students participating in extra-curricular activities; *Safford Unified School District v. Redding*, 557 US 364 (2009), explaining that a warrantless strip search of a student could be performed by school officials upon suspicion of danger or of a "resort to underwear" to hide drug evidence.
16. Kupchik and Ward, "Race, Poverty, and Exclusionary School Security."
17. Nicole L. Bracy, "Circumventing the Law: Students Rights in Schools with Police," *Journal of Contemporary Criminal Justice* 26 (2010): 294; Aaron Kupchik, *Homeroom Security: School Discipline in an Age of Fear* (New York: New York University Press, 2010), 11.
18. Kupchik, *Homeroom Security*, 8.
19. Patrick Lopez-Aguado, *Stick Together and Come Back Home: Racial Sorting and the Spillover of Carceral Identity* (Berkeley: University of California Press, 2018), 3–4 (discussing the attachment and enforcement of racialized gang labeling in spaces of incarceration and the transmission of the resulting labels and logics to contexts outside of those spaces); see also Victor Rios, *Punished: Policing the Lives of Black and Latino Boys* (New York: New York University Press, 2011), 44–46 (discussing processes of criminalization).
20. Rob Nixon et al., "Trump Targets MS-13, a Violent Menace, if Not the One He Portrays," *New York Times*, March 2, 2018.
21. Victor E. Kappeler, "A Brief History of Slavery and the Origins of American Policing," *Police Studies Online*, January 7, 2014, https://plsonline.eku.edu/insidelook/brief-history-slavery-and-origins-american-policing.

22. Patrick Wolfe, "Settler Colonialism and the Elimination of the Native," *Journal of Genocide Research* 8, no. 4 (2006): 387–409.
23. Ruth W. Gilmore, *Golden Gulag: Prisons, Surplus, Crisis, and Opposition in Globalizing California* (Berkeley: University of California Press, 2007), 28.
24. Kathleen M. O'Toole, "The Garda Inspectorate: Driving Collaborative Reform Through a Model of Equilibrated Governance" (PhD diss., Dublin, Ireland: Trinity College, 2018).
25. David W. Parker, Melanie Holesgrove, and Raghuvar Pathak, "Improving Productivity with Self-Organised Teams and Agile Leadership," *International Journal of Productivity and Performance Management* 64, no. 1 (2015): 112–28.
26. Matthew R. Kutz, "Toward a Conceptual Model of Contextual Intelligence: A Transferable Leadership Construct," *Kravis Leadership Institute, Leadership Review* 8 (2008): 18–31.
27. Joseph Carens, *The Ethics of Immigration* (Oxford: Oxford University Press, 2013), 133.
28. As Amartya Sen has argued in *A Theory of Justice* (London: Allen Lane, 2009), we do not always need to know what the correct account of justice is to know when we can make an improvement in justice from the nonideal circumstances we find ourselves in. That said, we still need to work out what ideal justice would involve to know the strength of people's complaint against injustice. See Zofia Stemplowska, "Nonideal Theory," in *A Companion to Applied Philosophy*, ed. Kasper Lippert-Rasmussen, Kimberly Brownlee, and David Coady (Oxford: Wiley-Blackwell Publishing, 2017).
29. Criminal Alien Gang Member Removal Act, H.R. 3697, 115th Cong. (2017), https://www.congress.gov/bill/115th-congress/house-bill/3697/text/ih.
30. Victor Rios, *Human Targets: Schools, Police, and the Criminalization of Latino Youth* (Chicago: University of Chicago Press, 2017), 19.
31. Robert Garot, *Who You Claim: Performing Gang Identity in Schools and on the Streets* (New York: New York University Press, 2010).
32. Martin Jankowski, *Islands in the Streets: Gangs and American Urban Society* (Berkeley: University of California Press, 1991).
33. Howard Becker, *Outsiders: Studies in the Sociology of Deviance* (New York: Free Press, 1963).
34. Rios, *Human Targets.*
35. Angela Harris, "Gender, Violence, Race, and Criminal Justice," *Stanford Law Review* 52, no. 4 (April 2000): 777–807.
36. Avery Gordon, *Ghostly Matters: Hauntings and the Sociological Imagination* (Minneapolis: University of Minnesota Press, 1997).

CHAPTER 5 (Eyes in the Back of Their Heads 2.0)

1. Although experts disagree about the extent to which children's online exposure is to blame, they concur that children are at serious risk: 20 percent of students have been diagnosed with serious mental health challenges such as depression

and eating disorders, while suicide rates have increased 30 percent for boys, and 100 percent for girls, in just the past decade. See "National Survey Confirms that Youth are Disproportionately Affected by Mental Disorders," National Institute of Mental Health, September 27, 2010, https://www.nimh.nih.gov/news/science-news/2010/national-survey-confirms-that-youth-are-disproportionately-affected-by-mental-disorders.shtml; Traci Pedersen, "Teens Disproportionately Affected by Mental Disorders," *Psych Central*, October 6, 2015, https://psychcentral.com/news/2010/09/29/teens-disproportionately-affected-by-mental-disorders/18922.html; Lindsay Holmes, "Suicide Rates for Teen Boys and Girls are Climbing," *Huffington Post*, August 04, 2017, https://www.huffingtonpost.com/entry/suicide-rates-teen-girls_us_59848b64e4b0cb15b1be13f4.

2. Emily Suski, "Beyond the Schoolhouse Gates: The Unprecedented Expansion of School Surveillance Authority Under Cyberbullying Laws," *Case Western Reserve Law Review* 65, no. 1 (2014): 63–119.
3. Stopbullying.gov, "Laws & Policies," last modified September 8, 2017, https://www.stopbullying.gov/laws/index.html.
4. Suski, "Beyond the Schoolhouse Gates."
5. See, for instance, "Jury Verdicts and Settlements in Bullying Cases," last modified December 2017, https://www.publicjustice.net/wp-content/uploads/2016/02/2017.06.12-Spring-Edition-Bullying-Verdicts-and-Settlements-Final.pdf.
6. "Analysis of School Shootings," Everytown Research, https://everytownresearch.org/reports/analysis-of-school-shootings/.
7. "Issues and Controversies: Bullying," *Facts on File*, Infobase Learning, August 18, 2015, http://www.wtps.org/cms/lib8/NJ01912980/Centricity/Domain/745/Issues%20And%20Controversies%20article.pdf.
8. "Real-Life Success Stories: Reviews and Testimonials," GoGuardian, https://www.goguardian.com/success-stories.html.
9. This does not include other forms of student surveillance that are independent of students' computers or tablets, such as: video surveillance inside and outside schools and on school buses; RFID-enabled student IDs that can track student attendance, student meal purchases, and students' locations within the school building or on the bus; and facial recognition software attached to digital video cameras.
10. "Real-Life Success Stories."
11. "Real-Life Success Stories."
12. Zach Spitulski, "How Content-Based Filtering Helps Shape Student Behavior," *GoGuardian Blog*, April 06, 2018, http://blog.goguardian.com/how-content-based-filtering-helps-shape-student-behavior.
13. School Network and Computer Lab Management Software, Impero Software (US), https://www.imperosoftware.com/us/; see also "Support Positive Digital Citizenship Through Real Time Monitoring," *Impero Software Blog*, April 30, 2018, https://www.imperosoftware.com/us/blog/support-positive-digital-citizenship-real-time-monitoring/.

14. "White Paper: Digital Citizenship: A Holistic Primer," Impero Software and Digital Citizenship Institute, October 28, 2016, http://www.digitalcitizenshipinstitute.com/wp-content/uploads/2016/10/digital-citizenship-a-holistic-primer-v2-1.pdf.
15. "Keyword Detection Libraries," Impero Software, https://www.imperosoftware.com/be/products/education-pro/keyword-libraries/.
16. See, for instance, the network administrator's testimony on p. 2 of Impero Software's "Impero Education Pro Case Study Spencerport Central School District US," https://www.imperosoftware.com/us/resources/case-studies/spencerport-central-school-district/.
17. "Support Positive Digital Citizenship," Impero Software; "Student Suicide and Self Harm Prevention," GoGuardian, https://www.goguardian.com/suicide-self-harm-resources.html; Larry Magid, "School Software Walks the Line Between Safety Monitor and 'Parent Over Shoulder,'" *Forbes*, April 14, 2016, https://www.forbes.com/sites/larrymagid/2016/04/14/straddling-the-line-between-spying-and-protecting-students.
18. "Frequently Asked Questions (FAQs) for Educators and Parents," Gaggle, https://www.gaggle.net/frequently-asked-questions.
19. Natasha Singer, "How Google Took Over the Classroom," *New York Times*, May 13, 2017, https://www.nytimes.com/2017/05/13/technology/google-education-chromebooks-schools.html.
20. "Frequently Asked Questions," Gaggle.
21. "Round Rock Independent School District: Gaggle Success Story," Gaggle, https://www.gaggle.net/success-stories/round-rock-independent-school-district/.
22. "SchoolVue EMS eSafety and IT Asset Management," SchoolVue, https://www.crosstecsoftware.com/schoolvueems.
23. "SchoolVue EMS eSafety," SchoolVue.
24. "Impero's Confide System Explained," *Impero Software Blog*, March 13, 2017, https://www.imperosoftware.com/uk/blog/imperos-confide-system-explained/.
25. "Detecting Radicalisation and Extremism in Schools: Impero," *Impero Software Blog*, March 13, 2017, https://www.imperosoftware.com/uk/blog/detecting-extremism-and-radicalisation-in-schools/.
26. Kendra Gravelle, "Schools Examine Privacy Issues with 1:1 Initiative," *Narragansett Times*, June 11, 2017, http://www.ricentral.com/narragansett_times/schools-examine-privacy-issues-with-initiative/article_e4ffa9b8-4d2d-11e7-a396-afa7c65c2324.html.
27. "School Policies and Regulations Expose Massachusetts Students to Risk of Serious Privacy Violations," ACLU Massachusetts, October 25, 2015, https://www.aclu.org/news/school-policies-and-regulations-expose-massachusetts-students-risk-serious-privacy-violations.
28. See Clive Norris and Gary Armstrong, *The Maximum Surveillance Society: The Rise of CCTV*, Vol. 2 (Oxford: Berg, 1999); Victor M. Rios, *Punished: Policing the Lives of Black and Latino Boys* (New York: New York University

Press, 2011); Walter S. Gilliam et al., "Do Early Educators' Implicit Biases Regarding Sex and Race Relate to Behavior Expectations and Recommendations of Preschool Expulsions and Suspensions," (Yale University Child Study Center research brief, presented at the US Administration for Children and Families 2016 State and Territory Administrators Meeting, Alexandria, VA, September 28, 2016); Caitlin Curley, "How Profiling in Schools Feeds the School-to-Prison Pipeline," *GenFKD*, August 03, 2016, http://www.genfkd.org/profiling-schools-feeds-school-prison-pipeline.

29. Faiza Patel and Meghan Koushik, "Countering Violent Extremism," *Brennan Center for Justice* (New York: Brennan Center for Justice, 2017): 17, https://www.brennancenter.org/sites/default/files/publications/Brennan%20Center%20CVE%20Report.pdf.
30. See, e.g., Thea Renda Abu El-Haj, "'I Was Born Here, but My Home, It's Not Here': Educating for Democratic Citizenship in an Era of Transnational Migration and Global Conflict," *Harvard Educational Review* 77, no. 3 (2008): 285–316, doi:10.17763/haer.77.3.412l7m737q114h5m; Thea Renda Abu El-Haj, Anne Ríos-Rojas, and Reva Jaffe-Walter, "Whose Race Problem? Tracking Patterns of Racial Denial in US and European Educational Discourses on Muslim Youth," *Curriculum Inquiry*, 47, no. 3 (2017): 310–35, doi:10.1080/03626784.2017.1324736.
31. "Keyword Detection Libraries," Impero Software.
32. Simon Hooper, "UK: Keyword Warning Software in Schools Raises Red Flag," *Al Jazeera*, October 04, 2015, https://www.aljazeera.com/indepth/features/2015/10/uk-keyword-warning-software-schools-raises-red-flag-151004081940435.html.
33. "U.S. Sees 300 Violent Attacks Inspired by Far Right Every Year," *PBS NewsHour*, August 13, 2017, https://www.pbs.org/newshour/show/u-s-sees-300-violent-attacks-inspired-far-right-every-year; "A Dark and Constant Rage: 25 Years of Right-Wing Terrorism in the United States," Anti-Defamation League, https://www.adl.org/education/resources/reports/dark-constant-rage-25-years-of-right-wing-terrorism-in-united-states.
34. Anya Kamenetz, "When a School's Online Eavesdropping Can Prevent a Suicide," *NPR*, December 23, 2016, https://www.npr.org/sections/ed/2016/12/23/504709648/when-a-schools-online-eavesdropping-can-prevent-a-suicide.
35. "There's More Than Homework in Students' Google Drive Microsoft OneDrive Accounts," *Gaggle Speaks Blog*, November 21, 2017, https://www.gaggle.net/speaks/theres-more-than-homework-in-students-drive-accounts/.
36. "There's More Than Homework," Gaggle.
37. The Massachusetts ACLU has found, for instance, that seventeen of the eighteen school districts they investigated reported having contracts with private vendors to view and use student data. See Kade Crockford and Jessie. J. Rossman, "Back to the Drawing Board: Student Privacy in Massachusetts K–12 Schools," ACLU Massachusetts, October 28, 2015, https://aclum.org/wp-content/uploads/2015/10/back_to_the_drawing_board_report_large_file_size.pdf.

38. Kamenetz, "School's Online Eavesdropping."
39. Kamenetz, "School's Online Eavesdropping." Those who receive threat alerts may not even realize that assessing individual students' risk is now part of their job. One IT director didn't know that his monitoring software analyzed for suicidal ideation, for instance, until he began receiving alerts about a student's browsing patterns.
40. "New Future Privacy Forum Survey Shows Parents Overwhelmingly Support Using Student Data to Improve Education; Concerns About Privacy and Security Remain," Future of Privacy Forum, September 21, 2015, http://www.futureofprivacy.org/2015/09/21/new-fpf-survey-shows-parentsoverwhelmingly-support-using-student-data-to-improve-education.
41. Crockford and Rossman, "Back to the Drawing Board."
42. Michael Goot, "Family Questions Student Privacy," *PostStar*, November 14, 2015, https://poststar.com/news/local/family-questions-student-privacy/article_4df061d2-f710-5d66-a817-a9d218a05aec.html.
43. Gilliam et al., "Early Educators' Implicit Biases."
44. Julia Angwin et al., "Machine Bias," *ProPublica*, May 23, 2016, https://www.propublica.org/article/machine-bias-risk-assessments-in-criminal-sentencing.
45. V. John Ella, "Employee Monitoring and Workplace Privacy Law," American Bar Association, April 2016, https://www.americanbar.org/content/dam/aba/events/labor_law/2016/04/tech/papers/monitoring_ella.authcheckdam.pdf.
46. Ella, "Employee Monitoring."
47. "Frequently Asked Questions," Gaggle. This stance is not confined to Gaggle. In its investigation of Massachusetts districts, the ACLU found that schools "almost universally claim that students do not have an expectation of privacy when using school networks" and two-thirds of the districts maintained that teachers and administrators "reserve the right to search or inspect [school-issued devices] without notice or consent." See ACLU, "School Policies and Regulations."
48. Barton Gellman and Ashkan Soltani, "NSA Infiltrates Links to Yahoo, Google Data Centers Worldwide, Snowden Documents Say," *Washington Post*, October 30, 2013, https://www.washingtonpost.com/world/national-security/nsa-infiltrates-links-to-yahoo-google-data-centers-worldwide-snowden-documents-say/2013/10/30/e51d661e-4166-11e3-8b74-d89d714ca4dd_story.html; "One Month, Hundreds of Millions of Records Collected," *Washington Post*, https://apps.washingtonpost.com/g/page/world/one-month-hundreds-of-millions-of-records-collected/554/.
49. "The Prevent Duty: Departmental Advice for Schools and Childcare Advisors," UK Department for Education, 2015, https://www.gov.uk/government/uploads/system/uploads/attachment_data/file/439598/prevent-duty-departmental-advice-v6.pdf.
50. "The Prevent Duty," UK Department for Education.
51. Paul Thomas, "Changing Experiences of Responsibilisation and Contestation Within Counter-Terrorism Policies: The British Prevent Experience," *Policy & Politics* 45 (2017): 305–21.

52. David Cameron, "British Values Aren't Optional, They're Vital," *Mailonline*, June 15, 2014, http://www.dailymail.co.uk/debate/article-2658171/DAVID-CAMERON-British-values-arent-optional-theyre-vital-Thats-I-promote-EVERY-school-As-row-rages-Trojan-Horse-takeover-classrooms-Prime-Minister-delivers-uncompromising-pledge.html.
53. Tahir Abbas, "The 'Trojan Horse' Plot and the Fear of Muslim Power in British State Schools," *Journal of Muslim Minority Affairs* 37, no. 4 (2017): 426–41.
54. Ruth Sherlock, Joe Daunt, and Sam Tarling, "Found: The Bethnal Green Schoolgirls Who Ran Away to Syria," *The Telegraph*, July 3, 2015, https://www.telegraph.co.uk/news/2016/03/18/found-the-bethnal-green-schoolgirls-who-ran-away-to-syria/.
55. "The Prevent Duty," UK Department for Education.
56. Vicki Coppock and Mark McGovern, "'Dangerous Minds'? Deconstructing Counter-Terrorism Discourse, Radicalisation and the 'Psychological Vulnerability' of Muslim Children and Young People in Britain," *Children & Society*, 28:3 (2014): 242–56; Aislinn O'Donnell, "Contagious Ideas: Vulnerability, Epistemic Injustice and Counter-Terrorism in Education," *Educational Philosophy and Theory* 50, no. 10 (2016): 981–997.
57. Paul Thomas, "Youth, Terrorism and Education: Britain's Prevent Programme," *International Journal of Lifelong Education*, 35, no. 2 (2016): 171–87.
58. Katy Sian, "Spies, Surveillance and Stakeouts: Monitoring Muslim Moves in British State Schools," *Race Ethnicity and Education*, 18, no. 2 (2015): 183–201.
59. "The Prevent Duty," UK Department for Education.
60. Joel Busher et al., "What the Prevent Duty Means for Schools and Colleges in England: An Analysis of Educationalists' Experiences," research report, Aziz Foundation, 2017, http://azizfoundation.org.uk/wp-content/uploads/2017/07/What-the-Prevent-Duty-means-for-schools-and-colleges-in-England.pdf; see also Thomas, "Youth, Terrorism and Education."
61. Thomas, "Changing Experiences of Responsibilisation and Contestation."
62. "Individuals Referred to and Supported Through the *Prevent* Programme, April 2015 to March 2016," *Home Office: Statistical Bulletin*, November 9, 2017, https://www.gov.uk/government/uploads/system/uploads/attachment_data/file/677646/individuals-referred-supported-prevent-programme-apr2015-mar2016.pdf.
63. Reza Gholami, "Counter-Extremism and Education: Bringing Together Emerging Research and Analytical Perspectives" (paper presented at conference on Counter-Extremism and Education), February 14, 2018, Birmingham University, UK.
64. Natasha Duarte, Emma Llanso, and Anna Loup, "Mixed Messages? The Limits of Automated Social Media Content Analysis," Proceedings of the First Conference on Fairness, Accountability and Transparency, in *Proceedings of Machine Learning Research* 81 (2018): 106.
65. Faiza Patel, "Rethinking Radicalization," *Brennan Center for Justice* (New York: Brennan Center for Justice, 2011): 8.

66. See, e.g., Hal Abelson et al., to Elaine C. Duke, November 16, 2017, https://www.brennancenter.org/sites/default/files/Technology%20Experts%20Letter%20to%20DHS%20Opposing%20the%20Extreme%20Vetting%20Initiative%20-%2011.15.17.pdf; Aliya Sternstein, "Obama Team Did Some 'Extreme Vetting' of Muslims Before Trump, New Documents Show," *Daily Beast*, January 2, 2018, https://www.thedailybeast.com/obama-team-did-some-extreme-vetting-of-muslims-before-trump-new-documents-show.
67. danah boyd, "Social Steganography: Learning to Hide in Plain Sight," *Apophenia* (blog), August 3, 2010, http://www.zephoria.org/thoughts/archives/2010/08/23/social-steganography-learning-to-hide-in-plain-sight.html.
68. Natasha Lennard, "The Way Dzhokhar Tsarnaev's Tweets Are Being Used in the Boston Bombing Trial Is Very Dangerous," *Splinter*, March 12, 2015, https://splinternews.com/the-way-dzhokhar-tsarnaevs-tweets-are-being-used-in-the-1793846339.
69. Su Lin Blodgett and Brendan O'Connor, "Racial Disparity in Natural Language Processing: A Case Study of Social Media African-American English," *Proceedings of the Fairness, Accountability, and Transparency in Machine Learning Conference* (2017): 2–3, arXiv: 1707.00061.
70. Ben Conarck, "Sheriff's Office Social Media Tool Regularly Yielded False Alarms," *Florida Times-Union*, May 30, 2017, http://www.jacksonville.com/news/public-safety/metro/2017-05-30/sheriff-s-office-s-social-media-tool-regularly-yielded-false.
71. Nasser Eledroos and Kade Crockford, "Social Media Monitoring in Boston: Free Speech in the Crosshairs," PrivacySOS, https://privacysos.org/social-media-monitoring-boston-free-speech-crosshairs/; Charles Kurzman and David Schanzer, "Law Enforcement Ranks Anti-Government Extremism as Most Prevalent Terrorist Threat," Duke University Sanford School of Public Policy, June 25, 2015, https://sanford.duke.edu/articles/law-enforcement-ranks-anti-government-extremism-most-prevalent-terrorist-threat.
72. See, e.g., Libby Nelson, "The Hidden Racism of School Discipline, in 7 Charts," *Vox*, October 31, 2015, https://www.vox.com/2015/10/31/9646504/discipline-race-charts; Derrick Darby and John L. Rury, "When Black Children Are Targeted for Punishment," *New York Times*, September 25, 2017, https://www.nytimes.com/2017/09/25/opinion/black-students-little-rock-punishment.html; Thomas Rudd, "Racial Disproportionality in School Discipline: Implicit Bias is Heavily Implicated," Kirwan Institute, February 5, 2015, http://kirwaninstitute.osu.edu/racial-disproportionality-in-school-discipline-implicit-bias-is-heavily-implicated/.
73. Katie Zavadski, "Alabama School District Hired an Ex-FBI Agent to Monitor Students on Social Media," *New York Magazine*, November 3, 2014, http://nymag.com/daily/intelligencer/2014/11/alabama-schools-hired-ex-fbi-to-monitor-students.html.
74. Bethany Barnes, "Targeted: A Family and the Quest to Stop the Next School

Shooter," *The Oregonian*, June 24, 2018, https://www.oregonlive.com/expo/news/erry-2018/06/75f0f464cb3367/targeted_a_family_and_the_ques.html.

75. Barnes, "Targeted."
76. Malena Carollo, "The Secretive Industry of Social Media Monitoring," *CSM Projects*, http://projects.csmonitor.com/socialmonitoring.
77. Leslie Regan Shade and Rianka Singh, "'Honestly, We're Not Spying on Kids': School Surveillance of Young People's Social Media," *Social Media & Society* 4, no. 2 (2016), doi: 10.1177/2056305116680005.
78. Timothy Snyder, "Resist Authoritarianism by Refusing to Obey in Advance," *Literary Hub*, April 28, 2017, https://lithub.com/resist-authoritarianism-by-refusing-to-obey-in-advance/.
79. Faiza Patel and Rachel Levinson-Waldman, "Monitoring Kids' Social Media Accounts Won't Prevent the Next School Shooting," *Washington Post*, March 5, 2018, https://www.washingtonpost.com/news/posteverything/wp/2018/03/05/monitoring-kids-social-media-accounts-wont-prevent-the-next-school-shooting/?utm_term=.2525287611a3. Cruz was not identified as the author of at least one of the posts until after the shooting.
80. Other issues we asked about were considerably less divisive. For example, 86 percent of parents and 95 percent of educators agree that *parents* should monitor their teens' social media accounts.
81. Desmond U. Patton et al., "Accommodating Grief on Twitter: An Analysis of Expressions of Grief Among Gang Involved Youth on Twitter Using Qualitative Analysis and Natural Language Processing," *Biomedical Informatics Insights* 10 (2018): 1–9.
82. Howard Gardner and Katy Davis, *The App Generation: How Today's Youth Navigate Identity, Intimacy, and Imagination in a Digital World* (New Haven, CT: Yale University Press, 2013), 10.
83. Abigail Hauslohner, "Hate Crimes Jump for Fourth Straight Year in Largest U.S. Cities, Study Shows," *Washington Post*, May 11, 2018, https://www.washingtonpost.com/news/post-nation/wp/2018/05/11/hate-crime-rates-are-still-on-the-rise/.
84. Tom Rudd, "Racial Disproportionality in School Discipline."
85. Mark Berman and Marwa Eltagouri, "Parkland Suspect Detailed Plans in Chilling Videos: 'I'm Going to Be the Next School Shooter,'" *Washington Post*, May 30, 2018, https://www.washingtonpost.com/news/post-nation/wp/2018/05/30/parkland-shooting-suspect-detailed-plans-in-videos-im-going-to-be-the-next-school-shooter/; Joel Rose and Brakkton Booker, "Parkland Shooting Suspect: A Story of Red Flags, Ignored," *NPR*, March 1, 2018, https://www.npr.org/2018/02/28/589502906/a-clearer-picture-of-parkland-shooting-suspect-comes-into-focus.
86. "Suicide," National Institute of Mental Health, May 2018, https://www.nimh.nih.gov/health/statistics/suicide.shtml.
87. A discussion of the different types of privacy, including "informational privacy"

and "expressive privacy" (discussed below), can be found in Judith Wagner Decrew, *In Pursuit of Privacy: Law, Ethics, and the Rise of Technology* (Ithaca, NY: Cornell University Press, 1997).

88. For a discussion of developmental rights, see John Eekelaar, "The Emergence of Children's Rights," *Oxford Journal of Legal Studies* 45, no. 6 (1986): 161–82.
89. Cruz had posted "I want to be a professional school shooter" online, although the FBI was unable to connect his post to Cruz himself.
90. Lauren Musu-Gillette et al., *Indicators of School Crime and Safety: 2016*, NCES 2017-064/NCJ 250650 (Washington, DC: National Center for Education Statistics, US Department of Education, and Bureau of Justice Statistics, Office of Justice Programs, US Department of Justice, 2017): 33.
91. Matthew J. Mayer and Michael J. Furlong, "How Safe Are Our Schools?" *Educational Researcher* 39, no. 1 (2010): 24.
92. Bryan R. Warnick, *Understanding Student Rights in Schools: Speech, Religion, and Privacy in Educational Settings* (New York: Teachers College Press, 2013).
93. Langdon Winner, *Autonomous Technology: Technics-out-of-Control as a Theme in Political Thought* (Cambridge, MA: MIT Press, 1978); Lawrence Lessig, *Code: And Other Laws of Cyberspace*, Version 2.0 (New York: Basic Books, 2006), http://pdf.codev2.cc/Lessig-Codev2.pdf.
94. On the troubled history of textbook selection, for instance, see Texas Freedom Network Education Fund, "Writing to the Standards: Reviews of Proposed Social Studies Textbooks for Texas Public Schools," *Reports from the Texas Freedom Network Education Fund* (Austin, TX: TFNEF, 2014), http://tfn.org/cms/assets/uploads/2015/11/FINAL_executivesummary.pdf.
95. Michel Foucault, *Discipline and Punish: The Birth of the Prison* (New York: Pantheon Books, 1977).
96. Jonathon Penney, "Chilling Effects: Online Surveillance and Wikipedia Use," *Berkeley Technology Law Journal* 31, no. 1 (2016): 117; Jonathon Penney, "Internet Surveillance, Regulation, and Chilling Effects Online: A Comparative Case Study," *Internet Policy Review* 6, no. 2 (2017): 22, https://policyreview.info/articles/analysis/internet-surveillance-regulation-and-chilling-effects-online-comparative-case.
97. Virginia Eubanks, *Digital Dead End: Fighting for Social Justice in the Information Age*, reprint (Cambridge, MA: MIT Press, 2012).
98. Virginia Eubanks, *Automating Inequality: How High-Tech Tools Profile, Police, and Punish the Poor* (New York: St. Martin's Press, 2017): 12.
99. Eubanks, "Digital Dead End," 105.
100. Eubanks, "Digital Dead End," 105.
101. This is one of the hallmarks of the new General Data Protection Regulation (GDPR) enshrined in European Union law, which has highlighted the need for more data control and privacy protections for users of private platforms.

102. Diana E. Hess and Paula McAvoy, *The Political Classroom: Evidence and Ethics in Democratic Education* (New York: Routledge, 2015), 4
103. Shaowen Bardzell, "Feminist HCI: Taking Stock and Outlining an Agenda for Design," *Proceedings of the SIGCHI Conference on Human Factors in Computing Systems (CHI '10)* (New York: ACM, 2010): 1301–10.
104. See Ceasar McDowell, "Crisis or Opportunity? A Dialogue on Democracy, Inclusion, and Community" (presented at the Thirteenth Annual Ikeda Forum for Intercultural Dialogue, Ikeda Center for Peace, Learning, and Dialogue, Cambridge, MA, October 27, 2016), https://www.youtube.com/watch?v=OKXzJ8hwjlI.
105. For a theory of democracy as "world-building," see Hannah Arendt, *The Human Condition* (Chicago: University of Chicago Press, 1958); Harry C. Boyte, "Constructive Politics as Public Work Organizing the Literature," *Political Theory* 39, no. 5 (2011): 630–60, discusses citizens as "co-creators"; see also Danielle Allen, *Education and Equality* (Chicago: University of Chicago Press, 2016).

CHAPTER 6 (Particular Schools for Particular Students)

Bari Academy is a pseudonym, as are names of school staff, parents, and students. This case study is adapted from a longer article about this school: Terri S. Wilson, "Contesting the Public School: Reconsidering Charter Schools as Counterpublics," *American Educational Research Journal* 53, no. 4 (2016): 919–52.

1. Suzanne Eckes refers to these schools as "havens;" Nina Buchanan and Robert Fox term them "ethnocentric" charter schools. See Suzanne Eckes, "Haven Charter Schools: Separate by Design and Legally Questionable," *Equity & Excellence in Education* 48, no. 1 (2015): 49–70; Robert Fox and Nina Buchanan, *Proud to Be Different: Ethnocentric Niche Charter Schools in America* (Lanham, MD: Rowman & Littlefield, 2014). Examples of such schools include bilingual charter schools started by Latino community organizations, schools focused on native Hawaiian culture and language, and community-based Afrocentric schools.
2. For a profile of these different types of schools at the elementary school level, see Terri S. Wilson and Robert L. Carlsen, "School Marketing as a Sorting Mechanism: A Critical Discourse Analysis of Charter School Websites," *Peabody Journal of Education* 91, no. 1 (2016): 24–46.
3. Erica Frankenberg and Genevieve Siegel-Hawley make this point in a recent review of the literature on charter school segregation. See their chapter: "A Segregating Choice? An Overview of Charter School Policy, Enrollment Trends, and Segregation," in *Educational Delusions? Why Choice Can Deepen Inequality and How to Make Schools Fair*, ed. Gary Orfield and Erica Frankenberg (Berkeley: University of California Press, 2013), 129–44.

4. While charter schools in the central city enroll, in aggregate, similar proportions of non-White students as their districts (72% district; 67% charter), these students are often grouped into specific schools that focus on particular racial and ethnic groups. Source: Minnesota Department of Education, 2016–17 school demographic data.
5. Minnesota Department of Education 2016–17 school demographic data. The author compared district schools and charter schools located in the two counties (Hennepin and Ramsey) that encompass the central cities and largely overlap with the two major school districts. This excludes small alternative and extended-day programs (those with less than thirty students), as well as educational programs in hospitals and correctional facilities.
6. Stewart was quoted in Natalie Gross, "The Benefit of Racial Isolation," *Atlantic*, February 8, 2017.
7. Proficiency includes the percentage of students that meet or exceed standards on state assessments. In 2017, in the Minneapolis Public Schools that was: 43.6% (reading), 42.6% (math), 35.0% (science); in the St. Paul Public Schools, it was: 38.0% (reading), 35.2% (math), 32.4% (science).
8. Consider the data for African American or Black students who both qualify for free or reduced-price lunch and are classified as English language learners (ELL). In Minneapolis Public Schools, only 8.3% of these students were proficient in reading and 11.5% in math. St. Paul Public Schools is barely better: 11.8% proficient in reading and 15.6% in math. Statewide patterns are virtually identical, at 13.3% in reading and 15.5% in math. (All percentages calculated by the author using publicly available data from the Minnesota Department of Education, "Minnesota Report Card," 2016–17, https://rc.education.state.mn.us/.)
9. Mississippi Elementary School is also a pseudonym; school data is from the "Minnesota Report Card."
10. See Roslyn Arlin Mickelson, Martha Cecilia Bottia, and Richard Lambert, "Effects of School Racial Composition on K–12 Mathematics Outcomes: A Metaregression Analysis," *Review of Educational Research* 83, no. 1 (2013): 121–58; Sean F. Reardon, "School Segregation and Racial Academic Achievement Gaps," *Russell Sage Foundation Journal of the Social Sciences* 2, no. 5 (2016): 34–57.
11. Institute on Metropolitan Opportunity, *The Minnesota School Choice Project, Part I: Segregation and Performance* (Minneapolis: University of Minnesota Law School, February 2017), https://www.law.umn.edu/sites/law.umn.edu/files/metro-files/imo-mscp-report-part-one-segregation-and-performance.pdf_0.pdf.
12. Jomills Henry Braddock II, Robert L. Crain, and James M. McPartland, "A Long-Term View of School Desegregation: Some Recent Studies of Graduates as Adults," *Phi Delta Kappan* 66 (1984): 259–64; Maureen T. Hallinan, "Diversity Effects on Student Outcomes: Social Science Evidence," *Ohio State Law Journal* 59 (1998): 733; Douglas N. Harris, "How Do School Peers Influence Student

Educational Outcomes? Theory and Evidence from Economics and Other Social Sciences," *Teachers College Record* 112, no. 4 (2010): 1163–97; Rucker C. Johnson, "Long-Run Impacts of School Desegregation & School Quality on Adult Attainments," (working paper no. 16664, National Bureau of Economic Research, Cambridge, MA, 2011), doi: 10.3386/w16664; Reardon, "School Segregation," 34–57; Amy Stuart Wells, "Reexamining Social Science Research on School Desegregation: Long- Versus Short-Term Effects," *Teachers College Record* 96, no. 4 (1995): 691–706.

13. Franklin Heights is a pseudonym.
14. It is also worth asking about the civic costs of segregation for students who do *not* attend Bari—for the students in schools like Franklin Heights, from which Amina finally withdrew her son. What are the consequences of attending schools that drive away immigrant families and families of color, or that track their children into segregated classes? What will students in these schools fail to learn about the benefits of learning, working, socializing, and engaging with diverse others in shared civic life? It is possible that critics focus on the risks of segregation posed by Bari rather than by Franklin Heights because of the measures of disadvantage students face at Bari. Franklin Heights students, by contrast, are generally affluent and academically high achieving. But these critics' focus perhaps instead reflects racialized concerns about the integration of Muslim immigrants in the United States, and comparative indifference to the civic ills created by relatively isolated communities.
15. This school name is also a pseudonym. Demographic information adapted from: Aaliyah Hodge and Joe Nathan, *Minnesota Charter and District School Demographics* (St. Paul, MN: Center for School Change, 2017).
16. Ali A. Abdi, "Education in Somalia: History, Destruction, and Calls for Reconstruction," *Comparative Education* 34, no. 3 (1998): 332–34.
17. United Nations Educational, Scientific, and Cultural Organization, *World Education Report* (Paris: UNESCO, 1991).
18. Abdi, "Education in Somalia."
19. United Nations High Commissioner for Refugees, "UNHCR Report Highlights Education Crisis for Refugee Children," UNHCR, September 12, 2017, http://www.unhcr.org/en-us/news/press/2017/9/59b6a3ec4/unhcr-report-highlights-education-crisis-refugee-children.html.
20. Minnesota Public Radio, "Minnesota's Graduation Gap: By the Numbers," March 7, 2016, https://www.mprnews.org/story/2016/03/07/graduation-gap-by-the-numbers.
21. Cawo M. Abdi, *Elusive Jannah: The Somali Diaspora and a Borderless Muslim Identity* (Minneapolis: University of Minnesota Press, 2015); Cawo M. Abdi, "The Newest African-Americans? Somali Struggles for Belonging," *Bildhaan: An International Journal of Somali Studies* 11, no. 1 (2012): 12.

22. Sandra E. Black, "Do Better Schools Matter? Parental Valuation of Elementary Education," *Quarterly Journal of Economics* 114, no. 2 (1999): 577–99.
23. Abdi, *Elusive Jannah.*
24. Reva Jaffe-Walter, *Coercive Concern: Nationalism, Liberalism, and the Schooling of Muslim Youth* (Stanford, CA: Stanford University Press, 2016).
25. See Nelson Flores, "What If We Talked About Monolingual White Children the Way We Talk About Low-Income Children of Color?," *Educational Linguist Blog*, July 6, 2015, https://educationallinguist.wordpress.com/2015/07/06/what-if-we-talked-about-monolingual-white-children-the-way-we-talk-about-low-income-children-of-color/.
26. Christia Spears Brown, *The Educational, Psychological, and Social Impact of Discrimination on the Immigrant Child* (Washington, DC: Migration Policy Institute, 2015), https://www.migrationpolicy.org/research/educational-psychological-and-social-impact-discrimination-immigrant-child; Maureen Costello, *The Trump Effect: The Impact of the Presidential Campaign on Our Nation's Schools* (Montgomery, AL: Southern Poverty Law Center, April 13, 2016), https://www.splcenter.org/20160413/trump-effect-impact-presidential-campaign-our-nations-schools.
27. Costello, "The Trump Effect."
28. Reva Jaffe-Walter and Stacey J. Lee, "Engaging the Transnational Lives of Immigrant Youth in Public Schooling: Toward a Culturally Sustaining Pedagogy for Newcomer Immigrant Youth," *American Journal of Education* 124, no. 3 (2018): 257–83.
29. Gary Orfield and Chungmei Lee, *Historic Reversals, Accelerating Resegregation, and the Need for New Integration Strategies* (Los Angeles: The Civil Rights Project, UCLA, August 29, 2007), https://escholarship.org/uc/item/8h02n114.
30. Lynnell Mickelsen, "Why White Progressives Should Stop Crying over Black Parent Choice and 'Segregated' Charters," *MinnPost*, March 5, 2018.
31. David Card, Alexandre Mas, and Jesse Rothstein, "Tipping and the Dynamics of Segregation," *Quarterly Journal of Economics* 123, no. 1 (February 1, 2008): 177–218, doi: 10.3386/w13052.
32. Allison Roda and Amy Stuart Wells, "School Choice Policies and Racial Segregation: Where White Parents' Good Intentions, Anxiety, and Privilege Collide," *American Journal of Education* 119, no. 2 (February 1, 2013): 261–93.
33. Parker Riley, "Watch These White Parents Go Ballistic Because Their Children Will Go to School with Black and Brown Kids." *News One* (blog), May 2, 2018.
34. Thomas C. Pedroni, "Acting Neoliberal: Is Black Support for Vouchers a Rejection of Progressive Educational Values?," *Educational Studies* 40, no. 3 (November 1, 2006): 265–78.
35. Maxine Mckinney de Royston and Alea Holman, "'We Want It All': African American Parents' Perspectives on School Choice and Orientations to the Education of 'Our Children,'" *Improvisation Within Structure* (Vancouver: American Educational Research Association, 2013).

36. Vanessa Siddle Walker, *The Lost Education of Horace Tate: Uncovering the Hidden Heroes Who Fought for Justice in Schools* (New York: The New Press, 2018); see Siddle Walker's discussion of Black teachers (Lucy Laney in particular) and NAACP members explicit discussions about the role of civic education in Black schools for pursuing justice.
37. Zora Neale Hurston, "Court Order Can't Make the Races Mix," letter to the editor of the *Orlando Sentinel*, August 1955, retrieved from *LewRockwell.Com* (blog), https://www.lewrockwell.com/1970/01/zora-neale-hurston/court-order-cant-make-the-racesmix/.
38. Davison Douglas, *Jim Crow Moves North: The Battle over Northern School Segregation, 1865–1954* (New York, NY: Cambridge University Press, 2005).
39. W. E. Burghardt Du Bois, "Does the Negro Need Separate Schools?," *The Journal of Negro Education* 4, no. 3 (1935): 328–35, https://doi.org/10.2307/2291871; W. E. Burghardt Du Bois, "Whither Now and Why," *Quarterly Review of Higher Education Among Negroes* 28, no. 3 (July 1960): 135–41; Gloria Ladson-Billings, "Can We at Least Have Plessy?: The Struggle for Quality Education," *North Carolina Law Review* 85 (June 1, 2007): 1279–799; Michael J. Dumas, "Sitting Next to White Children: School Desegregation in the Black Educational Imagination," (PhD diss., City University of New York, 2007); Kihana Miraya Ross, "Brown v. Board of Education Anniversary—Re-Segregate Schools Voluntarily for Black Students," *The Hill*, December 7, 2017.
40. David F. Labaree, *Someone Has to Fail: The Zero-Sum Game of Public Schooling* (Cambridge, MA: Harvard University Press, 2012); Walter Rodney, *How Europe Underdeveloped Africa* (Black Classic Press, 2011).
41. "Charter School Purpose and Applicability 1991," Minnesota Statutes 2018, section 124E:01, https://www.revisor.mn.gov/statutes/?id=124E.01#stat.124E.01.1
42. For the brevity of this commentary, I will accept the premise that test scores are an appropriate measure of academic achievement at Bari Academy as well as district schools, though research cites the shortcomings of standardized test scores and the persistent achievement gaps for English language learners, racial and ethnic minorities and students from low-income families (National Education Association).
43. Amy Gutmann, *Democratic Education* (Princeton, NJ: Princeton University Press, 1987): 287.
44. "Minnesota's Statewide Population by Race and Ethnicity, 2000–2015," Minnesota State Demographic Center (2015), https://factfinder.census.gov/faces/tableservices/jsf/pages/productview.xhtml
45. Harry Brighouse et al., *Educational Goods* (Chicago: University of Chicago Press, 2018).
46. Amanda Machado, "Is It Possible to Teach Children to Be Less Prejudiced?" *Atlantic*, March 31, 2014.

47. "Growing Racial and Ethnic Diversity in the Twin Cities Region Today," *MetroStats* (St. Paul, MN: Metropolitan Council, October 2014). Retrieved from https://metrocouncil.org/getattachment/bfc72287-2b88-49e0-96ea-2fa2ee2eb0d2/.aspx.
48. Zaretta Hammond, *Culturally Responsive Teaching and the Brain* (Thousand Oaks, CA: Corwin, 2014).
49. Cathy L. Nelson and Kim A. Wilson, eds., *Seeding the Process of Multicultural Education* (Plymouth, MN: Minnesota Inclusiveness Program, 1998), 149–56.
50. Solvejg Wastvedt and John Enger, "Minnesota's Teacher Shortage: Real, Complicated," *MPR News*, March 27, 2017, https://www.mprnews.org/story/2017/03/27/minnesota-teacher-shortage-real-but-complicated.
51. Josh Moss, "Where are All the Teachers of Color?" *Harvard Ed. Magazine*, May 14, 2016, https://www.gse.harvard.edu/news/ed/16/05/where-are-all-teachers-color.
52. Anya Kamenetz, "The Evidence That White Children Benefit from Integrated School," *NPR*, October 19, 2015.
53. Paul Wellstone, "Sheet Metal Workers Speech," September 1999, retrieved from https://www.wellstone.org/legacy/speeches/sheet-metal-workers-speech.
54. The school opened in the fall of 2005.
55. The school's actual name translates as "haven" in the Somali language.
56. Although nowhere does Wilson mention racism or stigma. But see: (1) https://www.pri.org/stories/2016-08-05/shared-exclusion-and-discrimination-are-uniting-somali-refugees-and-black-lives; (2) http://www.dw.com/en/somali-americans-allege-discrimination-in-us-counterterrorism-policies/a-18710323; (3) https://www.thetoptens.com/most-racists-states-us/minnesota-542707.asp; (4) http://www.presspubs.com/white_bear/news/article_91be021c-11b4-11e8-9f08-6fe03b861ff5.html. The problem is much bigger than the Twin Cities. For instance, the Minnesota chapter of the Council on American-Islamic Relations filed a federal civil rights complaint against the St. Cloud school district in 2011 concerning a hostile educational environment. See https://www.pbs.org/newshour/education/how-one-minnesota-school-district-handles-a-rising-immigrant-population; in that same year there was a Federal Civil Rights investigation concerning discrimination against Somali pupils.
57. A majority of the White population claim German and Scandinavian ancestry, and they also settled Minnesota in ethnic concentrations before whiteness became a more convenient substitute; "Minnesota Ranked Second-Worst in US for Racial Equality," CBS Minnesota, http://minnesota.cbslocal.com/2017/08/22/minnesota-racial-inequality/.
58. Sarah Lahm, "As Integrated Schools Disappear, Minneapolis Somali Families Fight to Keep Theirs," *Progressive*, December 21, 2017, http://progressive.org/public-school-shakedown/as-integrated-schools-disappear-minneapolis-families-fight-t/.

59. See my *Equality, Citizenship and Segregation* (New York: Palgrave Macmillan, 2013) for a detailed analysis of these issues.
60. In addition to the all-too-common labor market discrimination and racial profiling by the police, racial covenants were also common throughout much of the twentieth century in the Twin Cities, and real estate and home buyer behaviors are still largely informed by the thinking that "good schools" are in overwhelmingly White and affluent neighborhoods.
61. See, e.g., Camille Zubrinsky Charles, "The Dynamics of Racial Residential Segregation," *Annual Review of Sociology* 29, no. 1 (2003): 167–207; Peter Rich, "White Parental Flight and Avoidance: Neighborhood Choice in the Era of School District Desegregation" (working paper, Cornell University, Ithaca, NY, 2016), accessed via http://www.peter-rich.com/workingpapers/.
62. Abby Norman, "Why White Parents Won't Choose Black Schools," *Huffington Post*, October 15, 2015.

CHAPTER 7 (Politics, Partisanship, and Pedagogy)

This case is a work of fiction account inspired by the authors' work in schools and the work of Diana Hess and Paula McAvoy, *The Political Classroom: Evidence and Ethics in Democratic Education* (New York: Routledge, 2014).

1. William J. Talbott, "What's Wrong with Wishy-Washy Teaching of Political Philosophy?" (paper presented at the American Philosophy Association Pacific Division Meeting, Portland, Oregon, March, 2006): 6.
2. John Dewey, "The Crucial Role of Intelligence," *The Social Frontier* 1, no. 5 (1935): 9.
3. Thomas D. Fallace, "The Origins of Classroom Deliberation: Democratic Education in the Shadow of Totalitarianism, 1938–1960," *Harvard Educational Review* 86, no. 4 (2016): 506–26.
4. Robert B. Westbrook, *John Dewey and American Democracy* (Ithaca, NY: Cornell University Press, 1991), 506–7.
5. Dewey, "The Crucial Role of Intelligence," 9.
6. Ann P. Haas, Philip L. Rodgers, and Jody L. Herman, *Suicide Attempts Among Transgender and Gender Non-Conforming Adults* (New York and Los Angeles: American Foundation for Suicide Prevention and The Williams Institute, UCLA School of Law, 2014).
7. Diana Tourée, "The Unclear Future of Trans Rights Under Trump," *Broadly Vice*, November 9, 2016, https://broadly.vice.com/en_us/article/8x4nxk/the-unclear-future-of-trans-rights-under-trump.
8. Joellen Kralik, "'Bathroom Bill' Legislative Tracking," National Conference of State Legislators, July 28, 2017, http://www.ncsl.org/research/education/-bathroom-bill-legislative-tracking635951130.aspx.
9. It is important to note that there are no federal laws that explicitly protect trans identity and the term *sex* is now legally constrained to dichotomous chromosomes.

10. Erik Eckholm and Alan Blinder, "Federal Transgender Bathroom Access Guidelines Blocked by Judge," *New York Times*, August 22, 2016, https://www.nytimes.com/2016/08/23/us/transgender-bathroom-access-guidelines-blocked-by-judge.html.
11. sj Miller, Cris Mayo, and Catherine A. Lugg, "Sex and Gender in Transition in US Schools: Ways Forward," *Sex Education* 18, no. 4 (2018), doi: 10.1080/14681811.2017.1415204.
12. Although as of this writing, they remain on the US Department of Education's website under the heading "Resources for Transgender and Gender-Nonconforming Students"; US Department of Education, Office of Elementary and Secondary Education, Office of Safe and Healthy Students, *Examples of Policies and Emerging Practices for Supporting Transgender Students* (May 2016), https://ed.gov/about/offices/list/oese/oshs/emergingpractices.pdf.
13. American Civil Liberties Union, "Know Your Rights: Transgender People and the Law" (2017), https://www.aclu.org/know-your-rights/transgender-people-and-law.
14. Dominic Holden, "The Education Department Officially Says It Will Reject Transgender Student Bathroom Complaints," *BuzzFeed*, February 12, 2018, https://www.buzzfeed.com/dominicholden/edu-dept-trans-student-bathrooms.
15. Masen Davis, CEO of Freedom for All Americans, personal email correspondence, 2018.
16. "Homophobic and Transphobic Violence in Education," UNESCO, https://en.unesco.org/themes/school-violence-and-bullying/homophobic-transphobic-violence.
17. Diana E. Hess, *Controversy in the Classroom: The Democratic Power of Discussion* (New York: Routledge, 2009).
18. See Elisabeth Meilhammer, *Neutralität als bildungstheoretisches Problem: Von der Meinungsabstinenz zur Meinungsgerechtigkeit* (Paderborn: Schöningh, 2008); Wolfgang Sander, "Bildung und Perspektivität—Kontroversität und Indoktrinationsverbot als Grundsätze von Bildung und Wissenschaft," *Erwägen Wissen Ethik* 20, no. 2 (2009): 239–48, 274.
19. See Diana Hess and Louis Ganzler, "Patriotism and Ideological Diversity in the Classroom," in *Pledging Allegiance: The Politics of Patriotism in America's Schools*, ed. Joel Westheimer (New York: Teachers College Press, 2007), 131–38.
20. See, for example, Russel Berman, "How Bathroom Fears Conquered Transgender Rights in Houston," *Atlantic*, November 3, 2015, www.theatlantic.com/politics/archive/2015/11/how-bathroom-fears-conquered-transgender-rights-in-houston/414016/.
21. *Carcaño v. McCrory*, 203 F.Supp.3d 615 (M.D.N.C. 2016).
22. Daniel Trotta, "US Transgender People Harassed in Public Restrooms: Landmark Survey," *Reuters*, December 8, 2016, https://www.reuters.com/article/us-usa-lgbt-survey/u-s-transgender-people-harassed-in-public-restrooms-landmark-survey-idUSKBN13X0BK; "Police Departments," National

Center for Transgender Equality, October 3, 2017, https://transequality.org/police-departments; Emanuella Grinberg and Dani Stewart, "Three Myths in the Transgender Bathroom Debate," *CNN*, March 7, 2017, https://www.cnn.com/2017/03/07/health/transgender-bathroom-law-facts-myths/index.html; *National Consensus Statement of Anti-Sexual Assault and Domestic Violence Organizations in Support of Full and Equal Access for the Transgender Community*, National Task Force to End Sexual and Domestic Violence Against Women, April 29, 2016, https://endsexualviolence.org/where-we-stand/statement-of-anti-sexual-assault-domestic-violence-organizations-in-support-of-equal-access-for-the-transgender-community.

23. "Character Education," Wake County Public School System, https://www.wcpss.net/character-education.

CHAPTER 8 (Bending Toward—or Away From—Racial Justice?)

This is a fictionalized case inspired by our own experiences in classrooms and schools, as well as those of other classroom teachers and educators.

1. Karen Manheim Teel and Jennifer E. Obidah, *Building Racial and Cultural Competence in the Classroom: Strategies from Urban Educators* (New York, NY: Teachers College Press, 2008).
2. McArthur's "Universal Corrective Map of the World" up-ends, literally, European cartographers' placement of the Northern Hemisphere at the top of the world map. Some scholars argue that the choice to situate Europe and North America at the top and center of the map has psychological and political consequences, including seeing the south as subordinate to the north, and seeing Europe and North America as having outsized importance. See Nick Danforth, "How the North Ended Up on Top of the Map," *Al Jazeera America*, February 16, 2014, and Nicole De Armendi, "The Map as Political Agent: Destabilising the North-South Model and Redefining Identity in Twentieth-Century Latin American Art," *St Andrews Journal of Art History and Museum Studies* 13 (2009): https://ojs.st-andrews.ac.uk/index.php/nsr/article/view/206/215.
3. Katie Lemke and Anya Rosenberg, "Case Final" (unpublished case, 2017).
4. I use this as a stand-in for a variety of difficult topics that are traditionally taught in biased or inaccurate ways. It is in fact true that Columbus and other Europeans engaged in genocidal violence against the native peoples and sought to destroy them and their culture. While we might disagree, ideologically, on whether to include this in curricula, no serious historian would disagree that these facts are true.
5. To push the metaphor even further, these challenges have deep roots in habits of mind and habits of everyday life that support the sociocultural inequality in our society.
6. Robin DiAngelo, "White Fragility," *International Journal of Critical Pedagogy* 3, no. 3 (2011): 54.

7. "Anti-Prejudice Activities," Racism No Way, http://www.racismnoway.com.au/teaching-resources/anti-prejudice-activities/.
8. See Australian Curriculum Assessment and Reporting Authority (ACARA) at www.acara.edu.au, as well as www.australiancurriculum.edu.au. Although we are glad that Indigenous issues are now curricular mandates, we would note that ACARA omits key sociopolitical concepts such as "native title rights to ancestral land, self-determination . . . and long-term effects of colonisation." See Kevin Lowe and Tyson Yunkaporta, "The Inclusion of Aboriginal and Torres Strait Islander Content in the Australian National Curriculum: A Cultural, Cognitive and Socio-Political Evaluation," *Curriculum Perspectives* 33, no. 1 (2013): 11.
9. Peter Read, "The Return of the Stolen Generation," *Journal of Australian Studies* 22, no. 59 (1998): 8–19.
10. "Australia as a Nation," NSW Education Standards Authority, https://syllabus.nesa.nsw.edu.au/hsie/history-k10/content/805/. Emphasis in the original.
11. Sam Duncan, "'It Was Bloody Disgraceful': Outrage Over Stolen Generation School Play That Saw Year 6 Students 'Dress Up as Nuns and Act Out Abuse on Aboriginal Children,'" *Daily Mail Australia*, August 17, 2017, http://www.dailymail.co.uk/news/article-4796456/Outrage-school-play-stolen-generation.html#ixzz4xFywhK6X.
12. Clarissa Bye and Sarah Swain, "School Play on Stolen Generation Shows Children Abusing Others," *Manly Daily*, August 17, 2017, https://www.dailytelegraph.com.au/newslocal/manly-daily/footballer-among-parents-walked-out-from-northern-beaches-school-play-on-stolen-generation/news-story/c3148d03883b126d3304b5d739fb2780; Kevin Donnelly, quoted in Stefanie Balogh and Joe Kelly, "Ideologues 'Have Captured' School History Curriculum," *The Australian*, August 24, 2017, https://www.theaustralian.com.au/national-affairs/education/ideologues-have-captured-school-history-curriculum/news-story/957908af8797b7f7fa49c631588f81f1.
13. Helen Vnuk, "When Their Kids Starred in a Kids Stolen Generation Play, These Mums Weren't Angry. They Cheered," *MamaMia*, August 17, 2017, https://www.mamamia.com.au/stolen-generation-school-performance/.
14. Clarissa Bye, "Schools to Cop Lesson in Bias," *Daily Telegraph*, August 18, 2017. https://www.dailytelegraph.com.au/news/nsw/stolen-generation-play-controversy-schools-will-be-coached-in-avoiding-political-bias/news-story/db8e96566be6dae70a5bad3636ebe1a3.
15. Trevor Marshallsea, "How a School Play About Aboriginal History Set Off a Row," BBC News Australia, August 21, 2017, https://www.bbc.com/news/world-australia-40972348.
16. David Brooks, "Good Leaders Make Good Schools," *New York Times*, March 12, 2018, https://www.nytimes.com/2018/03/12/opinion/good-leaders-schools.html.
17. Darnisa Amante, Stacy Scott, and Lee Teitel, "Beyond Desegregation: Promising Practices for Creating Diverse and Equitable Schools" (paper presented at the

RIDES Conference, Harvard Graduate School of Education, Cambridge, MA, May 30, 2018).

18. Paolo Freire, *The Politics of Education: Culture, Power and Liberation* (South Hadley, MA: Bergin & Garvey, 1985), 122.
19. See Avi Mintz, "Helping by Hurting: The Paradox of Suffering in Social Justice Education," *Theory and Research in Education* 11, no. 3 (November 2013): 215–31.
20. Paulo Freire, *Pedagogy of the Oppressed (30th Anniversary Edition)* (New York: Continuum, 2000), 49–50, 57.
21. *SPLC Report: US Education on American Slavery Sorely Lacking*, Southern Poverty Law Center, January 31, 2018, www.splcenter.org/news/2018/01/31/splc-report-us-education-american-slavery-sorely-lacking.
22. "The Lincoln-Douglas Debates 4th Debate Part I: Mr. Lincoln's Speech," TeachingAmericanHistory.org, Ashbrook Center at Ashland University, 2018, teachingamericanhistory.org/library/document/the-lincoln-douglas-debates-4th-debate-part-i/.
23. See, for example, Phillip W. Magness and Sebastian N. Page, *Colonization After Emancipation: Lincoln and the Movement for Black Resettlement* (Columbia: University of Missouri Press, 2011).

CHAPTER 9 (Talking Out of Turn)

This is a factual case that describes real conflicts over teacher speech in schools across the United States, as well as court decisions that define the limits of teachers' First Amendment rights.

1. Mackenzie Mays, "A Teacher Wore a Black Lives Matter Pin to Class. Now He is Banned from a Clovis School," *Fresno Bee*, December 3, 2016, http://www.fresnobee.com/news/local/education/article118591388.html.
2. "Guiding Principles," Black Lives Matter, http://blacklivesmatter.com/guiding-principles/.
3. Mays, *Fresno Bee*.
4. Mark Maynard, "Interview with Mika Yamamoto," MarkMaynard.com, February 12, 2017, http://markmaynard.com/2017/02/5th-grade-charter-school-teacher-mika-yamamoto-fired-from-michigans-renaissance-public-school-academy-where-she-was-the-only-teacher-of-color-claims-she-was-told-by-her-principal-the-community/.
5. Maynard, "Interview with Mika Yamamoto."
6. Joshua R. Miller, "Kansas Teacher Claims Conservative Views Led to Loss of Job," Fox News, June 12, 2009, http://www.foxnews.com/story/2009/06/12/kansas-teacher-claims-conservative-views-led-to-loss-job.html.
7. Miller, "Kansas Teacher."
8. *Mayer v. Monroe County Community School Corporation*, 2006 US Dist. LEXIS 26137 (S.D. Ind. 2006).
9. *Mayer v. Monroe County*, 2006.

10. *Mayer v. Monroe County Community School Corporation*, 474 F.3d 477 (7th Cir. 2007).
11. Kimberly W. O'Connor and Gordon B. Schmidt, "'Facebook Fired': Legal Standards for Social Media–Based Terminations of K–12 Public School Teachers," *Sage Open* 5, no. 1 (March 2015), doi:10.1177/2158244015575636.
12. *Connick v. Myers*, 461 US 138 (1983).
13. *Garcetti v. Ceballos*, 547 US 410 (2006).
14. O'Connor and Schmidt, "'Facebook Fired.'"
15. *Boring v. Buncombe County Board of Education*, 136 F.3d 364 (4th Cir. 1998).
16. *Webster v. New Lenox School District*, no. 122, 917 F.2d 1004 (7th Cir. 1990).
17. *Webster v. New Lenox School District.*
18. Diana E. Hess and Paula McAvoy, *The Political Classroom: Evidence and Ethics in Democratic Education* (New York: Routledge, 2015).
19. Mackenzie Mays, "A Teacher Wore a Black Lives Matter Pin to Class. Now, He is Banned from School," *Miami Herald*, December 3, 2016, http://www.miamiherald.com/news/nation-world/national/article118686918.html; Maynard, "Interview with Mika Yamamoto."
20. Merle Curti, "Changing Issues in the School's Freedom," *Social Frontier* 2 (March 1936): 167.
21. For a more detailed historical account of these trends, see Jonathan Zimmerman and Emily Robertson, *The Case for Contention: Teaching Controversial Issues in American Schools* (Chicago: University of Chicago Press, 2017), 8–43.
22. *Wieman v. Updegraff*, 344 US 183 (1952).
23. Alexander Meiklejohn, "Teachers and Controversial Questions," in *Alexander Meiklejohn, Teacher of Freedom*, ed. Cynthia Stokes Brown (Berkeley, CA: Meiklejohn Civil Liberties Institute, 1981), 214.
24. Meiklejohn, "Teachers and Controversial Questions," 210.
25. Quoted in Carlos Miller, "Educators Face Blowback for Protesting Iraq War in Schools," RawStory.com, Feb. 9, 2006, https://www.rawstory.com/news/2005/Educators_face_blowback_for_protesting_war_0209.html.
26. Miller, "Educators Face Blowback."
27. Miller, "Educators Face Blowback."
28. *Mayer v. Monroe County* (*Mayer* II, 2007).
29. Justin Tosi and Brandon Warmke, "Moral Grandstanding," *Philosophy and Public Affairs* 44, no. 3 (2016): 197–217.
30. Tosi and Warmke, "Moral Grandstanding," 201–5.
31. "Education Programs May Have a 'Disposition' for Censorship," Foundation for Individual Rights in Education, September 21, 2005, https://www.thefire.org/education-programs-may-have-a-disposition-for-censorship/.
32. "Democratic v. Republican Occupations," Verdant Labs, http://verdantlabs.com/politics_of_professions/index.html.
33. Michael Kazin, "Howard Zinn's History Lessons," *Dissent* (Spring, 2014), https://www.dissentmagazine.org/article/howard-zinns-history-lessons.

34. Constance Flanagan, "Young People's Civic Engagement and Political Development," in *Handbook of Youth and Young Adulthood: New Perspectives and Agendas*, ed. Andy Furlong (New York: Routledge, 2009), 293–300.
35. Mark A. Pike, "Faith in Citizenship? On Teaching Children to Believe in Liberal Democracy," *British Journal of Religious Education* 30, no. 2 (2008): 120.
36. Michael Hill and Lian Kwen Fee, *The Politics of Nation Building and Citizenship in Singapore* (London: Routledge, 1995), 35; see also Beng-Huat Chua, *Communitarian Ideology and Democracy in Singapore* (London: Routledge, 1995); Simon Long, "The Singapore Exception," *Economist*, July 18, 2015, https://www.economist.com/news/special-report/21657606-continue-flourish-its-second-half-century-south-east-asias-miracle-city-state.
37. "About Us," Ministry of Education, Singapore, https://www.moe.gov.sg/about.
38. Li-Ching Ho, "'Freedom Can Only Exist in an Ordered State': Harmony and Civic Education in Singapore," *Journal of Curriculum Studies* 49, no. 4 (2017): 488.
39. "About Us."
40. Mark C. Baildon and Jasmine B.-Y. Sim, "Notions of Criticality: Singaporean Teachers' Perspectives of Critical Thinking in Social Studies," *Cambridge Journal of Education* 39, no. 4 (2009): 407–22.
41. Li-Ching Ho, "'Don't Worry, I'm Not Going to Report You': Education for Citizenship in Singapore," *Theory and Research in Social Education* 38, no. 2 (2010): 217–47.
42. Li-Ching Ho, Theresa Alviar-Martin, and Enrique N. P. Leviste, "'There is Space, and There are Limits': The Challenge of Teaching Controversial Topics in an Illiberal Democracy," *Teachers College Record* 116, no. 5 (2014): 1–28.
43. *Social Studies Syllabus for Upper Secondary*, Ministry of Education, Singapore (2016), https://www.moe.gov.sg/docs/default-source/document/education/syllabuses/humanities/files/2016-social-studies-(upper-secondary-express-normal-(academic)-syllabus.pdf.
44. Li-Ching Ho, "Sorting Citizens: Differentiated Citizenship Education in Singapore," *Journal of Curriculum Studies* 44, no. 3 (2012): 403–28.
45. Ministry of Education, Singapore, *Social Studies Syllabus for Upper Secondary*, 15.
46. Jasmine B.-Y. Sim, Shuyi Chua, and Malathy Krishnasamy, "Riding the Citizenship Wagon: Citizenship Conceptions of Social Studies Teachers in Singapore," *Teaching and Teacher Education* 63 (2017): 92–102.
47. See also Mica Pollock, "Standing Up Against Hate," *Teaching Tolerance* 56 (2017): https://www.tolerance.org/magazine/summer-2017/standing-up-against-hate.
48. *Plyler v. Doe*, 457 US 202 (1982).
49. Oxford Dictionaries, s.v. "white supremacy," accessed April 24, 2018, https://en.oxforddictionaries.com/definition/us/white_supremacy.
50. Mica Pollock, *Schooltalk: Rethinking What We Say About—and To—Students Every Day* (New York: The New Press, 2017).

51. Mica Pollock, "Three Challenges for Teachers in the Era of Trump," *Answer Sheet* (blog), December 9, 2016, https://www.washingtonpost.com/news/answer-sheet/wp/2016/12/09/three-challenges-for-teachers-in-the-era-of-trump/.

CHAPTER 10 (Educating for Civic Renewal)

1. For a more detailed discussion of the clash between present-day democratic control over schools and future-oriented civic education, see Meira Levinson, *No Citizen Left Behind* (Cambridge, MA: Harvard University Press, 2012), chapter 7.
2. For an explanation of how to create "micro" cases and commentaries based on the originals that can be read even more quickly, see Meira Levinson and Jacob Fay, eds. *Dilemmas of Educational Ethics: Cases and Commentaries* (Cambridge, MA: Harvard Education Press, 2016), chapter 7.
3. We gratefully acknowledge Judith Pace, Gina Schouten, Heather VanBenthuysn, Beth Rubin, Harry Brighouse, Terri Wilson, Paula McAvoy, Doris Santoro, Eric Shed, Noah Heller, and Jane Lo for sharing their ideas.

Acknowledgments

We collectively owe profound debts of gratitude to the many colleagues, friends, students, family members, and other gracious volunteers who talked out ideas for this book and its design, tested case studies, recommended and helped us recruit commentators, responded to conference presentations and public lectures, supported our course development and teaching, and pushed our thinking along the way. There are far too many of you to name individually, but we trust you can see your contributions written into the pages of these chapters (and the sheer existence of the book!). This book reflects in particular the deep intellectual imprints and support of the Harvard Graduate School of Education and the Edmond J. Safra Center for Ethics at Harvard University. We both value our time in these stimulating and caring environments. We are also grateful for support from the Spencer Foundation.

Jay Lee, Arielle Ticho, Nithyani Anandakugan, Sarah Mehrotra, and Chris Fisk provided outstanding research and copyediting assistance at crucial junctures in the book's development and completion. Nancy Walser has been a cheerleader for this project at Harvard Education Press since our first book together, *Dilemmas of Educational Ethics: Cases and Commentaries* (2016), and we are thankful for her consistent support of this effort, as well. We also appreciate the HEPG team effort by Laura Cutone, Christina DeYoung, and Rose Ann Miller.

We had the opportunity to test out a few of the ideas in this book in print. We gratefully acknowledge permission from *On Education* to include portions of Meira Levinson and Ellis Reid, "The Paradox of Partisanship," *On Education* 1 (March 2018), www.oneducation.net/no-01-march-2018/the-paradox-of-partisanship/, and permission from ASCD to include portions of Jacob Fay and Meira Levinson, "Teaching Democracy in Polarizing Times," *Educational Leadership* (November 17, 2017): 62–67.

We each owe some individual debts of gratitude. Jake's thanks are due, first and foremost, to Sarah Fay. I am grateful for your steadying presence in my life, always and simply putting one foot in front of the other no matter what comes our way. I would also like to thank my parents, Stephen and Laurie Fay, for the weeks upon weeks of childcare that enabled me to write and edit this book while you both learned anew how to put one foot in front of the other. You were all indispensable supports for me during this project. Finally, I would like to thank my coeditor, Meira Levinson, for all the conversations that this book has started and will continue to start, as well as for making sure that this project came to be despite both of our busy schedules and full lives.

Meira has pulled virtually her entire family into conversations about these cases over the past few years. Rachel and Ariel Levinson-Waldman, Cynthia and Sanford Levinson, and Susan and Ian Lipsitch participated with good cheer in and contributed fundamental insight to discussions of civic educational ethics over meals, email, and frequent telephone conversations. Marc, Rebecca, and Gabriella Lipsitch deserve particular thanks for enduring my mental and physical absences as I worked on the book, and for humoring my many dinner table forays into civic educational ethics. They could probably teach full seminars about educational ethics at this point. It gives me great pleasure to continue the family tradition of acknowledging Rebecca and Ella as thoroughly splendid human beings, and Marc as everything a spouse could ask for and then some. Finally, I am thrilled that Jake was game for launching this book project even as he was both completing his dissertation and entering fatherhood. I value our partnership on this book and much else.

This book is dedicated to the memory of Brendan Randall, who was Meira's constant and indispensable thought-partner during the first years of the Justice in Schools project, including the genesis of the normative case study approach. Brendan also pushed both Meira's and Jake's thinking about the opportunities and challenges of achieving inclusive, democratic schools in ideologically, culturally, and religiously contested contexts. At the time of his death, he was in senior leadership at the Interfaith Youth Core, working with college campuses across the country and developing into a leading scholar in religion and education. Brendan's presence and insights are woven into the warp and weft of this book; we hope he and those who knew and loved him best would agree.

About the Editors

Meira Levinson is professor of education at Harvard, where she also serves as graduate fellowship program codirector in the Edmond J. Safra Center for Ethics and as co-convener of Harvard Graduate School of Education's Civic and Moral Education Initiative. A normative political philosopher and former middle school teacher, Levinson writes about civic education, multiculturalism, youth empowerment, and educational ethics. Her work has been supported by the Radcliffe Institute for Advanced Study, the Spencer Foundation, the National Academy of Education, and a Guggenheim Fellowship. Her books include *The Demands of Liberal Education* (Oxford University Press, 1999), *Making Civics Count*, coedited with David E. Campbell and Fredrick M. Hess (Harvard Education Press, 2012); *No Citizen Left Behind* (Harvard University Press, 2012), and *Dilemmas of Educational Ethics: Cases and Commentaries*, coedited with Jacob Fay (Harvard Education Press, 2016). She is currently working to develop a field of educational ethics, modeled after bioethics, that is theoretically rigorous and policy- and practice-relevant.

Jacob Fay is a visiting assistant professor of education at Bowdoin College. His research synthesizes philosophical theories of injustice with insights from developmental psychology to propose a novel approach to theorizing about injustice. He was co-chair of the *Harvard Educational Review*, a member of the 2013–14 Spencer Foundation Philosophy of Education Institute, a 2016–17 Edmond J. Safra Center for Ethics Graduate Fellow, and a 2017–18 Edmond J. Safra Center Ethics Pedagogy Fellow. He is coeditor with Meira Levinson of *Dilemmas of Educational Ethics: Cases and Commentaries* (Harvard Education Press, 2016). Previously, Fay taught eighth-grade history at the Dwight-Englewood School in Englewood, New Jersey.

About the Case Study Contributors

Sara Calleja is the PK–5 literacy program coordinator for the Andover (Massachusetts) Public Schools, having formerly served as an assistant principal, literacy coach, and classroom teacher in grades 1, 3, and 5 in New York City and the greater Boston area. Sara earned an MA in curriculum and teaching from Teachers College, Columbia University, and an EdM in school leadership from Harvard Graduate School of Education, where she was a recipient of the Leadership in Education Award.

Nick Fernald teaches English as a second language and social studies in the Boston area. Prior to becoming a teacher, Nick earned his master's degree at Harvard Graduate School of Education, where he was the recipient of the Leadership in Education Award and studied teaching, curriculum, and urban education.

Tatiana Geron is a PhD student at Harvard Graduate School of Education studying ethical decision-making in education reform. Prior to her doctoral studies, Tatiana taught middle school English language arts, social studies, and English as a second language in the Boston Public Schools and in Crown Heights, Brooklyn.

Heather Johnson is a doctoral student in the EdLD program at Harvard Graduate School of Education and a resident fellow at Jobs for the Future. She previously worked as director of the teacher education program at the College of the Holy Cross, as a middle school teacher, and at the Rhode Island Department of Education.

Toni Kokenis is pursuing a career in child welfare, building on both her experience in nonprofits and state agencies and her JD from Northeastern

University School of Law, EdM in human development and psychology (child advocacy track) from Harvard Graduate School of Education, and MA in sociology from Stanford University.

Garry S. Mitchell is a doctoral student at Harvard Graduate School of Education analyzing issues related to discipline and control in schools. He previously worked as a middle school English and history teacher in New York City.

Ellis Reid is a doctoral student at Harvard Graduate School of Education. Previously, Ellis worked as the associate director for a college access program in the San Francisco Bay area.

Nicolás Riveros works for J-PAL North America as a technical adviser. He holds an MEd degree from Harvard Graduate School of Education and a master's degree in political science from Universidad de los Andes, Colombia.

Terri S. Wilson is an assistant professor in the School of Education at the University of Colorado Boulder. Her research focuses on the intersections (and tensions) between individual choices and the "public goods" of education, including equity, justice, and democratic participation. She previously worked with community organizations and public schools in St. Paul, Minnesota.

Index